Out in Front

POLISH
IGHTER PILOT'S
RAMATIC
IR WAR

OUT
IN
FRONT

WITOLD
'LANNY'
ANOWSKI

Published in 2014 by Fighting High Ltd,
www.fightinghigh.com

British Library Cataloguing-in-Publication data. A CIP
record for this title is available from the British Library.

ISBN – 13: 978-0992620745

Designed and typeset in Adobe Minion 11/15pt
by Michael Lindley www.truthstudio.co.uk

Printed and bound in China by Toppan Leefung.
Front cover design by www.truthstudio.co.uk.

Contents

Foreword

The book title *Out in Front* has significant meaning to my father's story. Firstly, when the Germans invaded Poland in September 1939, my father was at Deblin cadet school as an instructor and was ordered to take a group of cadets out of Poland, south towards Rumania. Secondly, as flight commander and deputy squadron leader of 302 (Polish) Squadron he often led 302 into battle. Thirdly, and most significantly, during his posting with the 56th Fighter Group of the USAAF, the American pilots of his squadron, the 61st, would remark that they felt safe when 'Lanny' was in front, as he would guide them out and steer them back safely. There were a few occasions when on completion of their missions, as the squadron turned for home, the whole of the 61st Squadron would form up behind the 'Polish flight' with the request: 'Take us home Lanny.'

This volume tells the story of a truly remarkable and inspiring man, my father. He taught and influenced me through all the years we had together and, still to this day, motivates me through his philosophy of life. These pages have been sitting in a box in a cupboard for fifty years and now are here for all to read and enjoy his life and stories, as I have.

My earliest memory of my childhood is my mother sitting on the shared balcony in Fair Green Court, Mitchum, madly typing away on her typewriter, the words of the manuscript as dictated directly to her by my father. This was the early 1960s, the recollections of his life were fresh in his mind and I always said my father was like an elephant – 'He never forgets!' I remember visiting the Polish Air Force club in Earls Court, London, where my father was still treated with contempt by the other high-ranking Poles in the club, but he never let it faze him as he was so proud and really didn't care what they thought.

All throughout his later life, after his air force days, he would be in contact with various authors, helping with research for their books. Authors like Danny Morris who wrote *Aces and Wingmen*, and Roger Freeman who penned *The Mighty Eighth* among other titles, and he also gave lectures at various venues on his flying exploits, to some of which I used to accompany him as his 'sound effects engineer'. But the occasions I enjoyed the most were when we went to air shows together – for example, when he was invited by Duxford Imperial War Museum to set up his table with his models and he would be introduced over the tannoy so that the aircraft enthusiasts would know he was there and where to find him. He would proceed to sign his autograph on their programmes and he would have a tin of sweets for the children, who would crowd around the table to listen to his stories or see his models, some of which had electric motors to turn the props. He was keen to talk to anyone who was interested and loved to interact with aircraft enthusiasts. It was at Duxford that he was reunited with Hub Zemke and other pilots of the 56th Fighter Group, having not seen them since the war.

We would often attend the 'Friends of the Eighth' meetings in Bury St Edmunds, which is where he first met Roger Freeman, who introduced himself with a remarkable story that I would like to tell, as it shows the influence my father had on people. Roger, as a young boy, lived by Boxted airfield and in the early mornings when the Thunderbolts would warm up their engines, Roger would cycle down to the end of the runway where the 'Jugs' started their take-off run. He would sit on the fence watching them roar off into the sunrise, and there was one he would always wait for. This Thunderbolt had a distinct red and white emblem on the front and he would madly wave at the pilot, who would always return the gesture. My father remembered the boy sitting on the fence and it was a warm reunion of pilot and watching fan after all those years and I recall it brought a tear to my father's eyes!

My father would often champion a cause he believed in; with his fighting spirit he would inspire others in their endeavours to do the same, urging them never to be afraid to take on the big guns to get satisfaction. This has always been my philosophy, ingrained in me by him, and I have often applied this in my life.

His legacy lives on. I am truly overwhelmed with the number of people worldwide who are fascinated by his story, his very distinct personal insignia and his Thunderbolt, even down to arguments and varied opinions on many aircraft enthusiast forums on the colour of the mark 'M' Thunderbolts. There have been radio-controlled flying models of his Thunderbolt made and, as I write this, I am in contact with two aero modellers who built a RC flying Thunderbolt, taking part in a national competition in America, and this beauty has a 9-foot wingspan! Truly amazing!

There is no denying that he was a rebel through and through, always fronting injustice or what he believed to be erroneous, which got him into trouble on many an occasion – but he would always stick to his guns. A born fighter, he would often prove people wrong with the strength of his resolve and his spirit. For example, following the collapse of vertebrae in his spine and a bone-replacing operation due to cancer, he was told that he would never walk again by the consultants at the London hospital he was in. But after going home, within seven months he was in the back garden pushing a lawn mower around!

Life around this man was never boring, or without a controversy or two; I never knew what was coming next by phone or post or turning up on the doorstep.

So, this book is our family's way of sharing with you some of the stories and experiences of the greatest influence in my life, my father the Polish fighter pilot.

What he and every other brave Allied pilots did during that awful time in history, was so that we don't have to. I have the greatest admiration and respect for them all. I hope you enjoy this book and the story within as much as we as a family have. The fact that you are reading it helps to keep my father's memory and legacy very much alive.

Krys Lanowski

Chapter 1

Poland

Lwow, where I was born in 1915, was situated in south-east Poland and occupied as part of the Austro-Hungarian Empire (now annexed as part of Russia). The remainder of Poland was controlled by Russia in the east, and Germany in the west. During those times in the First World War, Lwow was constantly the centre of military activity and frequently came under siege. On the day I was born heavy guns could be heard in the distance outside the town. An interesting note about Lwow is that it was one of the cities in Poland that was very anti-establishment and was against the government leadership from Warsaw, which was effectively a military junta. Later in my military career when the Polish air force was undergoing a 'revolt' (their words) against the leadership, the main people involved originated from Lwow or the surrounding area.

By the time I was three years old the town was again under siege and fighting was taking place in the streets. Of all moments it appears I chose this particular time to leave home! I apparently prepared myself suitably, taking along my favourite toys and set off to go and live with my grandmother. As soon as my absence was discovered (the maids reduced to tears for their negligence) my mother ran frantically along the streets, dodging from door to door to evade stray bullets and snipers, as she searched the area. Later I was discovered safe and sound at my destination some distance away, having arrived completely unscathed and oblivious to any danger. It was an awful fright I'd given my mother and not the only one during this period. I had quite a determined nature – described as sheer devilry – at this early age, obviously having already acquired my mother's love of freedom of thought and action that she sought to instil in her children (myself and later my younger sister). This particular little escapade of mine prompted my father to send my mother and me to the safety of the mountains in Zakopane (where the peaks reach 10,000 feet), and there we lodged in the home of a peasant family named Btachut, of the Goral (mountain people), who were exceedingly kind and hospitable to us.

My father – Leon Lach – was born in Poland of a reasonably well-off peasant family. He had possessed an exceptionally clever mind, self-educated until he finally entered Krakow University (one of the most famous in the centre of Europe, dating back to 1365). He finished his studies as a Doctor of Law. I recall from my early days that he spoke at least five different languages fluently and was in the process of learning others; it was his particular hobby and one he could master with ease. He began his business career as an accountant in one of the largest banks in Lwow. When we moved to Zakopane he gained a transfer to the Krakow branch. But within a short period he was offered a directorship at the Zakopane office and consequently we were able to move into our own home. Having such a brilliant mind he very quickly established himself and soon held several directorships in various other sizeable companies.

My mother, Elizabeth Gerlich, was born in Breslau, Germany (following the Second World War it was annexed as part of Polish territory and renamed Wroclaw). She came from an upper-class German family and was one of twelve children. An engineering designer in his day, her father had been commissioned to design and build powered flour mills. (I recently learned that the name of Gerlich for his architecture and buildings is still remembered in Hamburg today.) Her upbringing had been strictly controlled. So much so, that it had only succeeded in making a rebel of her. When she married my father (an action not considered acceptable to her family) she determined that her own children would be guided and encouraged to develop their own spirit and willpower, an experience denied to her. She kept to her resolve, which was to prove a source of inspiration to me as I grew up. Even so, she was extremely firm and strict with me, particularly as a boy more so than towards my younger sister. As a result of a misdemeanour my punishment would always come swiftly and with the desired effect (an action I did not appreciate at the time but later realised how beneficial it proved to be). Her greatest desire for both her children was that we should travel the world (in this respect, for me at least, her dream became a reality), although it wasn't possible for her to be with me, in the West, to realise it.

Mother had a sensitive nature, was very creative and possessed a great love of the arts. Her softheartedness showed itself in extreme generosity towards her friends and especially to those less fortunate who found themselves in difficulty. She literally emptied the larder for any hungry beggar who called, and from one particular artist friend who, with his family, was on the point of starvation, she commissioned from him three portraits of our family simply to assist him over his critical period. I later discovered, when I met him by chance in 1938, that he had by that time attained fame as a distinguished portrait painter, which gave her immense gratification. Another attribute was that of a very determined woman who would not hesitate to fight for the rights of her children. This, and her own personal patriotism to Poland, was proved by endangering her own life and liberty on the outbreak of the Second World War for our own sake and that of our Polish birth. She converted to the Catholic faith upon her marriage and took Polish nationality. After her father's death, her mother and one sister also came to live in Poland, near Lwow, choosing to do so in preference to living under a regime whose attitude and policies they could not agree with. They were her only contacts with her own family as the remainder of the Gerlich family stayed in Germany and these we never saw or contacted.

Although she had adopted Catholicism, nevertheless she had very definite ideas about churchgoing and attitudes towards religion and life. She naturally imparted these notions to us (her children), but we were free to form our own conclusions, and she did not permit anyone else to thrust religious doctrine upon us in an effort to sway our beliefs. As a result of all this, in later life while serving in military service with the Polish Air Force, particularly during the Second World War in England, the Polish priests and I differed on many occasions concerning the duty of Polish airmen under wartime conditions. My mother considered ordinary daily tasks an important offering as a prayer. She was against compelling us to attend church every Sunday, and simply wouldn't agree with an attitude (quite common) of going in the expectation of being forgiven one's sins of the last six days. Not when there was obviously no special will to make a determined effort in the following six days. Neither would she be present simply for the sake of appearances.

We were encouraged to cultivate many friendships, including those of the opposite sex, while we were free and unattached. Once married there must be no diversions! It therefore horrified her that her own marriage failed and my father's 'attachments' caused her great distress and heartache.

She loved life and beauty and, being herself artistic, believed beauty could be found where one chose to seek it.

As a sincere and honest person she had no notion of politics or intrigue. They just didn't exist for her. What she did understand and wished to impress upon us was simply that people wouldn't always appreciate the truth when it was spoken. Therefore it would likely as not gain us more enemies than friends. But the important point was to continue on the right path, no matter what the temptation. One's enemies could then be faced without fear. We were important as human beings with our feelings and beliefs, and above all should be loyal and true and keep one's honour. During the many decisions throughout my life her words, which were imbedded in me, assisted in my attitude. In such cases I never doubted for one moment that I was right to continue with the task facing me – which was not always a happy one.

Whatever she had passed on to us was based on her own experiences and personal attitude to life. She was content to live by these basic principles and when the crisis came (Germany's attack upon Poland, an action that hurt her deeply) she was equally prepared to endure the suffering for them, whatever the outcome. Her courage and belief enabled her to survive a German labour camp during the Second World War.

She never wished us to have conflicting loyalties and for this reason her native tongue, German, was never spoken in the family, and we were not allowed or even encouraged to learn one word of it. We were Polish, and there was no question at all to whom our allegiance and honour lay – only to Poland.

This recalls a very similar situation during the 1950s after I had received British nationality (in 1949) and had joined the Royal Air Force the following year. At a later stage the British Intelligence authorities apparently became apprehensive in case pressure should be applied to me through my mother in Poland. What would my reactions be? There was no doubt in my mind whatsoever, but as though in answer to their (British) uncertainty, when she had heard from me of my new status and military position in this country she immediately wrote without hesitation or regard for her personal position, in complete understanding and acceptance that my loyalty and every endeavour now lay towards my adopted country. Accepted, too, without question, what this would mean – particularly at that time during the Stalin era – that we could not hope to be reunited in the foreseeable future.

....

We lived well in Zakopane and enjoyed our life among the Goral population, a most interesting and colourful people of the mountain region. It didn't take long before I acquired their most distinctive accent. It had a song-like quality, fascinating to listen to, but embarrassing to possess if you were actually from a town or city and returned there to live – as I did later on.

The Goral were blond, fair skinned and handsome, with a very happy and lively character and an enormous sense of humour, contagious to anyone in their company. They wore beautifully embroidered clothes of vivid hues, and their sleighs and horses were just as colourfully decorated.

The children learned to ski almost as soon as they could walk, with the result that the Goral were reputed skiers. The most well known among them were soon roped in to joining the Polish Army Ski Regiment formed and camped in the locality. In 1938 I was to train with the regiment for the winter sports activities. Skiing was, in fact, the easiest, cheapest and most convenient form of transport, especially for the children going to and from school. So naturally I was quickly initiated into the art and my love of skiing began to develop from this period.

Zakopane itself became the centre of the health resort, mainly for tuberculosis sufferers. Poets, artists, writers and musicians all flocked to Zakopane's mountain region to benefit from the pure air. The town was very soon considered to be the 'St Moritz' of Poland, famed for its winter sports and the amenities it offered.

In winter there was the normal skiing for all grades of skiers and the more difficult areas of the Alps for the experts. There was also the bob-sleigh run, high ski jump (where top ski jumpers from all over the world came to compete), the funicular and cable railways (the latter took you to the slalom and downhill runs), winter horse racing and skijoring, a hot-spring swimming pool that was open all the year round, ample hotel facilities, restaurants and the usual nightclubs. In summer one could enjoy mountaineering, horse racing and the Grand Prix Racing Car Mountaineering Run.

My mother particularly enjoyed watching the ski jumping, both while the competitors practised and competed. I recall seeing in those days the world champion Norwegian brothers Sigmund and Birger Rudd. The Polish ski jump champion was Stanislaw Marusarz. He was at least ten to fifteen years my senior but, even so, it was from this period that my friendship with him first began, and was to last many years, during which time I, too, became a winter sports competitor for Poland.

As a small boy, though, my interest was fixed firmly on the grand prix car racing and by the time I was sent back to Lwow (which was part of the grand prix mountain route) to continue my school studies my ambi-tion, though more of a dream, was already to become a famous racing driver myself! These men were all heroes in my eyes, without exception. The more daring and death defying they appeared, the greater the heroes they became for me.

Once the family became established in Zakopane my parents enter-tained a great deal. On my father's side, business associates and scholars, and on my mother's, friends who were artists and sportsmen – in the latter instance they included racing drivers! So it was more or less inevitable that eventually I would be taken around the course in one of these 'magnificent machines'. I had returned to Lwow by this time and was in my teens, my excitement at such an invitation was almost un-containable. I had taken to haunting the pits for days to watch the mechanics at work on the cars. The maintenance to keep them in per-fect condition was more a family affair, unlike what one would expect to find. Besides the mechanics, there were the drivers plus their girlfriends or wives. Everyone gave a helping hand and it was the women's job to apply the spit and polish and elbow grease until the cars were shining immac-ulately. It might also have been a music festival for the amount of singing and gaiety that surrounded these occasions while the polishing was done. The tramlines in Lwow were sealed with tar for the grand prix. For four or more days beforehand they made practice circuits very early in the morning between 5 and 6.30 a.m. It was impossible to sleep during this period of noise and excitement. In any case, invariably everyone was out and about to watch the cars roar past through the town. They were Bugatis, Alfa Romeos, Mercedes Benz and the many names of the world-famous drivers I have long since forgotten. But not, for instance, Hans Stuck and Rudolf Caracciola, who were then the top racing drivers in the world. Stuck was the German champion and Caracciola, I believe, began racing with the Italians and later transferred to the German team.

I have never lost this boyhood dream and desire to be a racing driver, so consequently it became an unfulfilled ambition that has remained with me.

I have also never forgotten the smell of the castor oil they used, and the memories it can evoke. For it so happened that when I first started to fly in 1935, at Luck Flying School, the very same oil was used on the First World War engines we were flying. It was the only oil that could be used on these engines. The reason was that the piston remained station-ary and the cylinders rotated. The mixture (petrol, air and oil) needed to enter through the centre of the engine and only castor oil did not dissolve by the chemical action of petrol.

My sister was born in Zakopane and as children we were brought up in the atmosphere of famous people who were constant visitors to our home – mostly writers, artists, travellers and sportsmen. We were urged to circulate among the guests and listen to the various topics of con-versation. During these early years I was encouraged to acquire a sense of adventure and subsequently was sent to fetch special white sheep cheese from the Valley of Five Lakes high up in the Tatra mountains. The top resembled a plateau that could only be reached by vertical steps of steel rings jutting out from the rocks, making the journey very danger-ous, especially to a young boy! It took me all day to journey there and back and I looked upon it as a challenge. I might also spend the whole day travelling to the top of the mountains with a coach driver. Providing my mother was assured I had been given food, she did not worry about these excursions of mine!

As my sister grew up it became obvious that she had inherited my father's abilities and fine brain. Unlike myself, she suffered no difficulty at all with her lessons or to stay at the top of the class. She was forever absorbed in some book or other improving her studies, whereas school and learning were just sheer hard work for me. Unless I found a particular interest in a subject – such as drawing, at which I held my own in the entire two years I spent at high school – I let the rest go very much by the board. I was, in fact, extremely and unashamedly lazy! Consequently my teachers were convinced I was a complete dunderhead. However, one particular professor made the grave mistake of expressing this opinion in a letter to my mother. Never was a teacher more surprised than when she turned up next day to demand an explanation. She didn't doubt for one instant that I was lazy, but it was an impossibility that I was stupid! To prove it I was hauled out before the blackboard to unravel the mysteries of a set of problems. Although I hated maths above all else, I was greatly inspired by her imperious attitude, and in dire fear of the consequences I came up with the correct answers in record time – to the amusement of my class colleagues and the astonishment of the learned professor. He was then warned against indulging in any further fancies of my 'supposed' stupidity, which would cost him his post as this she would see to personally through the school governors. He didn't doubt this for one moment and neither did I! From then on I was 'coached' up to my ears, however much I loathed it or tried to escape my lessons.

It was soon after that our life as we knew it collapsed. My father's work occupied much of his time, but what personal life he had he would devote very little of it to the family. My parents' marriage was the exact opposite of everything my mother believed in, which caused her dreadful distress. As children we grew up with this knowledge and in the disagreeable atmosphere of constant arguments. Eventually, my father involved himself and my mother's business in financial ruin, which came as a complete shock to her. At this time I had just entered high school and soon began to suffer a great deal of unpleasantness as a result of our devastating position. My mother thereupon sent me back to my home town,

Lwow, to enable me to continue my schooling in comparative peace. I lived there with relatives until she, my father and sister finally came to join me.

For a time we tried to resume our life together as a family, but it was impossible without the full co-operation and interest of my father towards this end. The distress and torment my mother was subjected to by his attitude and behaviour, together with the constant arguments, had long since killed my feelings or respect for him. It was inevitable, therefore, that finally he and I would face each other and one of us would have to leave. I was sixteen when this moment came. As a travelling salesman – which he had now become – it had been his habit to spend days or even weeks away from home. While he was absent, although we had very little, the atmosphere in the home was happy and calm. His return (which my mother looked forward to out of the love she bore him) would quickly erupt into fits of temper once he began to feel the responsibilities of home life. With the knowledge of his true financial position – and while we frequently wondered where the next meal was coming from – it seemed obvious to me at least, there would be very little difference with him as without him. As I knew he would, he used the opportunity of a 'showdown' with me as a reason for leaving her, but there were no blows exchanged between us. Had there been I would have undoubtedly lost. Yet I was angrier than I had ever felt in my life! The saddest aspect was the realisation for my mother that not only was he content to be the one to go, but had been planning to do so.

Inevitably the three of us had to adjust to a new life, and it was one of poverty that lasted until after I had left high school at the age of nineteen. Until our position finally began to improve this was a sorrow I carried, knowing I was unable to change the circumstances under which we lived. Meantime, as we had no visible means of support, we had to rely on the generosity and kindness of relatives and friends. This in itself was a very precarious state of affairs, inasmuch as we could not expect others to keep us. Fortunately my sister was provided daily meals at the home of her school friend. I went along to the local poor kitchen to eat there. It was a very unpleasant experience. Most of these poor people were adults, beggars or elderly folk. I was the only young boy among them and I hated going. But if I didn't I went hungry.

Immaterial to our own impoverished conditions, nevertheless my mother kept us spotlessly clean and tidy. We had very few clothes, unless we were occasionally given a garment. These were meticulously cared for and repaired by my mother to keep them looking in good condition – such as my one, and only, shirt, which was washed and pressed daily without fail ready for the next morning. My father's departure had naturally greatly hurt my mother, but we found that peace had finally descended into our everyday lives and we were able to experience happiness together, however simply. All thoughts of my intention to become an architect had now diminished. Fulfilling my responsibility towards supporting my mother and sister excluded any hope of a career that entailed the necessary years of study plus the finances this would involve. At such a time, in such a circumstance, it was impossible to plan a future until I completed high school.

When I was thirteen or fourteen (just prior to this major upheaval) I had started to take an active interest in various sports. The friends I had were members of one or more of Lwow's four sports clubs. I spent a great deal of time in their company, particularly with those who were the team swimmers. And it was at this period that I learned to swim.

Just outside the town was a lake and part of it converted to a lido for the public and swimming clubs who also used it for competitive events. The swimming team members of all four clubs created a very friendly atmosphere. Each club was distinguished by a different colour costume and 'linen' swimming cap. Once I had had my 'ducking' they took me under their wing completely and my swimming training began in earnest. I wasn't 'allowed' to swim at all unless under the instruction or direction of one or another of them. Not even for pleasure! It was out of the question to play around! When they trained I trained (even though I wasn't a member) and when they relaxed, my swimming was still supervised, but all to very good effect. This training cost me nothing, and continued for several years. By the time I was sixteen I had become a club member. Every available moment I spent at the lido, including at weekends and immediately after school hours, which was very early afternoon. It kept me occupied with an active interest, especially from the time my father left us.

I put in a good deal of training, and once I had joined the club and become a team member I began competing against older and more experienced swimmers. The hard work and determination paid off by the success it gave.

As a club member one could participate in various sports such as water polo, ice hockey, skiing, and swimming of course. While still a junior I became the captain of the Senior Water Polo Team. I also concentrated on improving my skiing. I did this during the winter months in the surrounding hills of Lwow, making myself practise cross-country running (skiing) with the ultimate ambition of competing in this field also. My mother wasn't too happy about this last choice in ski sports. She would have preferred something less exhausting and it particularly horrified her to witness my condition after a long period of ski running – not a pleasant sight or experience to undergo. This was caused by the initial period during which cramp would tie in knots every muscle you possessed until the body could finally take the pressure demanded.

Within two years I had become the District Junior Ski Champion. As a member of the club ski team I also competed against senior sportsmen until finally I represented Lwow against the opposing team and town of Mukachevo in Czechoslovakia (now annexed by Russia, as was my own town, Lwow). Again I had worked hard to achieve this position during which time I had transferred to one specific club who were willing to supply me with the necessary equipment for ski training and practice (I was already in their swimming team and their water polo captain). This assisted me greatly in attaining the position of District Champion.

Besides a new swimming pool that had been built in Lwow – with a massive sheet window that was lowered in summer for open-air use and closed in winter and the pool heated, enabling it to be utilised all year round – a new ski jump had been erected for the town. It was now possible to jump 50 metres – 160 feet. This my mother would have much preferred I had taken up rather than cross-country skiing. Since our days in Zakopane she had taken a delight in watching the jumpers 'fly like a bird'. I have previously mentioned that from early days I had been friends with Marusarz (our Polish ski champion), and another such friend was Motyka, who was our famous long-distance ski runner. Their interest was an enormous help to my skiing, and I learned a great deal from them on how to control and govern my own ski training. This was to become important to me later on in the Olympic ski camp.

But for the time being I was being pressed to try ski jumping, particularly by my mother. It wasn't difficult to learn the basic rudiments of jumping, especially from my friends, the experts! Yet the thought of doing it terrified me, though I didn't care to admit it. I kept the intention of making the initial jump (goaded on by these experts) from my mother hoping to surprise her once I had made it – without mishap! On the morning of the attempt she presented me with a beautifully made new white ski suit that she had secretly been working on. Later she turned up at the ski jump, which was too much of a coincidence!

I was terrified and it was all too obvious to everyone. A combination of fear and overwhelming excitement reached a climax once I had climbed to the top of the ski jump. I had borrowed a special pair of broad skis and had even begun to feel quite professional until I got there. I was horrified to see how small and distant everything was, and how misleading when others jumping made it look so simple and perfect.

I stood there petrified, unable to move for well over twenty minutes, convinced every ounce of courage had deserted me. My heart thudded painfully, but I forced myself to remember all I had been told to hold a good flight position. There were spectators there to watch the ski jumping practice! At last I found the courage to move. After gathering speed down the slope their faces became just a blur – then I was flying in the air with the valley 200 or 300 feet below me. I was conscious of feeling utterly alone and dependent upon myself, such as I had never experienced before. Other than the wind whistling past my ears I was impressed by the silence and its suddenness once I had become airborne. Then the snow-white run seemingly rose to meet me and I became again conscious of faces – the broad skis touched down and I held on to complete the run in good style, without falling! The excitement and exhilaration I was experiencing left me almost without breath, and I felt great satisfaction and triumph at having conquered the fear. My mother was delighted I had made it, though admitted she had been clenching her hands, willing me to jump while I had stood 'rooted' at the top. My friends, of course, were all thoroughly enjoying the joke – all in good humour.

The following day was a competition and I intended to participate, so I now practised along with the others. As a result my companions were soon having to drag me away from the jump – as I went down again and again – for my own 'safety'! But next day I took part with them in the competition. I certainly couldn't hope to come anywhere but last in line for distance, but at least I managed not to fall and thoroughly enjoyed this new experience.

As it is important to begin jumping very young and also takes precedence over other forms of skiing, this was one recreation I could only enjoy as a relaxation from my other sports. But the feeling of flying was incomparable with anything I had known before, with the combination of speed, take-off and flight – freedom of spirit, mastery of one's fate and solitude were words inadequate to the actual experience. Yet if I had to pinpoint a specific time that initiated my love of flying – this, undoubtedly, was it.

My club manager of the ski section later enticed me (with four older club members) to undergo a special course to qualify as an umpire in ski sports, including ski jumping. When I qualified I became the youngest judge of ski competitions in Poland.

With regard to school sports competitions I had also taken up rifle shooting and represented my school in the championships. By this time I had concentrated a great deal of my time on sports rather than my studies. Which, being a very lazy student, was exactly as I preferred it to be, books and learning taking very much second place in my activities.

Surprisingly, my family began to realise that my rise in sports greatly assisted our financial and social position – which had deteriorated so drastically. We were now even able to feel less of a burden to those who supported us. Assistance came in the form of help towards my expenses as a club member or town sports representative, and through the club manager who found me a remunerative temporary post during the vacations, either teaching skiing in winter to holiday tourists or as a sports organiser in summer in a boys' reform school. The ages of the boys there ranged from thirteen to sixteen years old and some were not that much younger than myself. It wasn't long before they realised that my success as an amateur sportsman was due solely to my own hard work and determination, and as sports were particularly popular such achievements gained their respect – and co-operation!

Socially my rise in popularity was also a good thing for us as a family, more for my mother and sister perhaps than for me. I preferred spending my time with my sports friends, who made no such distinctions providing you trained well and worked hard. My mother now found she was receiving attention and invitations again and carefully chose her friends from among them. This was a little difficult for her as her nature was generous to the extreme and she bore no grudge or ill-feeling towards anyone, and therefore failed to understand completely their contempt for poverty that had hurt her so deeply.

The rules of my high school barred one from competing privately or belonging to any sports club. Consequently I did as others had done and adopted a pseudonym. I used the name Lech – a minor transformation from my own name of Lach (later to be changed to Lanowski) – which hardly deceived the school authorities. They simply closed their eyes and pretended not to recognise me!

I was suddenly forced to apply myself in earnest to my lessons and studies, having failed my matriculation examinations. I was able to sit them a second time in the autumn. This time I passed, after a great deal of coaching plus a little 'fiddling' on the part of one of the teachers on my behalf. The daughters of the family had pleaded for me that I should not be allowed to fail a second time and so the miracle was accomplished! My future had now to be seriously considered. As previously mentioned, I had wanted to be an architect. This was no whim, but a profession of the family on my mother's side.

At school I was given the opportunity to design the tableau for the matriculation ceremony. The background denoted futuristic (that is, present-day) building, which produced astonishment, and a sprinkling of displeasure, from the school authorities but was accepted none the less.

To qualify as an architect meant five years at college, and without financial support it was out of the question. We were determined not to beg from the family relatives. The art professor at school had tried to assist. He had invited the town's opera house designer to see my work, as I had been in charge of the school theatre (worthy of note as much money and thought had been given to its upkeep). I had undertaken all the designing and painting of the backdrops – scenics and props etc, plus all the lighting. The visiting designer set me to work on a mural and side wings for his examination and inspection. He was immensely pleased with the resulting work and without hesitation offered me the post as his assistant at the opera house in Lwow. All might have been well had I any inclinations at all towards music and the arts in the theatre world. The truth was I hadn't. I had occupied myself with the school theatre simply as an extension to my art classes. The thought of being 'caged up' in that massive opera house whose activities I found most boring anyway had no appeal to me and I despaired at having to contemplate accepting the job. I was given time to think it over. But, perhaps, fate now took a hand.

I was much more inclined towards an active outdoor life. Yet it was impossible to expect a sports career to offer an adequate remuneration to support us. By this time I was already in the position and sufficiently competent, in my own sphere, to follow such a career and attain without difficulty the necessary backing. But as it was not a professional life, one could so easily become a pawn to a sporting club. I couldn't imagine myself accepting such a life. So, with the decision of my future to make I found myself with time on my hands during the recess period, and acutely aware it was necessary for my mother to have to feed me during the holidays.

Once again the organiser of the sports club came to our rescue. He arranged for me to attend a six-week course at the state-owned gliding school run by internationally famous Polish glider pilots. I'd never been interested in anything to do with flying or aircraft before, as some of my friends were, so this holiday came rather as a surprise. Though hardly in my line, if nothing else it would ease the situation at home and I was always willing to learn a new 'sporting' activity!

Chapter 2

First flight

Due to the lateness of the application I was a week late in arriving at the school, by which time those ahead of me had already been fully instructed concerning the flight itself. Without much ceremony and a few helpful tips I found myself in the cockpit of a glider waiting to be catapulted forward. I wasn't in the least convinced I knew how to control the thing, but I took comfort in the fact that I was only expected to skim the ground on this first flight so I couldn't come to much harm! The aircraft was clipped to the ground at the tail and with a student standing by to release it at the word 'Go!', An elastic rope was stretched on either side by three trainees under the direction of the instructor. The pull on the rope determined whether the plane became airborne or just grazed the surface. At the given signal to release the glider I found to my horror I was suddenly airborne, a deliberate intention of my colleagues by giving a final last 'extra' pull. As the craft soared upwards my first reaction was to push on the stick – more in alarm than for any real purpose. I immediately found myself heading nose first towards the ground! Self-preservation made me pull the stick back and up she went again. While I was suffering every conceivable feeling of fright my delighted companions were cheering madly down below. After some desperate moments that seemed to last ages my fear began to subside sufficiently to allow me to get the feel of the movement. Quite suddenly I had started to enjoy myself and I had also become aware of the silence, which had a calming effect exactly as I had experienced before on the ski jump. It completely drained the fear from me. By sheer instinct – rather than instruction – I gently eased the glider down until she slid along the ground and stopped.

All in all I had given a pretty good performance of a kangaroo! But the episode had already taught me quite a bit. On each consecutive flight my interest in this new sport grew. By the end of the course one felt a sense of achievement; flying had begun to intrigue me, as any new activity that offered a challenge did. I therefore treated it in a competitive manner, with a will to succeed, just as I applied to any other sports contest. With the result that by the end of this fascinating unusual holiday I had finished the course as the number one student, which satisfied my competitive spirit!

I didn't exactly consider this to be the end of my flying activities. In fact, I had become quite determined to follow it up if I could find a way to do so. After returning home I found it impossible to forget the experience of gliding even more than anything I'd taken up previously; it engrossed my thoughts. Without any doubt in my mind I knew what I wanted to do. I had to fly – to become a pilot. But for a brief time I had no idea how to achieve this ambition.

This introduction to flying was the beginning of a career that was drastically to change my life from the course I had once assumed it would take. Particularly as I had never before even considered the thought of entering any kind of military service. Nor was there (to my knowledge) any regular family military tradition to induce, or perhaps compel, me to follow in their footsteps. But as from this period on my whole career and life was to be that of a regular soldier, primarily in the service of my country.

By some means (which I fail to recall) I learned of the opportunity to undergo a two-month flying course at a civilian flying school – the Air Flying Corps. It was most opportune in as much as it enabled me to fulfil my hopes of becoming a pilot without incurring any financial expenses providing, of course, I passed the necessary tests. These took the form of two medicals. One taken at Lwow – which served as a selection basis – was necessary to satisfy seven different specialists that there was absolutely nothing wrong with you physically. These medicals were so exacting that the percentage of successful candidates was just 10–20% from 200 applicants. The 20 then underwent the second medical at the military Central Medical Board (CMB) at Warsaw. Infinitely much stiffer to ensure not only that you were physically fit, but fit to fly, something quite different.

In a severe state of agitation I made myself sick worrying if I would be passed by the doctors. But I was. I owed a great deal to my sports activities for my excellent fitness. I was in no way sure or specifically aware of the opportunities flying could offer at that time. For the moment I was concerned first upon becoming a pilot and with this ambition I entered Luck Flying School.

Luck Flying School was run by military instructors, NCOs who thought they were super human beings and were determined to convince all of us of that fact. The aim was to induce the pilots to apply for entry to the Polish Air Force (PAF), although the final choice was yours whether you became a civilian or military pilot in the future. Apparently possessing the matriculation you could apply to Deblin Air Force Cadet College (equivalent to RAF Cranwell) to become a regular commissioned PAF officer and pilot. It was not necessary to be a pilot first before one applied, providing one had the necessary academic qualifications. Without these qualifications on the other hand, one could go through the ranks and become an NCO pilot, for which purpose there was a training school. We had not been at Luck long before we heard all kinds of hair-raising stories of what could happen to us in the air. On my first flight with the instructor, without warning he put her nose down in a vertical dive and we tore towards earth. Paralysed I watched the ground rushing to meet us, imagining I could already see the hole we were bound to make within seconds. But just as suddenly we were soaring up again – my insides still completing the dive. Sheer bravado wasn't enough for these types, they even picked out a particular spot and asked you to look down and state what you could see. Innocently you reported a church and a ceme- tery! 'Exactly, and that's where you'll finish up unless you really can fly!' would be the retort.

The aircraft were Henriots and Bartels; the former French and the latter Polish. The Bartel had rotating cylinders and ran on castor oil that coated the wings and fuselage after the day's flights. Love of flying was proved by having to scrape it off with special soap (and the surrep- titious use of paraffin – a very expensive method as we were informed when caught at it.) The smell of the castor oil recalled my earlier dream of becoming a racing driver for its sheer speed and excitement.

The first solo was the greatest moment during one's course. I was one of the first to go solo but had to convince myself I could land the plane before achieving any satisfaction. And even then successive flights could prove whether or not it had been a fluke. Then back with the instructors for cross-country flights, navigation, aerobatics (whatever the aircraft would stand) and forced landings – without engine etc – before you made the grade.

Officially there was no rivalry between us but it was inevitable we would compete against each other. One student was Stanislaw Skalski from Dubno (who years later was to become the Polish Air Force ace of the Battle of Britain). That same year Skalski and I were to join the Polish Air Force and enter Deblin Officer Cadet College together. As for the instructors at Luck we soon had them weighed up and considered some of them more cowardly than we were. One of them was so terrified of the sea he wouldn't even fly near it! At the end of the course came the presentation of your certificate qualifying you as a pilot. You would also be informed of your grading and I found I had finished the course as 1st Pilot.

Luck was one of two Air Corps (preparatory) Flying Schools set up in the early 1930s to initiate further interest in military flying and to acquire potential aircrew for the air force. Having once qualified and obtained a pilot's licence, those who chose not to enter the air force to become military pilots were automatically handed to one's local flying club. It became their responsibility to ensure the pilot was given the opportunity to keep up his flying by allotting him his quota of (free) flying practice hours, approximately two hours per month (thirty minutes for each flight), which was quite reasonable in the circumstances for the nominal number of civilian aircraft available (by no means modern aeroplanes).

In those days flying and everything connected with it was considered to be something super and it carried its own prestige value for those who flew. It also wasn't necessary to possess technical knowledge before being able to qualify as a pilot. What was normally an expensive sport or hobby, the Air Corps Flying Schools had made it possible for the average youth with any inclination to fly to be able to become a pilot, a) providing he could pass the stiff medical test in Warsaw; and b) without incurring any personal expense. Depending upon one's attitude to flying – whether taken seriously or not – the problems for the young aspiring aviator began after gaining his pilot's licence.

Until civil aviation expanded and developed, any hopes of a career in this direction was virtually impossible. Flying, as a profession, could only be achieved by entering the air force. This was providing there were openings for aircrew and one was acceptable to the standards required for these vacancies.

The course at Deblin Officer Cadet College took three years; upon graduation one became a regular commissioned officer. The course itself entailed no personal financial expense (a condition favourable to my situation, which I had to take into account). Once commissioned and in a squadron the rates of pay (including flying pay for aircrew) were excellent in comparison to any normal civilian career. Even after qualifying as an architect, for instance, I could not hope to earn as much for quite some time.

As a second lieutenant (pilot) in 1938/39 I received 440 zloty per month. After paying 80 zloty per month for a large modern flat in Krakow for my mother, sister and myself, and approximately 90 zloty for adequate food expenses (sometimes I ate at the mess), sufficient was left over for whatever else we required. An office clerk, with matriculation certificate, earned only about 110 zloty per month, so our rate of pay was on a level with an executive salary. An NCO pilot's rate of pay (including flying pay) for that of a corporal totalled that of an army second lieutenant. NCO pilots could afford matching cloth for their uniform and pay the same tailor that we (the officers) had. The only difference was the style as the cut and the finish were identical. Nine times out of ten they put the average officer's uniform to shame by their smart appearance.

On leaving Luck it was a matter of deciding whether or not I should enter into military service (a lifetime career), which previously I'd never considered. But within a couple of weeks I'd made my decision based on the situation facing me at that time.

The first thing I'd done on arriving home was to present myself as a fully licensed pilot to the head of the local aero club at Lwow, a captain (a military officer), to make arrangements for obtaining my free flights.

He assured me he'd do his best to ensure I would be able to fly.

The number of aero clubs prominent throughout Poland, although classified as civilian, chiefly owed their existence to military sponsorship, for – as I have indicated – the field of civil aviation and equipment was negligible. Most of these clubs were situated on military airfields whose production of pilots could be called upon as reserves for the air force. The membership invariably consisted of professional people, young men from wealthy backgrounds, and university students. A select group who experienced little, if any, difficulty to pursue or maintain their flying. Unhappily not so for those less fortunate, either socially or financially, who were equally entitled to flying practice having once qualified as pilots through one of the two ACF Schools. I met a couple of friends from Luck who experienced the difficulty just as I was doing. I walked miles to the aerodrome in the hope of being allowed to fly, and with only one or two exceptions encountered one disappointment after another at the constant excuses for there not being an aircraft available for me. The real reason was blatantly obvious – my qualifications as a pilot came low on their list in comparison to the social standing of their other members. You couldn't win against this kind of attitude. As a sportsman I had already learned – even by this time – to accept such blows. They merely served to strengthen my resolve. I had become obsessed with flying and during my training had realised flying came quite naturally to me. What had begun as only a challenging new sport had developed into something quite different. Instinct told me there was a thousand and one things flying could teach if I could only break through the barrier. Having once become a pilot I was determined to remain one. In civilian life in my present circumstances this was going to prove a practical impossibility.

Everything was pointing me towards a career as a military pilot, both to achieve my ambition and, at the same time, being the quickest and most substantial way to provide for my mother and sister.

Chapter 3

Deblin

As I have already explained, the exceptionally high medical standard was always the basic elimination of applicants, due to the requirements it demanded. Those of us who qualified and entered Deblin all held the aspiration to become fighter pilots. But not all were to have their goal realised, and for a specific reason. Apart from the elimination by the CAAB/CMB for any form of flying, either military or civilian, this also largely accounted for why the number of vacancies available for 1935 at Deblin Cadet College was not filled.

In 1933 Deblin was opened, for the first time since 1926, to accept approximately twenty trainees. The following year forty vacancies were made available. By 1935 they wanted to double this amount but there was 'some doubt' concerning the actual number of fighter pilots required. As a result of this hesitancy insufficient advertising was given and there was an inadequate number of applicants from which to choose. It wasn't long before we discovered that in the opinion of some military commanders the emphasis should be on bomber aircraft; therefore bomber pilots and particularly navigators were considered as a priority. So following our entry to Deblin they rushed through a further quota of approximately thirty, totalling eighty candidates in all.

At the end of the first year – the pilots by that time having completed the initial flying period – the authorities decided to select on flying ability and transferred about thirty-five to the role of navigator. The selection proved immensely difficult after the initial 20 per cent; that is, those who would not have made good pilots anyway. The balance was so equal that they decided upon a ruthless method based on petty discipline even

of the most insignificant nature. For instance, a friend of mine with a
half university diploma in forestry was a very good chess player (his name
incidentally was Sawicki) and enjoyed playing chess by memory. We were
in the midst of pre-briefing on the airfield just before the flying exercise. Ostrowski, our CO (who we later nicknamed Spy), was giving the
briefing. He suddenly noticed that he hadn't got Sawicki's attention
and promptly asked him to repeat what he had just said. Considering
the answer unsatisfactory Ostrowski informed him that this was the
end of his flying career. Sawicki was sent off to become a navigator.

By graduation of our year (1938) five of our number were to gradu-
ate as bomber pilots – but not necessarily by personal choice. As I have
said, it was everyone's aim to be a fighter pilot.

Two men came very near to expulsion and only escaped it by the intervention of the sports officer and the physician, Dr Letoft; the latter
liked us all very much! Both objected strongly and the balance was
weighed against the expulsion of the two culprits Skalski and Witold
Lokuciewski. The war proved their belief in these two as both turned out
to be exceptional pilots of the Second World War. Following the conflict
they both returned to Poland. After eight years of imprisonment under
the Stalin regime, Skalski in the Polish Air Force connected with the
Historical Department. Lokuciewski, also in the Polish Air Force, was
in charge of pilots' training. Both of colonel rank, they have visited Britain
again after many years, as official guests of the Royal Air Force.

There was another reason for these conversions, to enable the air force
to expand and develop (and presumably economise on the measure
meantime); the need for officers could be accommodated by drawing
upon the supply of surplus from the army and cavalry, who could well
afford it.

Unlike some other air forces (such as the RAF) the Polish Air Force
was under control and command of the army (for that matter right up
until the time we reached England and subsequently came under command of the British Air Ministry). Therefore, the army military authorities had the 'last word' concerning air force development; financial budget
covering all its requirements etc; and the nomination and dismissal of our
commander-in-chief. Army regulations were applicable to air force and,
as it can be imagined, were frequently out of keeping with the structure,

requirements and character of the air force and its personnel. And just as frustrating were the more personal regulations such as being unable to marry below the rank of captain. Whereas a young army or cavalry officer (second lieutenant) could not hope to support a wife and/or his family on his pay, his opposite number, an air force pilot of the same rank, could do so, by virtue of his additional flying pay. To some degree the rules, at a later date, were revised and I, for instance, was able to live off camp in a flat and support my mother and sister.

Both army and air force wore khaki uniforms, but to distinguish between the two, as air crew we wore light orange epaulettes and an orange band encircling our hats.

Deblin College also included a separate 'year' for the PAF Reserve, for members to train to become pilots.

Entering service as a regular, one became a military man for 100 per cent of one's life and not just on the basis of a contract for a specific period. You dedicated your entire life to your country. As the services had always been the guardians of Polish freedom, these terms were accepted automatically, and consequently the services were highly regarded by the public.

By the time I entered Deblin in 1935, the air force had already superseded the cavalry from its number one position in the public eye, something it had retained since the Middle Ages. Former achievements in international air contests had done a great deal to enhance the status of the air force. But the successful approach to air mindedness in a true military sense had been inspired by the endeavours of its present C-in-C General Rayski, who over the last years had worked diligently and with determination to expand and develop the air force and its aircraft industry (in the face of opposition from his superiors in the military high command). The result was that aircrew personnel enjoyed a particular place in the affections of the public and were treated as young gods (a position one either enjoyed or found embarrassing). In other words, the air force was undoubtedly the up and coming military body and the deterrent needed to maintain and secure Poland's freedom and safety; the onus to defend the country resided with the air force, and particularly on its aircrew. This knowledge one quickly realised soon after entering the service and training. Consequently one's mind was centred upon the time of getting posted to a fighter squadron to take up one's position; this was the ultimate aim.

For the first six months the rules demanded basic training at the army cadet school (most other military corps from all over Poland underwent this training, with the exception of the medical corps, engineers and the navy). Discipline was strictly controlled and proved one's personal abilities to oneself as well as to the military commanders. The six-month course ended with an experimental army regiment test, which nearly finished us all, including the horses. The aim was to discover exactly how much the human body could stand. Middle-aged and young alike had to take part – experienced soldiers and new recruits. Food for the test was based on army rations and rigidly watched; no other food was allowed.

We marched approximately 20 miles a day with full military battle equipment. Practically every day ended with a most realistic mock battle. Officers from colonel to company commander rode on horseback. Many of the horses died on the trek from the heat. Every time this happened a detailed report had to be made explaining why. Not long after these reports began the mileage per day was reduced and we breathed a sigh of relief. However, it proved to us that the horses were considered more important than the men!

In the final stage of the experiment the fullest show attack was performed near Warsaw. All possible equipment was used, including live ammunition from rifles, heavy machine guns and light artillery. Having thrown everything into this final test it was a remarkable achievement that there were no serious casualties. Every foreign military attaché present in Warsaw was invited to attend this finale and they came in full military uniform riding on horseback. (I particularly remember the Japanese attaché, my first experience of someone from the East, finding him most interesting and unusual!)

The experimental test proved immensely valuable for the military authorities, demonstrating what could be achieved and expected, especially in an emergency.

Before the end of the course the army commanding officers tried persuading me to change my mind about flying and instead stay at the college. What a comparison!

Deblin military college consisted of a main U-shaped building, with a severe-looking but immaculately clean entranceway, and a large dining hall situated at the back and centre of the U. Immediately above this hall were the 'silence' room for study and a PT hall. Three consecutive years of cadets occupied the main building, including our intake. The officers had their own separate mess and a small basement club nicknamed 'Piedelko' (Little Hell). Third-year cadets received their preparation for future social life in this den of iniquity! There was also an NCO and airmen's mess. A mile and a half away a separate building for the use of the college for lectures only, contained facilities for the air force primary subjects.

Cadets of the various years – first, second and third – were distinguished by the length of their hair. Or complete lack of it! First-year cadets had their hair completely shaved; in the second year they were permitted one inch of growth; in the third year one and a quarter inches. This system was also used as a psychological deterrent for bad behaviour, and the best form of punishment for second- and third-year cadets – for any misdemeanour one's hair would be shaved.

We continued our army training for the first year. Although only cadets, we could hold a rank equivalent to the army personnel and receive the same monetary allowance. We were also entitled to fifth-grade flying pay held over throughout the entire three years and payable on promotion, with some deductions. This enabled us to furnish and equip ourselves for our future career as air force officers. To compensate for the nominal financial arrangement received during training, a few of us took to photography and turned out some astonishing photographs – one scene or subject superimposed on another. Photographing aircraft crashes was strictly forbidden so naturally we engineered them – the photos sold like hot cakes! This all helped to fatten our budget and the proceeds secured a good night out in Warsaw!

Tuition under my first Deblin flying instructor did not last long. He had come from Luck Flying School where we had first met him as one of the NCO tutors. As soon as he began to accuse me of landing badly our relationship was doomed, particularly as it was unwarranted for 'he' was actually handling the controls on these occasions. To ensure we parted company I raised my hands and placed them on top of my head,

with the result that following the usual accusation he found himself
thrown out of Deblin by the station commander. We heard he went to
a parachutist school, where we met him again later on.

My next coach – a young corporal – was the best aviator and instructor
I could have hoped for, and who promptly began to teach me the real
meaning and enjoyment of flying. He was one of those superb pilots with
the gift of inspiring his pupils to attain the highest form of expertise. I
soon discovered he displayed an acute sense of humour and devilry
during low-level flying. It was a mania with him to fly as close to the
ground as possible and this meant the wheels touched the ground as we
skimmed along. No moving object or creature was safe from his attack;
yachts on the river were a speciality to be ditched by the wind of our propeller. Unsuspecting peasants working in the fields were rounded up into
a group then scattered in all directions as we hurtled towards them in a
dive. We picked remnants of hay from the aircraft after landing from
the small flattened haystacks left in our wake, and found holes made by
the stones little boys had thrown at us. On every flight I assured my
friends it would be my last – they certainly wouldn't see me alive again!
But from that time low-level flying became my ambition and delight;
the experiences under the corporal's tuition and the inspiration he gave
me to fly as well – and better – than he did proved invaluable during the
Second World War.

Being a pilot on entering Deblin I found no difficulty in keeping on
top of the flying requirements. The majority of flying instructors were
NCOs from the rank of corporal and the training and discipline were
rigorously strict. Both the cadets and the authorities aimed at the highest results possible for the college. This competitive system induced one
to achieve the greatest personal rating. Everyone dreaded to be told he
wasn't up to standard. Each one was determined to be a 'fighter pilot'.

In summer, to take advantage of the best weather conditions with the
minimum wind, we flew in both early morning and late afternoon.
Morning take-off was at 7.30 a.m. A compulsory sleep of two hours followed midday lunch, then take-off again was at 4 p.m. As there were only
two circular flying areas, realised to be insufficient to accommodate the
whole of the school flying programme, two or three satellite airfields
were therefore opened, which we travelled to by heavy diesel lorries.

On one particular return journey from one of these airfields a crowd of us were watching a French Potez biplane executing aerobatics when suddenly the pilot got himself into difficulties and the aircraft went into a flat spin. The young pilot, one of the reserve cadets, had climbed out of the cockpit and was sitting on the fuselage too terrified to jump. He managed to give an account of what happened before he died on his way to hospital. Thereafter a compulsory first parachute jump was ordered for all pilots at Deblin, given under the tuition of a civilian parachutist. As it was feared we may try sky diving, a maximum three-second count was stipulated. But by the time it came to our year we were already taking bets on who would hold out the longest, though none of us felt particularly brave! The situation wasn't improved when we discovered our instructor to be the former NCO we had had thrown out of Deblin. We were supposed to land on the airfield and went up to make the jump five at a time. Convinced I was too cowardly to parachute he tried to push me out before we had even passed the target. I jumped and my four colleagues followed me out, leaving him to face the music when he landed. There was hardly a breeze worth mentioning and we were able to practise our amateur sky diving without being observed. It was an entirely pleasant experience and I recall landing fully upright in a soft ploughed field. The most daring of us received his winnings and we then trudged back to camp. When we got there we were asked why the aircraft seemed to have taken so long to take off. We said it was the weight of our fear bogging it down! I don't think any of us would have made really good parachutists – we weren't joking!

During my free time I began resuming my interest in sports. In the winter a friend of mine named Klawe taught me sabre fencing, which I enjoyed. In summer I swam and won most of the short-distance air force competitions at 100, 200 and 400 metres. I sometimes practised cross-country running as a preparation for winter sports. There was also the opportunity to shoot, as one of the officers had formed a shooting club. We made our own ammunition for the pistols to cut down expenses and used empty shells from the practice range, remaking them time and time again. I occupied myself a great deal assisting with the formation of this club and in return was coached by the officer, who taught me a lot about shooting. He suggested we build a special range of six automatic silhouettes for .22 fully automatic colt pistols and we practised constantly, firing three rounds of six shots in eight seconds, three lots of six shots in six seconds, and the same rounds again in four seconds at a range of 22 yards, which was a special Olympic competition. I needed 162 rounds a day for this and we succeeded in obtaining this amount from a nearby ammunition factory– free of charge – for testing the shots. As a result of all this practice I went on to win the 1938 Polish championship.

In the summer of 1937 we were sent to the mountains for gliding and the following winter for skiing. This was to enable us to retain our physical condition while we relaxed from flying. I was approached to train a team of cadets from Deblin to enter the forthcoming marathon (a long-distance ski race) called the Pilsudski Legion Route, a very arduous run of over 30 kilometres in the Carpathian mountains where the legion had fought their battle. The competition was open to all Poles from all walks of life. I gathered a team together, but other than a skier from Wilno, Aleksandrowicz (a second-year cadet), and me, the rest of the team had no experience of competitive running.

Difficulties kept cropping up. The sports officer consistently failed to supply us with the necessary equipment, although I discovered he was more than sufficiently reimbursed with funds, and he finished up being floored by the college commanding officer for being 'obstructive' towards my team. Then there were the poor cadets themselves who were finding it impossible to cover more than half the distance of the course during training, being pushed to their limits due to lack of time for preparation that should have begun at the beginning of summer. So the project had to be abandoned. Instead, Alexsandrowicz and I were sent to a small, newly established, camp to train for and enter the Inter Service Championship (Winter Sports) early in 1938. We both specialised in cross-country and had both participated in competitions prior to joining the Polish Air Force, although we had never met previously to pit ourselves against each other.

Some of the competitors were the excellent skiers (soldiers) from the Goral in Zakopane who I had known when I had lived there as a young boy. The sports captain – an army officer – was an odd chap, not exactly unlikeable, but he seemed to have decided from the outset that I didn't ski well and wasn't worth bothering with as a hopeful contender for the championship. So I decided to conceal my true running speed until the actual competition. Although I didn't win the race (the first places were won by the Goral soldiers), I beat all competing officers from the cadet school. The army captain was so surprised he couldn't understand how I'd managed it. I said I wasn't quite the novice he'd thought I was!

To my knowledge this was the first really serious attempt to prepare and train a military team for winter sports championships, hence the setting up of this small preparatory camp. As a result of beating my colleagues I was chosen to go to the Military Olympic Camp (in the winter of 1938/39), for the world championship to be held in February 1939, as the Polish Air Force representative. Meantime, the air force authorities in Warsaw decided I should also enter as a competitor for the pentathlon. Out of the five sports required – shooting, fencing, swimming, running and horse riding – I had no experience of the latter. I had ridden bareback as a youngster but that was all. So, in a short while, I was sent off to train at the cavalry regiment occupying a nearby fort situated at the junction of two large rivers, the Wista and the Wiepsz. Without any doubt, I'd never been so terrified in my life as I was astride a horse and it was obvious even to a child! My training was rigorously conducted and I could only pray for the opportunity to arise one day whereby I could return the compliment and demonstrate the 'joys of flying' to my cavalry instructors! They made sure they did a thorough job of my tuition. As an accompaniment to horse riding I took the opportunity of practising skijoring (being horse-drawn on skis over snow), an exhilarating experience and much more in my line. In Zakopane it was a very popular competition.

Since I had been participating in various sports and competitions, with reasonable success, it wasn't difficult to realise I was receiving deferential treatment, as I had experienced previously in the civilian sports club before joining the Polish Air Force. The reasons were understandable: sports, purely for its own sake, played a very prominent part in military activities, and the ambition was to hold the cream of sportsmen within the air force and particularly have them based at Deblin, where the college had fast become the centre of the air force sporting functions. But for me it was a hobby and an outlet for relaxation purposes, providing it did not interfere with my career as a fighter pilot. Therefore, it never occurred to me there might be another reason behind the deference shown. With a shock I discovered this later.

During our third year at cadet school the air force received a boost to its morale in the form of a uniform created specifically for air force personnel. The uniform was based on the British 'best blue' with slight variation, i.e. we had gilded buttons eliminating the necessary polishing! Officers (air crew) wore a specially designed small bayonet (12 inches long) with ivory handle on the right thigh, held in place by two small straps. New officers were entitled to wear one after the first year's holiday on the full dress uniform when they were then also eligible to wear white gloves. The new working uniform was a battledress top, tracksuit trousers, black beret and black knee-length leather overcoat – the latter an expensive item that came in very useful later on when we found it necessary to sell in order to survive while escaping from Poland. On the other hand, it could virtually be your death warrant, signifying your military status to the occupying forces, particularly the Russians. The reason for the change to air force blue was the growth of popularity the service now enjoyed and to distinguish its separate identity from the army.

To complete our fighter pilot training (from those selected – in our opinion the lucky ones) we were sent for advance fighter training to Grudziądz in the north of Poland during summer 1938. Prior to this course I had become chief cadet; while it lasted – not for the entire year as it might have done – it had its compensations At Grudziądz we were able to fly continually, without studies, and had the finest instructors on this final course.

We all did so well that when the general chief of the Polish Air Force, General Rayski, visited us he was astonished and immensely pleased at our high flying standard. He was the honoured guest at dinner that day and as chief cadet I sat next to him and endeavoured to entertain him suitably. Inexperienced in various military matters, nevertheless I soon found myself making a few simple suggestions on affairs concerning the air force and forwarding questions about the 'feelings' within the service, things that affected those of us (cadets as future flying personnel) to a large degree. However, our chief took it all very well. For what seemed quite a long moment he sat there contemplating me, then with a large smile he leaned towards me in confidence and said quietly: 'My dear child, if you think that as Chief of the Polish Air Force I have any say in these matters, I regret you are very much mistaken.' At the time his words puzzled me and I did not understand them fully until many years later, when I learned just how much were his endeavours on behalf of his air force in the face of immense opposition and hostility from his superiors.

At Grudziądz we were forbidden alcohol in any form or we would be scratched from the course and returned to Deblin, in which case one lost the chance of becoming a fighter pilot. A way round the ban was soon devised by drinking a very large vodka and orange (looking identical to a squash drink) through a straw. Highly embarrassing for the demur young lady companion served with the wrong drink!

The King's Castle, the local restaurant and bar, was the favourite haunt of the air force and cavalry officers and cadets of both schools. The cavalry personnel exercised extraordinary demands and orders between themselves. To either refuse or withdraw from one of these inexplicable commands was naturally unheard of and a complete disgrace for the person concerned. On the other hand if we (air force cadets) became involved with a cavalry officer our honour was equally at stake even though we could not call upon such age-old traditions. Any attempt to embarrass us individually (which they were apt to try on the younger service) meant the only hope was to foil the effort. In the following incident the captain concerned unwittingly came close to costing me my career as a fighter pilot.

On this occasion I came face to face with an extremely elegant cavalry officer – a captain – complete with monocle in the bar of the King's Castle, which was out of bounds. I was a non-drinker anyway, but for some reason I had been there and suddenly he entered. Immediately he halted and viewed me through his monocle with obvious relish. 'Ah,' he said. 'The air force! We drink', perfectly aware I shouldn't. He called for two vodkas and handed one to me. Convinced I would finish up under the table I prayed for luck. We raised our glasses – he clicked the heels of his beautifully polished boots – spurs jingling – and we drained the glasses in a gulp. The barman was under the impression it was the beginning of a duel and both he and I stared in horror as the gallant captain crushed the glass in his mouth! Sheer self-preservation prompted me to throw mine quickly into the fireplace. It was now my turn to propose the toast and I ordered two more vodkas. 'To the cavalry, the most famous of all forces,' I declared, holding the drink aloft. I clicked my not so immaculate heels. But before he could drink I gave him an order using the cavalry procedure, which he dared not refuse. 'Przysiad' (squat), and he obeyed. 'About face – march.' He waddled forward waiting for the order to halt. I turned and ran!

Air-to-air shooting was the most important activity of the course. There was a competition for first place. There had been other contests and very little to choose between us overall and this would decide the issue; the most difficult of all. The aircraft we flew was a P7 (designed by Pulawski) single-seater, with a single (British) engine and two Hotchkiss (British) sub-machine guns synchronised to shoot through the propeller between the blades. There were five targets to shoot, the 'white drag' (15 feet by 3 feet) towed by an aircraft. Four colours and one neutral (which I chose) were used to ascertain the score when the bullets hit the drag. The excitement grew daily as in an air race, the colours fought over out of superstition. With our best girl's stocking bound round our head worn under the helmet and pockets stuffed with lucky charms. And, of course, the inevitable sideline gambling!

The most important rule was that having twenty-five rounds per sub-machine gun, if you fired less than that amount (due to the gun jamming), you could reshoot. The left machine gun jammed mostly (invariably after ten rounds as I noticed), possibly due to the very difficult system of synchronisation between the guns and the speed of the propeller. To correct this jamming we were given a wooden hammer to use to give the gun a sharp crack! We soon found it was useless and felt like using it to clout the instructors instead for suggesting it.

As I watched those competing ahead of me I worked out my own system to combat the problem. I arranged with the armourer to load ten rounds only on the left gun and the remaining forty on the right. I was convinced I was then able to shoot a full fifty rounds. I could even afford to make four attacks instead of the usual two – generally after two attacks you had nothing left to fire except one jammed machine gun – as nothing in the rules forbade it! After completing shots on three targets from the five I was pleased with the result and my instructor puzzled at how well I was doing! I suggested he had a go himself – it was easy. When he landed up with a jammed machine gun he said he still didn't know how I did it and I shrugged it off without telling him. At the end of the competition (which I won) I told my colleagues what I'd done, to their amazement. As the rules hadn't stipulated that twenty-five rounds had to be loaded on each gun I hadn't cheated and they considered it great fun. They just hadn't thought of it themselves.

Successfully completing the course we returned triumphant to Deblin. We were now feeling very pleased with ourselves and had nothing to be ashamed of as competent pilots. We still had a great deal to learn, but in moments like these inevitably felt we knew it all. The competitiveness had drawn us very close in friendship. We became a unit, thinking and feeling alike, something we realised at the beginning of our third year when, as 'one person', we refused to obey an order of our squadron commander, a thing unheard of in the history of the college. We were placed under house arrest for three months. But we didn't intend to give in and were determined he must go.

Any serious occurrence within the college was observed by both press and public as a consequence of the status of the air force. Two of our year were sons of generals who would, at least, give us a sympathetic hearing, if we found it necessary to approach them. Instead, we achieved our objective by using our power as duty officers (the responsibility of the third year). We exhausted the younger cadets (about 100) at midnight with impossible tasks and energetic PT until they were in no fit state to fly next day. Although we were threatened by the CO it made no difference and eventually the squadron commander's resignation was tendered and finally accepted. It had been no whim on our part; he had earned our dislike and disrespect and the authorities had chosen to ignore it.

The maximum graduation marks obtainable were ten for each of the various subjects, listings and military classifications, such as education (assorted subjects), presentation, attitude towards the forces, discipline etc. If for any reason they considered – or one gave them cause to consider – any indication of a reactionist attitude to be observed and cautioned, this was reflected in the marks one was given.

Although I knew I couldn't possibly be among the top of the class for educational subjects, I knew there could be no doubt that I had obtained the maximum in flying and sport. As regards to marks for anything else I wasn't in the least worried. Providing I was the top pilot, it was the only thing I cared about. Without doubt everyone knew exactly how I felt. All in all I considered my marks were not 'that bad' and adequate for me. With reference to the controversial balance 'book' I said I might as well get rid of the 'blasted thing' and that I was completing the signing for the 'benefit of my friends', as they had wanted, and not for the college authorities!

Once it was signed Captain Penc said that 'probably' I would like to know my position on the promotion list – said with more than a hint of putting me in my place (he knew what we had been doing was right and justified but he wasn't in the position to show it and consequently behaved according to his position and status). My name certainly wasn't among the top ten in the overall listing. As he couldn't fence with me directly regarding the grievances we held, his intention was to use my position rating to prove to me I wasn't anything special. He opened the large book containing the complete list of names and indicated the number 44. My overall position was 44th out of 92, which included the navigators' and NCO officers' schools. I was also rated the number one pilot of the 1938 promotion year – which satisfied me.

The listing was under my new name of Lanowski, an action of mine that hadn't improved my standing one bit in the eyes of the military authorities. In the opinion of some higher officers I had done a thing unheard of by changing my name, and certainly something considered sufficient justification to warrant strong disapproval. By this time, in any case, my name was indelibly marked for future reference as someone to be watched closely as a rebel and possible troublemaker. To alter one's name required a particular procedure, complying with set regulations and rules, special authority and permission; it was stricter in every way than in Britain for instance. According to the rules I had grounds to change from my father's surname by virtue of his past actions, but an insufficient reason – and more to the point a rebellious one – in the opinion of my commanding officers. With the help of my mother I had 'composed' my own surname! We decided to keep the L and played around with various ideas until we had formed a name to our own liking – hence Lanowski. We'd certainly never heard or saw it written before, or since.

So, taking all into consideration, the squadron commander obviously considered I should feel somewhat 'subdued' at finding myself so far from the top of the list. In fact, I was quite happy to be somewhere in the middle and thought it the best place to be. Hardly the point of his argument, though. Suddenly, I recalled that this number, 44, was significant in Polish literature, attached to the famous Polish writer Mickiewicz. I'd never had any memory for books but this fact flew into my mind and I laughed and remarked what a fantastic coincidence; how could I wish for a better number for the significance it held, what better connection! The interview ended sharply.

In explanation, Mickiewicz, in one of his well-known books of prose, mentioned his 'name' was Forty-Four. It had consistently puzzled scholars and public alike and no one knew, or could even discover, what it actually meant. He had lived during the days of great musicians and writers such as Chopin etc, and at the time of Russian occupation, Siberia and concentration camps. He had been considered a 'revolutionary' writer. And today there is a revival of Mickiewicz rebellion in the Polish writers' circle and among students.

A day or two prior to graduation day I was having a chat with the sports officer, Lieutenant Osuchowski, who inadvertently let it slip that he anticipated seeing me back at Deblin in the very near future. Shocked at this remark I pressed him to explain and he finally admitted that it was 'already decided' to have me posted there, particularly after I had returned from the Olympic Camp (for the world championship). He was even willing to bet on it to convince me! I said angrily that nothing would get me back there even if I had to use every possible means I could find. The intention was, to all outward appearances, that I would be posted to Deblin in the capacity of flying instructor, but the ulterior motive behind it was to ensure I was freely available to compete in future championships and competitions. The mere thought of this future prospect sounded like a posting to Siberia! My career as a fighter pilot would be jeopardised for one of sport – beneficial to the service no doubt, for prestige purposes, but not for me personally! To be a good all-round sportsman was sheer hard work, enjoyable solely as an interest and not as my chosen career. Flying, on the other hand, came naturally to me after being initiated into it (by pure accident) and I had an obsession towards fighter flying. Moreover, I objected to having my future career determined for me, especially when it was totally opposed to the one I had chosen. The fact remained that I was in a very precarious position and could easily lose a great deal. My recent activities were not likely to be forgotten either! All I could do was wait and meet the issue when it came. My best opportunity was to use my ability in sports as a competitor of the air force (as they intended) to my own advantage to secure my position in a fighter squadron, which was all-important to me.

In the main, our feelings regarding the college was that we all felt we were leaving the finest flying school in the world. We were departing with the ambition of becoming leaders and were expected to do so. Nevertheless, recent exposures concerning financial appropriations provoked disgust and did nothing to further the example of leadership from the authorities concerned.

After the war I learned from General Rayski (at that time our C-in-C) that he had known nothing of the cause of the unrest at Deblin. He was shocked at my disclosures. Apparently, whatever he had succeeded in discovering was nothing like the truth. In his book written after the war, he considered there may have been cause for our grievances. But plainly he did not know the whole story.

On promotion day we all stood on parade listening to our names being announced to receive our wings and promotion diploma. My new name being used for the first time caught me completely unawares. Lanowski was called and for a minute there was a puzzled silence as no one stepped forward. Then suddenly my friends gave me a hefty push 'Lanowski! Witold, you fool, that's you!' The graduation was celebrated as a national day with all the press present, one's relatives and friends invited and attended by public personages. A massive ball ended the day and vodka flowed like water to mark the occasion. At last we could each join our squadrons – for us this meant a 'real' fighter squadron – to begin our careers.

This promotion proved to be the 'vintage' year of the Polish fighter pilots, established by achievements and personal success (rate of 'aces') of its pilots during the coming years. In the Second World War we had the highest result and the lowest losses (average 20 per cent) killed in action of the entire Polish Air Force!

Chapter 4

Fighter pilot

In September 1938 I arrived at the regimental camp of 121 Fighter Squadron in Krakow with ten of my friends from graduation. We all had to live on the camp in the unmarried officers' quarters. Only married personnel were allowed to live off site. The quarters themselves were an experience for all new entrants. One of the first things we discovered was the necessity to bolt the door of one's room, in order to keep out the 'ladies' who roamed the corridors. If you forgot they walked straight in uninvited, determined to stay.

On leaving Deblin we'd had tailored the best civvy suit we could afford, only to discover we were expected to wear our uniform both on and off duty, virtually without exception. This caused a problem when one was compelled to wear the uniform even in leisure hours. The public attitude to aircrew – especially among women (mothers and daughters alike) – amounted to adoration. Hospitality and social life was a benefit the uniform and the nature of our job automatically brought with it. Yet it required every bit of skill to successfully escape the over-anxious mothers of unattached daughters, however enchanting!

The resolution to this was to wear civvies, so we promptly ignored the rule expected of us, even if severely frowned upon for doing it. It was possible now, at least, to meet a girl under more natural circumstances and impress her without the use of the air force 'blue'. To allay her suspicions regarding our work or background one automatically 'adopted' a new profession. Only a fool would try to break his neck in an aeroplane! But we constantly ran the risk of recognition from other airmen. Once, as I walked out with a girlfriend who believed I was an 'architect', a squad from the regiment came marching towards us. As they drew level the NCO barked the order 'Eyes left' and gave me the most efficient salute. Obviously puzzled at my blank expression, he turned to stare at me in amazement that I hadn't returned the salute. I shrugged the 'so-called' recognition off as a case of mistaken identity. If it happened again I was sunk! But the deception was a form of relaxation we felt entitled to.

There was also another reason that prompted us to disregard the uniform regulation. As duty officer one was required to wear a service pistol (which we purchased for ourselves until we received a service supply). I'd bought a fully automatic Walther. But off-duty (and outside the camp) we were also compelled to carry firearms with our uniform. For this purpose my friends and I bought a baby Walther, which was not so conspicuous. Moreover, if an officer became involved in a dispute with a civilian and was insulted – rightly or wrongly – he was forced to use his pistol, with the obvious intention. He was then court-martialled and sentenced automatically to three months' 'honourable' confinement in Twierdza fort. Should he not exercise this 'right' to use his weapon (that is, on an unarmed civilian), he received his court martial with the same sentence, but was classified as 'dishonourable'. We hung up the firearm, together with the uniform, when we donned our civvy suit. The uniform retained its honour and we our self-respect and principles.

Life on the camp contained another pastime that contradicted the former attitude applied at Deblin and especially the advanced flying school at Grudziądz. It concerned the restriction on alcohol or, I should say, now the total lack of restriction. If anything the coin was reversed and drinking encouraged as a social practice in keeping with one's promotion and status in service life. With the result that we were free to enjoy ourselves without fear of losing our position as a fighter pilot. Presumably you were expected to know what you were doing and if your flying was affected or you killed yourself that was your own affair. I didn't drink, but that didn't mean I was against it. But in my opinion, it no more mixed with flying than it did with sports (the reason I hadn't taken to it in the first place). Apart from that, I couldn't afford it. The whole reversal of procedure would have been laughable if it hadn't been so dangerous and significant. It was an open invitation and membership card 'to join the club' whose members included those who considered flying as one big laugh – and life cheap.

To understand this attitude it is necessary to return to the earlier days of flying. The First World War saw the beginning of the Polish Air Force. Following the hostilities and the revolution against the Russian invasion, the air force stood still for many years including in the production and progress of its equipment and machines. During this time came the infiltration of officers from the cavalry. They brought with them to the air force their cavalry traditions and procedures, expecting to apply them to this new service. Only those who took flying seriously realised its potential, otherwise the general attitude was irrelevant to what the air force could offer or become in the future. It was, after all, considered second class to their own prominent service. They liked the high life and would indulge in schoolboy pranks. Flying offered such an opportunity to live it up and live dangerously. In many instances they were killing themselves in their aircraft as a result of sheer bravado or what they thought was fun. And just as often they treated the aeroplanes as they had done their horses, expecting them magically to bring them back home out of sheer instinct and horse-sense.

We called this generation of pilots Lesne-Dziadki – or Forest Gremlins. They enjoyed drinking and imbibed heavily even as pilots. One was expected to share their ideas of social life in preference to a private one of your own. Camp life, therefore, didn't exactly encourage a broader view and offered little but the prospect of finding relaxation by joining drinking parties or gambling with cards etc, unless you specifically followed a hobby or enjoyed an outdoor life of sports.

Nevertheless, we insisted upon building our own off-duty social life outside camp in our own way, by wearing civvy suits in order to relax as members of the public. We preferred our relationship with the 'outside world' to be on an equal footing. This, of course, didn't conform to the accepted rules (and defeated the objective of our commanders to keep strict control over our everyday lives). As an example of wearing a uniform and being compelled to use a firearm if caught in conflict with a civilian, after an evening out, a high-ranking officer hadn't hesitated to shoot dead a taxi driver who had 'presumed' to ask for his fare after driving his passenger to his regimental camp. The officer in question was the former famous fighter pilot Pawlikowski, who was later to become our OC Fighter Command in England. If the regulations incited such an action it was better to hang up the uniform during off-duty excursions – and this is what we did.

After the Spanish Civil War and the Abyssina–Italian war, the importance of air power was realised and the air force made progress as a military defensive power. This is when we came into the picture: young boys took this new dream to their hearts. On the other hand, the old boys suddenly got a shock and found themselves out of touch and sympathy with this completely new outlook towards air-mindedness, which had gradually been developed in the previous few years. One of the first things we experienced when we got out into the squadrons was opposition, and it wasn't hard to establish where this came from.

Those responsible for our flight training and practice – themselves of a different school to their superiors – gave of their utmost to perfect our piloting techniques and air tactics: dogfighting, formation flying, vertical diving, low-level manoeuvring, air-to-air shooting, etc. The standard was high – everything had to be perfect and one had to keep on top form continually. As soon as we arrived in Krakow, for instance, we were told we knew nothing anyway and had much to learn. You either swallowed this lack of appreciation of your 'ability' and got down to the job of absorbing everything there was to learn, or your flying suffered in the process.

But our immediate commanders had their difficulties with the higher officers. Our regimental commander, Colonel Lewandowski, consistently complained of the 'noise' created by our aircraft, particularly during vertical dives. Why was it necessary for us to make so much noise when we flew as he was unable to work! Captain Medwecki our wing commander – a very decent man and good leader – was forced to explain that this form of flying and practice was 'essential'. We were soon disputing the advisability of flying such a very tight formation, but our squadron commander, Captain Sendzielowski, enforced the procedure to the letter – as did other commanders – against the arguments put forward. Likewise, what we really hungered for was to be taught 'advanced' aerial tactics for war, based on those experienced in the Spanish Civil War. But such knowledge and methods were non-existent. The principle held by higher officers was that the days of fighter flying were over! Yet it became all too obvious later that lessons learned in Spain were exactly what the German Luftwaffe had applied and adapted in techniques used in their fighter squadrons. And far from being over, the days of the fighter pilot were just about to begin, and in deadly earnest.

Stated in historical records, and providing proof in such books as General Rayski's *The Truth about the Polish Air Force*, a fifth column was responsible for the 1939 September campaign catastrophe. Looking at it from a different view it was a fifth column older hierarchy 'from within', based on jealousy of modern advancement and of a younger generation who possessed an entirely different view from their own. Especially when those junior men (for the first time) questioned and opposed their ideas and behaviour. Instead of retiring on their merits (which many had demonstrated as the history of Polish aviation shows) and allowing younger and competent men to take their place (the one learning from the other), they had been purposely destroying not only themselves but also Poland, who suffered in the end for this short-sightedness. This progressive course was exactly what our commander-in-chief, General Rayski, had been endeavouring to do – with some degree of success – by retiring or ousting some men and replacing them with those of a more advanced outlook, beneficial to a modern air force. The policy was met with hostility in the belief that it was simply a means of depriving them of their position and status, unfortunately a character failing in the national make-up of Poles. Come what may they would hang on to their positions while progress passed them by.

Any form of opposition was considered reactionary and revolutionary, not to be tolerated and forthwith crushed and punished, even in their own circle. Yes-men attained key positions immaterial to whether they were suited to the post or not. By such means they were able to keep the Polish Air Force higher command between themselves, and again in France and thereafter in England. Even though – in the latter instance – they were only pawns to the British high command under whom we served.

Later, they shirked their responsibility for the inevitable catastrophe that resulted in Poland due to the policies of the high command and placed the blame where it suited them best. At the same time they took the credit for, and basked in the glory of, the enormous contribution by the individual performance of Polish heroes such as the pilots. The facts of the September 1939 conflict in Poland between the German and Polish air forces verify the effectiveness of the attitude and skill of Poland's young pilots, proving it to have been not such an 'easy campaign' as it has been described by some sources.

The participation and fighting attitude of Polish pilots and airmen under British command during the Second World War are well known. One didn't become a pilot of such flying ability and training as we had – acknowledged by our Allied counterparts – within a period of weeks or even over a few months. It stemmed from a fundamental basic training and attitude tried and tested, as we had been in our own country. If anything, the only member of the Polish high command justifiably entitled to take credit for the individual performances and achievements of Polish pilots and squadron commanders – particularly during September 1939 – belongs to our former C-in-C General Rayski, for his extreme efforts to build up the Polish Air Force as a protective weapon for Poland's defence and given at the expense of his career and position. The seed of the fighter pilot was sown by him; each merely blossomed and proved their worth under his successors when the great battle of the Second World War came.

Nos 121 and 122 Fighter Squadrons were equipped with the PZL P.11C fighter aircraft; 123 Fighter Squadron with PZL P.7s. Aeronautically speaking, I suppose I could say that the greatest love of my life was my relatively short attachment with the P.11C. She had been described as old-fashioned, antiquated and obsolete. All of which were true, of course, until you met her and knew her charms! Once you fell in love you never quite forgot the experience. Many times throughout the war, and after, I found myself pining for the opportunity to fly her again.

She was a small aircraft spanning 34 feet 8 inches and a length of 22 feet 11 inches. Her wings, which joined at the top of the fuselage in a wide V, were finely corrugated to increase her lift by expanding the flying surface, which was quite an ingenious idea for this type of aircraft. The construction was all metal with the exception of her propeller, made of wood. Her two machine guns were synchronised to fire through the propeller. Her maximum speed was 242 mph at 15,000 feet.

Comparing the PZLs P.11C and P.7 – which we flew in to fight the Polish campaign in September 1939 – against the PZL P.24C (for the Turkish Air Force) and the P.24F (for the Greek Air Force) that were being exported by the government to these countries right up until the day war broke out, the engines of the latter aircraft were 80 per cent more powerful than our own in the P.11. The P.24C had a much stronger engine, with a metal propeller of three feathers for adjustable pitch and four machine guns in the wings. The P.24F carried two 20 mm Oerlikon cannons and two machine guns in the wings.

There is no doubt at all that the PZL was one of the strongest aircraft I have ever flown, and so robustly built that no one could break her wings. During a vertical dive it was a constant source of amazement to watch her register maximum (dial) speed of 380 mph, then a further 50 mph by registering again from the beginning, which I personally did and perhaps even more by other pilots. How the engine never 'marched off' we failed to understand, but it never did. Her cockpit was open, of course, with a small glass windshield. So in winter you felt pretty cold, with frostbitten cheeks. She had a modern design for the petrol tank, which was situated behind the pilot seat enabling the tank to be dropped in an emergency, such as a fire.

One of the important factors of the plane's design was her undercarriage. The oleo shock absorbers were placed 'inside' the fuselage. From each ran a steel tape to the wheels – crossed diagonally – producing a pulling action rather than the normally designed up and down movement. This allowed the wheels to spread in a scissorlike motion, enabling her to perform a very heavy landing on rough surface in a minimum landing distance. It was possible to execute any aerobatic manoeuvre and she would fly quite happily upside down for several minutes.

Our training consisted of tight Vic formation, flying three to five aircraft. Individual aerobatics comprised ten to twelve pilots joining consecutive dogfights, in air-to-air (cine-camera) firing. Once a year, for a month's training, we were sent to the special testing area to practise with live ammunition air-to-air and air-to-ground firing, plus dive-bombing. We performed dive-bombing on the aerodrome itself (Krakow), thus giving our CO plenty of reason for complaints due to the noise.

One of the toughest elements we needed to perfect was to land within 100 metres. This invariably was the final exercise that finished the day's flying. The oblong landing area of 50 x 100 metres (approximately the length of a football pitch) was marked out between red flags. The PZL was the right aircraft for this purpose, due to the construction of her undercarriage. It seemed a practically impossible task to accomplish but with practice you could succeed. I did manage to do it 'accurately' once or twice. It proved an invaluable experience. Visibility was poor for the manoeuvre, with the radial engine and wings joining the fuselage right in front of you. When you came in, reducing your landing speed to the minimum possible, you flew with your wheels just a few feet off the ground for quite a distance before the actual touch-down point. The plane would be practically hanging by the power of the engine (which you needed to have). As soon as you reached the touch-down line you cut out the engine and she fell out of the sky with a heavy thud! But her construction could withstand the fall. The other important point was to break gently the maximum possible to avoid putting her on her nose – so as not to hurt the lady!

To an onlooker the aircraft presented the oddest picture at the latter stage of the manoeuvre, quite funny to watch – one moment flying just above ground, the next skimming along on her belly as if flattened. Then she proceeded to waddle along irritably, like some silly duck getting up from an almost squatting position, until she finally came to a stop. It had to be seen to be believed – for it was supposedly an impossible feat to achieve in the history of aviation, at that time, without completely wrecking the aircraft. Particularly as it was a fighter aircraft not designed and built specifically for aerobatics! In this respect it was comparable with the stunt executed by Zurakowski, namely his famous cartwheel, which nobody but he could do. He later flew the manoeuvre in a Meteor with rockets attached to the wings.

When the war came, the above exercise contributed largely in saving the PAF from destruction 'on the ground' by the German Luftwaffe. For as their war records show, they were unable to find us and were deceived (even temporarily, by those aircraft they did find and destroyed on our aerodromes) into believing they had annihilated all that we possessed. As it was, our pilots could land and operate in any small grass field attached to the little forests all over the country – which they did – and were perfectly hidden from view. During such operations the Polish Air Force became the peasant air force and one to be reckoned with in combat.

To ensure a really tight formation (which later proved a fatal mistake) some squadron commanders used the method of attaching string to the wings of the aircraft. Intent upon keeping the string intact the pilots were literally flying blind, relying on the leader for their flight path and position, especially when coming in to land. When an accident occurred (which was inevitable sooner or later, though fortunately not fatal) the practice was forbidden. It happened at another regiment and apparently the leader brought his formation in too low. One of my friends, Zumbach (later one of the 'few' flying with 303 Polish Fighter Squadron), hit an ambulance. As I have said, we were constantly disputing the advisability and logic of flying a tight formation with our own squadron commander. But during the September campaign he lost his life for just this reason: he was flying a tight finger three with two of our pilots and they were shot out of the air like sitting ducks. Fortunately one of them survived. What was equally horrifying was that it was our own artillery (army) that shot them down.

As the P.11 had no dual control all exercises were learned during briefing and actual practice. By such methods one grasped for oneself the 'trick' of the dogfight. At first I lost the mock dogfight on every occasion, which was very irritating. Then, quite suddenly, it clicked home. I realised the aircraft never made a perfect circle as you endeavoured to get on the tail of your opponent. It flew an oval. By pulling on the stick too much she began to shake, but give way slightly then pull again and she would follow, straighten up to get her speed then turn again, using the same method. From then on there was no difficulty and now I was winning. Also with a small aircraft like the P.11 she virtually turned on her tail, forming the smallest possible circle.

We were made to practise air-to-air shooting with the new system using cine-cameras. There had already been some fatal accidents and the reasons not fully understood. At briefings we were told to try one method and then another, but what it really amounted to was that without an instructor with you in the aircraft you were on your own to learn the hard way. The target sleeve (pulled by another aeroplane) was attached by a strong, long thin steel cable approximately 600 yards in length. The attack position was about 550 to 600 feet vertically above the sleeve. Unless you practised sufficiently you needed to tip your wing to check your vertical position; without realising it you could be either in front or behind the target. With both aircraft flying at the same speed (when diving from above), if you came in a little behind it was difficult to make a hit. But in the correct position you could catch it beautifully, coming to a perfect shooting position. There had been some mishaps, but, so far, no one from our regiment had been killed, as had other pilots we'd heard about. But I had a near miss, and at about the same time as another pilot from another squadron.

Being overambitious to make a proper attack I went a little too forward. Instead of forgetting about it and making a fresh start I began my assault from an incorrect position. I went down vertically and realised that I wouldn't slip in behind the target but actually straight on to it, or the cable it was attached to. I kicked my rudder hard and tried to slide in to miss both. There was a terrific explosion, which left me shaken. I'd hit the sleeve and as I glanced round at my right wing the sleeve, complete with cable, had wrapped itself around it, the end running beneath my undercarriage and trailing behind. The explosion I had heard convinced me I had snapped the cable.

I flew towards my deputy squadron commander's aircraft (who had been towing the target) to show him what had happened and as we had no radios in those days we used sign language to talk to each other. He wanted to know if I was all right. Fortunately I was! He then indicated we must land immediately, but first he intended to release the remainder of the cable, which both he and I believed was still attached to his aircraft. We then came in for landing.

He went first and I followed happily behind, the sleeve catching my eye as it flapped on the wing. I lined myself up for the normal approach from west to east between 20 and 30 degrees. In the field down below, the horse artillery regiment were practising. In my final approach, approximately 100 feet and descending, my aircraft was violently jerked to the right – almost pulling her out of the air. She was practically standing on her right wing and I noticed the target had disappeared. I instantly applied full throttle and straightened out. I then had time to glance down, wondering what on earth had happened to the target sleeve. I couldn't help laughing at what I saw going on in the field below me. The horses were careering in every direction pulling the guns behind them, the target flying straight down towards them.

The entire squadron was there waiting for me as I taxied towards the dispersal after landing. I wondered what was going to be said for a moment, but we were all busy examining the aircraft for damage for me to think too much about any reprisals; fortunately all we found was a cut in the leading edge from the steel cable. We discovered I'd been trailing the entire length of the cable (600 yards), which had a weight on the end of it as it hadn't snapped at all. As I came in to land it had naturally been dragging along the ground and, after hitting some high-tension cables, had become entangled causing an explosion and fracturing two pylons, thus depriving the surrounding area of electricity for the next twenty-four hours. The local authorities returned the cable to us by taxi a few days later!

I was a little surprised to find that I wasn't reprimanded at all. I concluded by their attitude – much nicer than I expected – that they were only too glad to see me alive after two such narrow squeaks!

The other pilot I spoke about had a similar accident to mine. In this instance the cable snapped when he hit it and embedded itself in his instrument panel after whipping past his head. The authorities realised by this time the reason for some of the fatal accidents. We were then informed we should have to be a little less 'ambitious' if we wanted to stay alive during these exercises. Very difficult in the circumstances with such a competitive atmosphere.

Chapter 5

Skiing and War!

All this added up to the fact that antique though the P.11C was when war broke out, the Luftwaffe didn't have it all their own way. This included the fact of not being able to find the Polish (peasant) air force on the ground, camouflaged in fields and forests. In spite of their superiority in numbers and the speed of their aircraft they found it a very difficult task to shoot the Polish pilots down. On the other hand, due to the training our pilots received, especially in air-to-air firing, once in a dogfight or attacking enemy bombers there was no difficulty on our side in this respect. These facts are borne out by the losses inflicted on the Luftwaffe during air battles over Poland. The historical records, especially from German Luftwaffe documents published recently – taking into account the amount of aircraft we had to use and the circumstances of the Polish campaign and its duration – show the losses for this period, and that our pilots had already attained the highest score of the 'entire' last war. These figures are as follows:

- The duration of the war in the air for the air force was fourteen days.
- In the Polish Air Force there were 1,786 officers; 3,800 NCOs; and 610 cadets, a total of 6,196. From this number 3,000 were fully trained aircrew available to fly at the outbreak of the war, in a total of 392 aircraft. In addition to this there were 100–150 reserve aircraft, including school trainers (which in fact were never used fully due to the breakdown of communications, direction and authority):
  158 fighters, i.e. 30 P.7s and 128 P.11Cs;
  150 bombers and reconnaissance aircraft, i.e. 36 Los and 114 Karas;
  84 observers.

- On 17 September 43 P.11Cs and P.7s landed in Rumania. In other words approximately one-quarter of the Polish Fighter Command.
- Polish fighter squadrons, including the fighter brigade and those in army co-operation units lost 50 pilots and 114 aircraft.
- In Germany Luftwaffe aircraft plus reserve totalled 1,785 (more superior aeroplanes than those we possessed).
- In the final score of the September campaign German losses are stated to have been:
   285 aircraft destroyed;
   279 beyond repair;
   734 flying personnel killed, missing and wounded.
- Polish Air Force records estimated only 126 enemy aircraft shot down by Polish fighters and bombers, with 10 probable and 14 damaged. In other words this is all they 'claimed'.
- The highest score was by the Poznan Fighter Wing (131 and 132 Squadrons), figures: 33 – 3 – 0. Second highest was Warsaw Fighter Wing (113 and 114 Squadrons) with Krakow 123 Fighter Squadron (who flew P.7s), figures:- 29 – 3 – 5.

During the days before war descended upon Poland we took life very much as it came in the fighter squadrons. All our ambitions concentrated on improving our flying technique as fighter pilots. While we had no time to feel bored, all the same we were in need of releasing the tension of flying, therefore we let off steam during our off-duty periods. To brighten up life on the station itself there would be a variety of activities in the quarters themselves. Target practice became a favourite pastime. The walls and ceiling took a lot of punishment on these occasions and the expense account for electrical fittings must have been costly. An inexhaustible supply of ideas to help liven things up excluded any hope of a quiet evening. Our friends in the Warsaw regiment played a form of Russian roulette, leaping from one parapet to another and it seemed feasible enough at the time!

We were fortunate to have in our wing kapitan, S. Skarzinski, an engineering officer, who due to his former flying days as a pilot of considerable repute had expert knowledge of maintenance. Any slight hesitation by a ground crew worker under his command concerning a mechanical fault in an aircraft was sufficient to send the poor chap back to school to relearn his lessons. Formerly Skarzinski had competed in international air competitions with success and had flown a small Polish aircraft to Africa and then across the Atlantic to South America. He was fortyish, slightly bald, and with a very cheerful personality. I had met him previously when I was a cadet travelling by train from Zakopane and we had discussed various topics and I'd found him immensely interesting. At Krakow I soon discovered he had a wicked sense of humour.

Answering a knock on my room door early one evening I found it was Skarzinski. Without any preliminaries he came straight to the point: 'Lieutenant, I would like you to present yourself at my rooms at 8 o'clock this evening.' I was by this time standing to attention but even so I ventured to ask the reason. He just said: 'Never mind, just come.' He then left, leaving me apprehensive as he very well knew. It was out of the question not to appear and as I dressed in my best 'blue' I couldn't help wondering what to expect. When I knocked on his door, at the appointed time, it was flung open and Skarzisnski stood in the doorway to greet me, a magnum of champagne under each arm. I was told to enter but whoever else was expected hadn't yet arrived. He said: 'I am very glad you have come, I am expecting two ladies presently, you will entertain one of them.' He then burst out laughing and added, 'Relax, Lieutenant, I assure you it will be a very pleasant evening.' I could only hope so!

While we waited for the ladies to appear I was able to study the many trophies he had collected on his travels to the African continent and the South Americas, which decorated the large room. The walls were covered with a collection of animal skins, spears and shields. I doubt I would have believed then that I might one day myself travel as extensively in relatively happy circumstances.

The evening was an amusing affair, with the two young ladies delightfully charming company and the supper excellent – all in all much better than I previously thought it would be. In fact the 'order' had turned out to be a very pleasant 'duty'!

A sense of adventure and constant competition dominated each pilot's persona, spurring him on with his own ambition to distinguish himself as a first-class pilot, if not the best. Inevitably air accidents occurred but were accepted as the price of experience. We had brought with us a fresh attitude and outlook to the squadrons – individualism, both on the ground and in the air. And in developing our own private and personal life as individuals we had also established an opportunity for relaxing, generally impossible under a military system. But although no direct reprisals were made we were well aware of the disapproval of our superior officers and commanders and as a consequence we were not so indoctrinated with the military organisation as our German opponents. We had no idea about the viewpoint or structure of, for example, the RAF or French Air Force.

When war in Poland broke out and the individual role of the fighter became necessary, our pilots automatically assumed the role without difficulty, applying it in the air as they had done on the ground. At a ratio of ten to one against us the whole battle was as personal (and even more so) as the Battle of Britain that came later. The results in terms of figures were excellent considering the equipment we had in comparison to the enormity of the German Air Force. This individual attitude took us to France and thence to England to continue the struggle. In France, particularly, we fought and flew without hesitation in French aircraft (the Caudron), which French pilots considered to be 'flying coffins' and would not themselves fly. The point being, of course, that they were better than nothing at all!

The Polish squadrons were comprised of officer and NCO pilots. The majority of flying instructors at Deblin College, for instance, were NCOs; my own instructor had been a senior corporal and I could not have hoped for a finer instructor, his flying ability unquestioned. Those NCOs in the fighter squadrons were just as irritated by the opinion and scepticism of the older generation of COs towards fighter flying as we were and just as maverick in their attitude, only they were not able to show it to the extent that we did in our off-duty hours. Until Deblin finally increased its output of pilots they were the backbone of the Polish Air Force. Likewise, during the Battle of Britain 50 per cent (if not more) of the fighter and bomber pilots, navigators and gunners were NCOs and their leadership indisputable when called upon.

Such was the case concerning the so-called problem of the Karas bomber, condemned by the older Polish officer pilots. They had been used to flying the old-type aircraft and their form of aviation (by the seat of their pants) without doubt was suited to the particular aeroplanes of their day. There was then no question of navigational aids, radio, or watching a collection of instruments. The cockpits were open and they flew by instinct and feel of their aircraft.

Then came the closed cockpit plus artificial horizon and all the paraphernalia of modern equipment necessary for the latest type of aircraft and they hated this form of flying. Consequently there were accidents and many lost their lives in this new bomber. A rumour very quickly spread that the Karas was hopeless, and they were subsequently handed over to the young corporals to fly. They flew them superbly, without any difficulty whatsoever, testifying to the airworthiness of the Karas and their own flying skill. This could only result in an inevitable split between the old and the new. Like ourselves as the younger generation of pilots, their attitude was akin to our own towards the need for a modern approach, therefore with the introduction of the new 'blue' uniform we had welcomed the oncoming change of perspective taking shape in the air force to determine its uniqueness, and with the promise of modern aircraft being introduced into the squadrons, around the time we took up our posts, an effective modern military air force was finally established.

The source of these changes came directly from our commander-in-chief General Rayski, the encouragement to achieve the high standard demanded by a modern air force taken as our ambition. One hoped for more transformation that would inevitably lead to the complete separation of the air force from army control, with fully fledged air force commanders understanding its requirements and maintenance and rid us of the restrictions and influence imposed by the army generals of the military high command. Our eagerness for the necessary reorganisation to take place was naturally met with hostility from our superiors, who were adverse to any form of progress. The climb to the top of the popularity poll by the air force had been achieved swiftly over the last few years – altogether too swiftly for some.

In only a few years, a series of events and coincidences had shaped my future without very much detailed planning by me. My interest in sport had led me to flying which, in turn, had resulted in my entry to Deblin College in 1935 to become one of the 'revolutionary bunch' of fighter pilots (the last intake of students to join the squadrons before the war began and who would distinguish themselves by their personal achievements during the Second World War). The three main groups of trainees from that time were those who entered in 1933 and graduated in 1936; in 1934, graduating in 1937; and in 1935, graduating in 1938. Possibly for the first time there came a regular supply of air force officers holding no previous army or cavalry commissions, who were all pure air force personnel with a natural ambition and enthusiasm for flying.

The one thing that had led me to flying in the first place eventually threatened my profession as a fighter pilot – a series of links in a chain resulted that governed my entire career and the effect it had upon my future life in 'civvy street' in Great Britain.

Within weeks of entering the Krakow regiment (121 Fighter Squadron) the order came from Headquarters for me to report to one of the army ski regiments camped in the mountains at Bielsko (Polish Silesia). I was to train for the World Ski Championship as the PAF representative. If I was chosen for the final team (after the training period) it would be an opportunity to represent not only the services, but Poland – an honour not easily dismissed. All the same, the whole prospect daunted me and I was desperately worried about the effect it would have on my career in a fighter squadron plus the fact that I would miss a great deal of training and practice flying. Once I dropped below standard my future in a squadron was automatically doomed. I had sufficient confidence in my own flying ability that my skills would not deteriorate, but it was impossible not to acknowledge the nagging doubt at the back of one's mind. I certainly could not refuse to go to the ski training camp and in my own interests it was now necessary I should go simply because my future and position as a fighter pilot depended upon the result. If successful in the coming winters sports championships, I hoped to be in the position to 'bargain' to remain in a squadron.

Before I left for Bielsko (for initial instruction before going to the Olympic training camp outside Zakopane) I discussed briefly my anxiety concerning my flying education with the wing commander, who understood the problem I faced. As he, himself, shared an interest in sport, he advised me not to worry and feel assured he would do what he could to assist me to catch up as soon as I returned to the squadron.

The army regiment consisted of many of the well-known skiers from the Goral, professional skiers in every sense but financial. All the competitors for the world championships were army personnel with the exception of myself. So if I was chosen for the team at the end of it all it would be quite an achievement for the air force – and for me! But I was obviously going to have a battle on my hands for the others were not going to relinquish the army honour that easily. I was going to have to prove I was more than 100 per cent worthy. So far Poland had not succeeded in coming within the first ten places in a cross-country championship. The Scandinavians excelled in this event. But we held our own in the academic skiing students, championships and the ski jump (in 1939 Kula won third place for Poland and it was believed that his young age at the time was the reason why he had only been awarded the bronze instead of the silver medal).

Our instructor for the coming months was an Austrian, Joseph Röhl. He spoke Polish very badly to begin with but it gradually improved during the time we were there. He had been commissioned by the authorities specially to train us for the world championship and was himself a famous skier; in the summer months he coached tennis to officers in the higher command. We soon discovered he was exceptional at his job and participated personally in every bit of the training – with the exception of the latter stage just prior to the actual championship – and it seemed almost impossible to keep up with him.

We took physical instruction four times a week for two-hour sessions, and until the snow came we did athletics, walking and running cross-country for long distances in preparation. Mountain rambling in the forests meant we could practise 'skiing' by riding on our boots on the dead fir-tree needles that covered the ground thickly; and we participated in various summer sports such as football and swimming. All the while, we were waiting for the snow to fall in the Tatra Mountains near Zakopane.

During our training we heard some disturbing news over the radio and in the press. A dispute concerning Teschen (Zaolzie) had come to a head between Poland and Czechoslovakia. Zaolzie was formerly a part of the Polish Empire that the Czechs had invaded and captured after the First World War during the time the Poles were busily occupied repulsing the Russian invasion of Poland. The Polish authorities had now decided to take back Teschen, if necessary by force of arms. I expected to be recalled to my unit at any moment as soon as it was realised the situation was indeed serious. But nothing happened and no order for my return came.

Soon after, I was amazed to see my wing land at Bielsko aerodrome a few miles from the army barracks. I immediately took the opportunity to visit my unit and arrived there in my tracksuit, which caused some haughty comments from my colleagues. There they were ready to fight and die if necessary and here came Lanowski in his running gear! I found they were fully equipped and armed, ready to fly against the Czechs.

While training with the army regiment I had made friends with a civilian, and I persuaded him during this crisis to take me to the disputed area on the back of his motorcycle. We arrived at the bridge spanning the River Odna, which separated the area in question from the frontier of Poland. Passing myself off as a reporter I succeeded in getting to the front of the crowd and as a result I was one of the first to cross the bridge at that time. The Czech and Polish forces faced each other either side of the bridge and the atmosphere was tense. A meeting then took place between the commanding general of the Czechoslovakian forces and our own Polish commanding general, Bortnowski, in the centre of the bridge. Apparently the Czechs were not in the least bit keen to resort to battle over Zaolzie, with the result that an agreement was reached to return the area to Poland, thus avoiding any unpleasantness. In my newly adopted professional capacity of a 'reporter' I was able to witness this meeting at close quarters and I took the opportunity of photographing the historic event.

Zaolzie was an area similar, for example, to Essex, and the entryway to the mountains at the border of Czechoslovakia. In my opinion the dispute had been ill advised and should never have been allowed to happen. The eventual invasion of both Czechoslovakia and Poland proved my conviction, if only to myself. Such a similar dispute had developed previously between Poland and Lithuania concerning Wilno. I was a comparatively young man but instinct caused me to believe that the antagonistic feelings between the two countries had been instigated by the Germans. I believed it was also now the case regarding Zaolzie between the Czechs and Poland. An attempt to drive a wedge between our two countries – and a successful one at that. Germany was in the position to occupy Czechoslovakia in the secure knowledge that Poland would be in no frame of mind to offer the Czechs any assistance.

In 1934 I had visited Czechoslovakia as a ski competitor and realised the extent of German influence in the country, especially among the forces (with whom we were competing). I was astonished to find all the Czech military personnel spoke German as though it was their native language. I met a professor from Prague during this time and discussed with him the relationship between our two countries, which was becoming increasingly unfriendly. Neither he, as a member of the older generation, nor I as the younger man, understood the reason for it. Every indication pointed towards government policy, justified by the behaviour of my Czech sports opponents. But the professor dismissed my suspicions as groundless.

With the wedge between the countries securely created, the German plan worked very well. In the eventual invasion by Germany the Czechoslovakian air force high command hesitated to order their pilots to fly their aircraft and equipment to Poland, with the result that only four Czech aeroplanes (on their pilots' own initiative) escaped, and one of these landed in Krakow aerodrome in March 1939 while I was duty officer. The pilot and navigator of the aircraft that touched down on our station had brought with them many aviation books and manuals in the hope of assisting us, probably with some idea that more of their aircraft might manage to escape. They were convinced Poland was next in line for invasion, something by this time we were also sure of. When I say 'we' I refer to the military personnel in preference to the civilian population. It was impossible not to imagine we would be attacked and we later had proof of the German intentions. I was immensely impressed by the exceptionally good condition and upkeep of the Czech aeroplane that had landed. Many Czech pilots (the majority seemed to be NCOs) did escape of their own accord, travelling by foot over the mountains to fight with us during our campaign in 1939. They too, then escaped to France as we Poles did and finally on to England to fight and fly with the RAF until their own squadrons were formed.

General Bortnowski, who had negotiated the settlement of Zaolzie, and I met again in England in 1946–47 when I took up employment in a small Polish factory. I was horrified to find that he, too, was in reduced straits ill-befitting his rank and past career as a general of the Polish forces.

Prior to Christmas we moved from Bielsko regimental camp to Zakopane. I travelled there by car with a racing driver friend from pre-PAF days who came to fetch me. We were billeted in a completely separate and very large pension (lodging), and we had every facility – as well as staff from cook to masseur. In all there were approximately twenty-five of us: five officers and nineteen soldiers and the coach, Röhl. Our real winter training was about to begin, all we waited for now was the snow to fall. We were not allowed in town unless special permission was granted, and then one's reason was scrutinised carefully. We retired each evening at 9 p.m. discipline as usual was strict. Finally the snow fell in the high mountains to everyone's delight, and we could really begin skiing at last. Straight after Christmas it fell in Zakopane itself, very heavy snow, and the training then began in earnest.

I considered it all to be super intensive, neither anticipating nor believing I could even endure or manage to cover such distances as we were expected to do – normally this was 20, 30, or 40 kilometres a day (150–200 per week). Rest day was Sunday, by which time one needed it! In accordance with the strict discipline exacted by Röhl, within a short while one of our best runners was thrown out of the team for drinking.

Come January it was time to reduce the team from twenty-four to eight members – two officers and six soldiers. The final championship team would comprise one officer and three men. The competition for the military team involved a run of 25 kilometres, with the officer carrying only pistol, compass and map, and the soldiers a rucksack (weighing 10 kilograms), and a rifle plus ammunition. At the halfway mark (12 kilometres) was a shooting range with red balloon targets, the teams firing at these from a distance of 110 yards (the officer was not required to shoot). If a soldier tired during the actual run the officer was allowed to carry his rucksack and rifle.

To prepare for all this we shouldered the complete pack during the runs, and likewise participated in the target shooting. Every bit of training was entirely devoted to this special cross-country race. No one was allowed to ski alone in the mountains or take part in any other form of skiing such as downhill or slalom in case of suffering any unnecessary injury, thus affecting the team's chances. Most of us specialised in cross-country running, but it was an irritation being unable to put in any practice for downhill and slalom, particularly as in the inter-services competition following the forthcoming world championship I was competing in all three events. The loss of practice inevitably hindered one's prospects, but there was nothing we could do about it, for the reason was obvious.

Röhl was indisputably an excellent trainer but this didn't stop me from neither liking nor trusting him. It was difficult to define what prompted this reaction in me for there was nothing specific I could put my finger on. I was convinced from the outset that it was more than just a clash of personalities, yet for a time it appeared this must be the only reason. The discord grew steadily between the two of us. Soon he was trying to fault me at every opportunity. If it was unjust or uncalled for, I didn't hesitate to stand against him, which naturally made things worse! I knew then that under no circumstances would he choose me for the final team. Moreover, the fact that I was a fighter pilot had apparently contributed a great deal to the 'atmosphere' between us. And when I was allocated with my own personal doctor (from the Central Medical Board, who was, in any case, only using me as a guinea pig for his experiments), Röhl's attitude changed from dislike, which I could appreciate, to hatred, which made me suspicious. Subsequently, when the foreign competitors finally began arriving just prior to the championships, I noticed he slipped away and went immediately to see the German civilian visitors accompanying their team. This somehow confirmed my mistrust.

A few years later I learned that he had been working for the Gestapo and this had been the reason for his presence in Poland. Although many had suffered through him, apparently he had helped some Poles. At the time of these pre-war competitions it was known that sportsmen had the best opportunity to work as 'agents'. I was discussing this with a friend of mine from my home town of Lwow (whose name was Sliwaki and who was one of Poland's best-known 800-metre athletic runners) when I met him again in France in 1939–40; he told me it was definitely the case. In about 1954 I found myself in Salzburg for a few hours and made some enquiries about Röhl (more out of curiosity) at the Austrian Ski Club. I had no sooner mentioned his name than the atmosphere became frigid and it was almost impossible to ascertain any details about him, either present or past! Finally I did discover through his sister, a dentist (whose address I had been given), that he was living in Hamburg.

I was in fine condition during my training at the Olympic Camp so it came as a complete shock to me to discover I was tiring and falling back after running only 20 kilometres! Both Marusarz and Motyka were both present in Zakopane and I immediately sought their expert advice. Without hesitation they advised an immediate complete rest of one week as I was in serious danger of overtraining. The championship was still four weeks away but nevertheless Röhl threatened to throw me out of the team. So far it had only been a battle of nerves between us and this seemed to him a sufficient excuse to get rid of me. As the matter would go before the military authorities I suggested the witnesses I would call on my behalf; he then backed down and agreed to the one week of rest. This was just the opportunity for me to visit my squadron and try to catch up on some of the flying I had been missing. Röhl raised every conceivable objection, as I expected he would, but I was equally determined I was going.

I hadn't flown for the past three months and I felt more than a little nervous at the effect this might have had on my flying ability. When I arrived at the squadron I was greeted with words to the effect of what the hell did I think I was, pilot – or sportsman? I had recently been asking myself this same question and I understood their reasons! Besides which, every day my name had appeared on the board for flying duties and, of course, I wasn't there to carry them out, and this was an irritation in itself for my colleagues. When I asked if I could do some flying before returning to Zakopane the next day it was thought my 'good living' would have affected my flying considerably and the squadron commander set a test to discover just how much! Meantime, my friends had already decided to enjoy the fun. Everyone had turned out to watch the display and just to add to the fun I was given an old P.7 for the exercise. The P.7 had the exhaust pipes coming from the piston all the way round and the fumes came straight at you behind the small windscreen protecting your face. The P.11C, on the other hand, had a cowling and the exhaust came out beneath the fuselage.

Having breathed nothing but pure sweet mountain air for the last few months, if anything was going to sicken me it was going to be the exhaust fumes – apparently part of the plan! I was to complete ten to twelve figures, flying between 7,000 and 10,000 feet. I climbed into the cockpit determined not to fail. It was even more important for my own morale than it was for them to judge my standard.

I executed the figures, spinning left and right, performing loops and blending each figure to the one before, which gradually brought me down to and within the specified distance of 200 yards. I couldn't afford any mistakes under such scrutiny. The ordeal terrified me and I found it tough due to lack of constant practice. Only my determination and ambition helped me to succeed. I landed, sick to my stomach from the fumes of the engine and the tension inside me. The squadron commander sauntered over and grudgingly admitted I had done 'quite well considering' – and perhaps I should go again. I looked and felt thoroughly nauseated – and they stood there waiting for me to retch. I had good friends!

Unable to refuse, I took off again, battling against the stench of the exhaust that was now threatening to cause me to give up and land immediately. I had to do even better than before to scotch any criticism. I eventually touched down, satisfied I had achieved my aim and the flights confirmed I hadn't, in fact, dropped below standard. I felt much easier in my mind to return to Zakopane that day and enter the last phase of training for the skiing championship.

For some years in the Polish Air Force the ultimate measure of one's flying ability had been dependent upon executing aerobatics to perfection. Prior to 1933–34, world flying events and aerobatics predominated in the attitude of the authorities. After the Spanish Civil War, fortunately the pursuance of this form of flying decreased to some extent, to concentrate on more military combat flying. All the same the 'old school' still prevailed, and was one reason why I had to prove my worth in this aerobatic exercise. Individual aerobatic 'aces' are born, not made. Aerobatics are without doubt essential, providing they are only a part of the rigorous training for fighter pilots. It serves no purpose on its own account other than for competition and as an excellent form of display. It is vital to know how to perform manoeuvres in the air for one's own safety. Fighter pilots especially were bound to find themselves in a difficult situation sooner or later, particularly in bad weather or, as in the war, when aerobatics are essential to outmanoeuvre the enemy. But they were by no means the be-all and end-all of flying. There are many tricks to the trade and just because you happen to know one doesn't mean you're going to win.

For example, Kapitan Kosinski was what I would call a born aerobatic ace, but that didn't mean he would be equally good as a fighter pilot on the front line. His speciality was flying upside down as close to the ground as one could get. At the last moment on coming in to land he would flip his aircraft over and touch her wheels on to the runway, a 'falling leaf' he performed exquisitely.

However, this bravado could induce a false mental attitude towards one's capabilities. Equally, it was a dangerous practice to expect a specialist in the aerobatic field to automatically become not only a fighter 'ace' but also an exceptional leader, and these were rarities. A true leader understood his responsibility and duty towards the personal safety of the pilots under his command, especially in times of conflict. In war it's bullets that fly – not only the birds.

In England, when I saw Kosinski again, his attitude to operational flying instinctively told me he would not survive. So it was no shock when later I heard he had been shot down, without any opportunity to put up a fight. But it was still a tragedy to lose such a talented flyer. It reminded me of the fate of Richthofen (but who had, of course, distinguished himself as a fighter ace) – it was possible to be too sure of oneself and be caught off guard. But so gifted was Kosinski, enabling him to become an intrinsic part of his machine during a magical display of aerobatics, that he astonished our British counterparts at his daring. Another such Polish pilot was Zurakowski and no doubt his aerial feat will long be remembered by visitors to Farnborough Air Display after the war, before he finally left for Avro Canada.

After arriving at an RAF station, Kosinski was shown the Hurricane aircraft flown by the squadrons. Canadian as well as British pilots were attached to the units. Expressing the desire to take a Hurricane up for a short trip he was naturally told he would first need to be converted to this type. But having already flown so many different aircraft in his career he would 'manage', he said, 'just for a short spin'. Still sceptical, but good-humouredly, the British pilots allowed themselves to be persuaded and agreed for him to 'have a go'. He suggested they would perhaps just show him the cockpit for reference. After a brief introduction to the controls he taxied out on the grass and to the surprise of everyone watching 'lined his aircraft up facing the empty space between the two hangars'. He took off and flew straight between the hangars and immediately having passed them went straight into a sweeping loop, completing the manoeuvre back down between both hangars only inches from the ground. His audience gasped in amazement, convinced he'd kill himself. The performance was all the more amazing because he had only just stepped into the Hurricane for the first time. But Kosinski didn't need more than the briefest acquaintance!

One of the watching Canadian pilots considered there was nothing difficult in this feat and felt compelled to show this Pole he was as good. Unfortunately, the Canadian boy had no idea with whom he was competing and when his aircraft hit the ground the machine simply disintegrated, killing him outright.

Back at the skiing championship the German competitors arrived early, one of the first. They were billeted quite near to us (the Polish team) but made it blatantly obvious they wanted to have no contact with us at all – other than Röhl who went to see the civilian members of their party. They refused to touch our food and brought their own cook along. I don't particularly recall that we thought their attitude especially strange, even though it was, after all, a sports competition. We just ignored their behaviour altogether.

When the rest of the teams showed up things became more interesting and in a short while I had found some friends among the various competitors and we instinctively formed a little group together to relax after the day's training. In the Finnish team there was a fighter pilot like myself and automatically he and I found a great deal in common. Then from the Hungarian team there was 'Bucki-Beckt' an officer from the famous Budapest Fencing Academy. He was the fencing champion of Hungary (who were at that time the world champions) and an instructor at the academy. And lastly came three from the Italian team, all from the Alp regiment, and wearing typical Tyrolean uniform – which together with their spontaneous sense of fun brightened up our group no end! Their names were Vinco, Fabre and Alberti. As soon as we discovered that Bucki-Beckt was thirty-five years old he was termed the 'old man' straight away. His 'great age' seemed incredible to us for the forthcoming competition! He also spoke French so we were both able to exchange views more broadly. But to our Italian friends and the Finnish pilot we used either a smattering of each other's language or fell back on 'sign language', frequently with highly amusing results! Without doubt we were the liveliest assortment in the entire camp and subsequently attracted the most attention, particularly while spending an evening in the local restaurants or cafes. Not surprisingly, perhaps, it wasn't long before we found ourselves in trouble. The accusations ranged from 'hard and frequent drinking' and 'high living' to 'not concentrating on the championship ahead' in preference to enjoying ourselves. If all the rumours were true we would have spent most of our time 'under the table'! The press joined in the attack and the whole thing got out of proportion. By no stretch of the imagination could coffee and orange squash be termed 'hard liquor' We obviously laughed just a little too loud and a little too often for some! Once the competitors returned to their own countries I wrote to both the Finnish pilot and Bucki-Beckt. I was immediately in trouble again and reprimanded strongly for corresponding with foreign military personnel. In 1940, while in France, I decided to write again to Bucki in Hungary through a French friend. I was immensely surprised to receive an answer from him, which I never really expected to get. I was relieved to hear that he was, at least, still alive.

Just prior to the opening of the world championship the weather turned nasty and it poured with rain. This was followed by warm weather, with the result that it made a ghastly slush of everything. It became necessary to bring snow down from the high mountains to build special tracks and repair the damage to the ski jump. We all assisted in this work to get it done in time for the competition. The opening ceremony was filmed, and as the only Polish Air Force representative I was placed in the foreground of the Polish section, but other than for the record this didn't indicate very much. Although I had successfully beaten my officer colleague from the army during our training practices, there was very little to choose between us. When Röhl made his final choice for the Polish team, as I anticipated I was placed as 'reserve'. Naturally it was a disappointment to me not to be representing Poland, but in the circumstances I had expected this decision for some time. What was important was that the Polish team should be well placed and they did not disappoint us. The Germans took first place, then – if my memory serves me correctly – came the Finnish team, with the Poles attaining third place. This was a first-class achievement for us and a most excellent performance against the seven other national teams. While it was never expected that the Germans would win the championship, there was no question whatsoever that without Röhl's superb training the Polish team would not have stood a chance against the opposing teams. As it was we had every reason to be proud of our successful placing.

The world championship had been the prelude to the 1940 Olympic Games, to be held in Garmisch-Partenkirchen. The next competition following the championship was the inter-services competition in ten days' time. Röhl's coaching and jurisdiction over us was now complete. I was to compete in the coming events as a representative of the air force in an individual capacity.

In the short time before the competition I put in as much practice as I could for the downhill and slalom events, but couldn't hope to train enough in only the few days available. The first race to take place was to be the cross-country event, and was the most important challenge for me personally out of the three in which I was competing. The majority of the cross-country competitors were those with whom I had trained for the world championship – including the army officer of the final Polish team who had attained third place for us. The toughest competition would be from two soldiers from the Goral, both superb skiers who would almost certainly take the first positions. I would be more than satisfied if I could beat my army colleague, especially as both Röhl and I knew I was capable of it, having done so in the past.

Friends Marusarz and Motyka were just as determined to assist me, for they had been irritated by Röhl's attitude during the previous training and disappointed for me. So they took it upon themselves to wax my skis for the race next day. The special waxes could either win or lose you the race, and there was the constant fear of one's skis being tampered with during the night for this particular event, a practice that was not unknown by any means. I literally slept on my skis that night – just in case!

Just before the race was due to begin in the morning my opposite numbers from the army – the officers – came to inform me that I stood no chance against them personally. I had spent my time previously enjoying myself with Bucki-Beckt when I should have been training (for the world championship) so what could I hope to achieve? One (who was to start in this race six numbers ahead of me – in other words three minutes faster) became particularly aggressive so I offered him a wager to allow him to prove his point. I promised him that not only would I beat his three-minute advantage, but would pass him and finish three minutes ahead.

In the midst of this rather heated discussion a small peasant boy had entered the hut where we were, wanting to speak to me. He handed me a coin that had been given to him by some woman outside. She apparently had been listening to the 'argument' and wished me to carry this 'lucky coin' during the race.

As it was expected, the first two places were secured by the Goral soldiers. However, I won my bet and took third place in the race, accomplishing what I had set out to do, and both Marusarz and Motyka were satisfied.

Both the downhill and slalom were going to be a different proposition, though, due to lack of practice. But I meant to do the best I could.

During this competition I was staying at the hotel belonging to the daughter of the Goral family of Blachut, with whom I had lived as a little boy with my mother when we first came to Zakopane in 1918. The father was a woodcarver and exceptionally clever. As I was now using my own personal skis, which were extremely old, we decided to strip them down completely and revarnish them before applying the waxes, to afford me maximum speed for the downhill slalom. I also fitted the rims with metal strips (as on the modern skis) to assist when cornering. The family were now giving me encouragement and moral support, though I couldn't rate my chances very highly.

I was out of luck for the downhill, having drawn number 54. This meant watching the run (piste) deteriorate with each competitor during as many minutes. (In those days it was the luck of the draw for everyone, both first-and second-class skiers.) Moreover, during a long wait the weather could always change and, of course, it did. The first numbers not only had fresh snow but beautiful weather; then it began to snow. By the time I made my run it was snowing steadily. Fortunately I had made myself a Perspex visor, which was as yet unknown in those days. (I don't remember where I got the idea from, I imagine from our air force equipment.)

I knew I would have to go flat out to win. I went fast – too fast, in fact, to take the turn properly. The only solution for me was to go through the two poles holding a blue banner. My ski sticks hit both poles, then my body and then my face. I flew into the air and rolled down, but somehow managed to recover quickly and finish the last 100 yards. When the time was checked there was no doubt that had I not fallen I would have won the race – as it was I had managed to come third.

I had badly pulled a ligament in my arm, which immediately depressed me as the next day was the slalom (the arms all-important in relying on your sticks for control). My friends were doing their best to cheer me up with the fact that I had done very well in the circumstances. But now I had even more cause to worry. Just as I was leaving with my friends to return to my hotel I was stopped by a woman (who looked in her early forties) who had pushed her way through the bystanders to the front. Her clothes were extremely fashionable, expensive and in good taste. She was well spoken, obviously from a good family, and educated. Therefore her overwhelming manner seemed all the more surprising, particularly as I had guessed she was most probably married. I was right, although I didn't know it at the time. She wanted to congratulate me on my run and seemed unusually distressed about the fall I had sustained. I tried to tell her not to worry about it but my assurances made little difference. During our brief talk I realised it was she who had sent me the 'lucky coin'. I later dismissed the entire encounter from my mind, accepting her behaviour as due to the excitement of the competition.

That evening the Blachuts made an all-out effort, massaging my arm to get it working properly for the following day's race. The weather was particularly fine and I was fortunate enough this time to get one of the first numbers. I succeeded in putting in a good run although not satisfactory enough to attain first place – instead I'd come second. But with this result there was no reason not to be pleased with my performance. As before, there was the lady to offer her congratulations and I was also in a happier frame of mind.

My overall position in the inter-services championship had earned me first place, a personal achievement and an important factor for me.

The reception for the prize-giving was held in Zakopane's largest hotel, the presentations made by the well-known cavalry officer commanding, General Wieniwa-Dlugoszewski. As I stepped forward to receive my last award (my fourth) for first place in the competition, he remarked humorously that he was thoroughly fed up constantly seeing me coming to receive them. He couldn't have felt more surprised than I did, in the circumstances, for having won them!

On leaving the hotel I was immediately confronted by the woman I'd met earlier, and looking even more attractive than previously in the day. She had a gift that she insisted – against my objections – that I accept. The box she gave me contained an expensive and beautiful cigarette holder made from bernstein (light amber from the sea) and gold. Obviously I couldn't just take it and walk away! She wanted to ask me something and I suspected my answer might appear rude, which I didn't particularly want it to be. On the other hand she didn't seem to me to be the type of person who made a habit of this behaviour. We went into the hotel lounge to talk. After a moment or two discussing the recent skiing she told me her husband was an important government official of the military high command. What she was proposing was an 'attachment' with me. In return she could be beneficial in advancing my career and position. She dismissed my suggestion that perhaps her husband may not feel disposed to approve of her interest in me or assist in the matter (as she inferred), expressing surprise that I should think it unusual in their social circle. Apparently these 'affairs' invariably proved mutually advantageous. In the manner she put it I believed her! It was no secret that in the sporting world (in this instance within our military command) this type of life existed, enabling one to advance one's career, both in sports and in promotion within the service, without too much effort or danger in the field. You were either a fool not to accept the opportunity and relied upon your own ability, or took up the offer to advance yourself. It seemed ironic that I was being given the chance to secure my position at a time when my career hung in the balance. But I didn't consider myself a fool for preferring to make my own way. I even surprised her by stating that my ambitions did not include a sports career so, with respect, there was nothing she could offer me that I could not achieve for myself. As far as I was concerned, the progress of my military career could only depend upon my ability as a pilot. It was obviously not the outcome she had wished it to be, and I politely took my leave.

Taking a broad view, my recent success in the inter-services competition amounted to a relatively small achievement in an overall career in international sports and, in ordinary circumstances, not very exceptional. But circumstances were far from ordinary. To begin with no one, except perhaps Hitler and the German high command, knew that in approximately six months' time war would break out. And I was also in the midst of a personal battle of my own to retain my flying career.

I had by no means disappointed the expectation of the air force authorities, who wished to push me further into sports. From my own point of view my hand was now strengthened (the only importance attached to the inter-services results being to have some kind of weapon to use for my own benefit). Facing me in a few months was the prospect of the 1940 Winter Olympics, when I would have no sooner resumed flying before being called away to begin another jaunt. There was also the pentathlon, the shooting championships and swimming. A continuous career in these fields required dedication and a driving ambition to succeed. While the rewards could be unlimited (particularly from within the military command), I've never claimed to have this dedication, even though when competing I have gone all out to train for the ultimate purpose of winning. But my character just wasn't compatible with the conditions in which competitors were required to live and train – I was too much of a rebel. Even under Röhl's direction the regime was murderous, and despite taking the punishment in order to prove myself, I'd never indulge in it continuously by choice. The thought of being forced into it as a future career horrified me! I have the greatest respect for all sportsmen and women who accept this challenging existence.

Since first beginning to take an active part in sports as a young boy I'd had to fight for every bit of training, knowledge, piece of equipment and success I had acquired on my own merits, being content to do so for the love of a hobby. In the very near future I could see myself becoming nothing more than a human sports machine, and already the enjoyment I had once found in sports was diminishing fast under the present circumstances.

Flying was not my hobby – it was my sole ambition and driving force. Hence the reason why I was prepared to fight every inch of the way to remain in the air – not as an instructor, but as an individual pilot in my own aircraft.

After I had returned to Krakow from competing in the winter sports championships I had sought permission to live off camp, which was granted under a relaxation of the rules allowing unmarried officers to rent civilian accommodation. I acquired a small flat in town in a street named 'Officers Parade' and brought my mother and sister from Lwow to live there. Several others from the regiment did likewise. It became necessary to relax the rule in order to make way for the fresh arrival of new officers to the squadrons.

By the end of July 1939 we were alerted that German photographic aeroplanes were violating our frontier near Czechoslovakia and part of our squadron was called for operational duty to intercept them. We took four aircraft with us and landed on a smallholding where we set up camp. Our only radios were Marconis, with a radius of 5 miles, and one of us had to remain on the ground to direct the other three aircraft on where to find the enemy. The full realisation of the superiority of our adversaries came when all we could do was to stand and watch them as they flew high above the ceiling of our own aeroplanes. We couldn't even get up to them! We were recalled to Krakow and another squadron took over 'to keep up the observation' while they blithely photographed our territory without disturbance.

Meanwhile, the battle between transmissions on German (Polish-speaking) radio and our own Polish radio stations was now in full swing. But listening to these broadcasts left us in no doubt that Germany was not bluffing, as our own authorities would have us believe. We received much information about enemy aircraft but no idea of their superiority in numbers. This increasingly tense atmosphere triggered a clamp-down on all movements and we were restricted to the immediate vicinity except with special permission. Part of the reserve force was also recalled.

As the weeks passed and the squadrons were not re-equipped with new aircraft, one's morale suffered as a result, not an ideal situation with an impending war ahead. The German propaganda on the radio could not be ignored or their intentions doubted. Yet it appeared no one particularly bothered about the state or fate of the air force and this attitude reflected upon the personnel. One was apt to live for today and hope not to die tomorrow! When the time came to fight you could only do your best with the aircraft available. And they were already years old and had completed thousands of flying hours, being in constant use. Not all fighter squadrons were even equipped with P.11s; some still flew the earlier type P.7s, despite these having put up one of the best defences during the September campaign. In the event, not every pilot would have the opportunity of doing what he was trained to do, with such a deficiency of aircraft compared with the continual rising number of aircrew.

Just prior to the war there were indications that the authorities were taking the situation more seriously than they had. Demonstrating Poland's precarious position, there was a call for national funds for the forces, which the public subscribed to. But this seemed useless in such a situation as who could we buy aeroplanes from – the enemy? There wasn't anyone else. They may just as well have made a call for suicide volunteers! In the moment of truth they found they already had these in the form of the cavalry – forty regiments against the force of the German panzer divisions, having failed to equip them with modern armament and tanks etc. Those from the cavalry who succeeded in riding close to a German tank, boarded it, opened the hatch and threw in a bottle of petrol, died with the enemy!

Prior to the war, Goering paid a visit to Poland for a large boar shoot and presented an outstanding aerobatic aircraft – a Jungmaster – to the Polish Air Force. His visit was obviously a last endeavour to persuade us to join forces with Germany and subscribe to their policy. At the time, I experienced the feelings of the Polish national character when I overheard two small boys discussing the impending war, their fanaticism even outstripping the hatred I felt towards the Germans at that time. Young though they were they spoke with a certain amount of logic and had a fierce unbending loyalty and patriotism for Poland. I knew then that nothing the Germans could do would stop us from fighting, however great the sacrifice.

More than anything I dreaded the thought of war on my mother's account. Although she held Polish nationality she had, nevertheless, been born in Germany, which made her position dangerous, although she would never admit it, even to me. The Polish government issued instructions that all German nationals should leave Poland and her own mother left for Berlin. Mother loved my flying and occupied her mind with this. She often expressed the desire to be able to fly with me one day, and loved to watch aerobatics and formation flying. When I knew I would be airborne I flew over the flats at a prearranged time to say hello.

A month before war broke out the posting I thought I had successfully escaped arrived, ordering me to Deblin Cadet College to take up the post of flying instructor. I couldn't believe it now of all times – it seemed sheer lunacy! I immediately telephoned the War Office in Warsaw in an endeavour to speak to the colonel who had been with me in Zakopane, but it was useless. They seemed to be in a panic already and he was no longer at his office and I was unable to reach him. I tried to argue my way out of it; every pilot would now be needed in the squadrons. But I was told I must obey the order. In utter desperation I finally invented a pain in my side, which took me into hospital where I underwent an unnecessary operation for appendicitis. The doctors were under the impression I was an alcoholic! Apparently I had refused to go to sleep under ether so they had to switch to chloroform. It was only when I explained I hadn't long returned from the Olympic Camp did they believe me. The excessive physical training I had undergone obviously made the difference, for as I didn't drink there just wasn't another explanation. While I recovered in hospital the news over the radio showed war to be very close and I began to wonder if my brainwave had been such a good idea after all. Karol brought my mother to visit me frequently and as each day passed I became more impatient, being kept in bed with nothing to do. I asked to be allowed to leave but the hospital authorities wouldn't hear of it. Finally I asked Karol to bring my clothes from home and to park his car outside the window of the small ward I was in on the ground floor. He came the next day and within the hour I was in my flat in Krakow; I'd made it out through the window! Unfortunately, my stomach wound was still partly open with infection. I trusted it wouldn't give me much trouble and would heal in a few days or so. We kept it bandaged cleanly and hoped for the best. At least it was better to be on hand than in hospital if war started soon – as it did, three days later.

At 6 a.m. on 1 September German bombers flew over Krakow and dropped their bombs, 48 tons of them. Their objective was the aerodrome, but they were also falling in the town, some landing in front of the flats without exploding. From the window I could see black smoke rising in the direction of the airfield so I went straight there. The German bombers had done their work very effectively; there wasn't much left of the camp. Every alarm or bell that was on site seemed to be ringing.

The first person I came across was the deputy regimental commanding officer Lieutenant Colonel Luzinski. He was sitting on a chair in the centre of the main road surrounded by rubble, completely stunned and seeming not to notice me. I had entered the main gate and on my right the guardroom was partly demolished. Wires and cables had been torn apart by the explosions, setting off the alarm bells. Civilian workers were running from one side of the camp to the other frantically trying to put out the fires. To the left of me the headquarters had been completely flattened and only half the officers' mess remained standing. Just as I reached the headquarters I could hear groaning coming from beneath the rubble. I started digging with my hands until I found the head and shoulders of one of the civilian employees, caught fast in the debris. He was obviously dying from his injuries and all I could do was to fetch him the water he asked for repeatedly. He died shortly after.

I returned to Lieutenant Colonel Luzinski, who was still sitting on the chair where I had first found him. He continued to look dazed and appeared surprised to see me. In answer to my question he told me that all the squadrons had left for the emergency airfield some days ago. The wing commander, Kapitan, Medwecki, was, I believe, the first to be killed as they took off from the emergency airfield to attack enemy aircraft. They'd literally flown straight into a German formation and didn't stand a chance. He wondered why I wasn't with the squadron and I explained

I'd been in hospital and had only just left. I suggested rejoining my squadron, 121, with his permission. In the course of this conversation my posting to Deblin was recalled and he said I must obey this instruction. He refused to listen to my objections and was quite adamant I should proceed to Deblin.

So I went home to prepare for my departure, although it seemed to me a pointless thing to do. I explained to my mother what had happened and we collected together a few of my essential personal belongings and albums that were important to me. Karol Radziwill came the next day to take me to the station by car. My sister had for some time been working and living in Warsaw, which left only my mother for me to say goodbye to. Neither of us could visualise the future any more than anyone else. So when I kissed her I didn't think that it would be the last time I would see her. I could see she was dreadfully distressed and heartbroken but she wouldn't permit herself to cry. She was very brave, as I had always known her to be. It was my last memory of her and one I proudly kept. When my sister visited me from Czechoslovakia in 1966, the first time I had seen her since 1939, she said that when Warsaw was bombed for the first time everyone was under the impression it was the Polish Air Force practising 'war tactics', until the fires began and they knew it was war and they were being bombed by the Germans.

The train took me to within 40 miles of Deblin, to a little town called Radom. Then everyone was told that was as far as the train would be going. The stationmaster informed me that Deblin had suffered heavy bombing – one of the worst in fact, and German magazines gave the proof of this. The German bombers were endeavouring to destroy a bridge crossing the River Wisla. Next day an engine would be going to Deblin with just one 'platform'. I got his permission to travel on it and suggested I slept the night in the train that had brought me to Radom. The following morning I sat beside my case on the 'platform' behind the engine, heading for the Wisla and, just before we reached it, the German bombers returned to have another go at the bridge. We stopped just in time and took cover. Fortunately we were lucky; they had missed the bridge completely but the tracks on the opposite side were damaged. We resumed our journey over the bridge and bumped up and down over the shell holes, rocking from side to side, but we carried on without stopping until we reached Irena, a small village near Deblin.

I left the station and walked along the narrow streets, which were completely deserted. The little houses seemed deathly silent and empty. Three horse-drawn peasant carriages then appeared, carrying coffins containing the bodies of dead villagers. Apart from the drivers there wasn't a soul in sight. The impact of this left me stunned. I made my way to the police station hoping to find someone there. A policeman sat typing at his desk. I enquired about Deblin, feeling that it, too, would be deserted. He said it was but added that someone came every evening, after the bombing stopped, to collect supplies of food and ammunition. I decided to wait for their arrival and walked outside the police station. There was a tiny deer standing not far away that had come from the forest. One of its delicate legs had been completely blown off. It stood looking at me, panting with pain-filled eyes. I couldn't even touch it I felt so shocked. It seemed to represent the horror and distress that hung over the little village of Irena.

When two air force officers arrived I explained who I was and went with them to where the personnel were camped from Deblin. I reported to the deputy commander, who was Captain Brzezina. He had been the CO of Grudziac before the Advanced Flying School had been transferred to Deblin soon after we left in 1938.

The camp was situated 15 to 20 miles from Deblin. I was billeted in a private house on one of the small farms, as the other officers were. The cadets – 300 to 400 of them – were sleeping out in the open air with the NCOs and instructors. The cadets seemed resigned to the situation around them; the instructors were keeping very much to themselves. There was no flying as the aircraft were only trainers. Every pilot was feeling deflated. Everyone was conscious of the confusion sweeping over Poland. It was fast becoming a music hall joke.

Captain Brzezina was a very quiet and competent CO. We had liked and respected him when under his command at Grudziac. He had very little to say during the following five days that we were camped near the forest and it was difficult to guess his feelings or how much he knew of the situation as each day passed. We were largely unaware of what was going on outside Deblin and the surrounding area. It wasn't possible to take part in flying against the enemy without the proper aircraft. We could only await instructions – and so we waited each day until news finally came through with the relevant orders. From the outset Brzezina's concern rested directly with the welfare of the cadets for whom he was responsible and he proved to have little time or sympathy towards any colleague whose attitude or behaviour interfered with this in any way.

I was still having trouble with the wound in my stomach from the appendix operation, which didn't seem to want to heal; it took quite a time before it finally did. Meanwhile, all I could do was to keep it clean, washing the bandages that I had each day. As usual I hated having nothing to do and when Brzezina asked me if I would like to do something to occupy myself I was glad to do so and I undertook the organisation of the cooking and food supplies as catering officer. At the end of five days Brzezina received orders to march towards Rumania and the southeast border. Just before we started off Brzezina suggested I might like to fly back a P.7 trainer aeroplane from an emergency airfield nearby. It seemed an odd request in the circumstances but it was an opportunity to fly and I took it. Once airborne I scouted around for a bit but there was nothing to see and certainly no enemy aircraft appeared. When I landed and reported to Brzezina he grinned in amusement and asked me if I felt better after being back in the air again. And he was aware I had wanted to remain in the fighter squadron. As for the aircraft, well it hadn't been needed of course.

Chapter 6

Escape

For the march towards Rumania the entire number of cadets were to be split up into three groups and I was to take charge of one of these, of about 100 cadets. I was also the catering officer and head cook and bottle-washer for my group, including the officers who accompanied us. The plan was to cover between 20 and 30 miles a day, depending on the stamina of the cadets, marching by night and sleeping during the day. Before setting out we sent ahead what lorries we had, carrying our personal belongings, and this left us with only one lorry spare. Brzezina detailed this for my use to transport the equipment and cooking utensils etc. As for our luggage that had gone on before us, we never did see it again. Although it arrived in Rumania, when we reached there it was an unpleasant discovery to find that others had claimed it as their own. I saw one officer wearing one of my jumpers bearing my initials, which had been made for me. But he insisted it was his and there was little one could do. It was obvious someone thought we would never make it to Rumania.

It was decided that I should travel on ahead to a certain point and there set up camp and have everything ready by the time the column arrived. I was also responsible for buying all the food, whatever could be found en route. Until now I had had the assistance of an elderly cook but had been told to leave him behind. This prospect terrified him. He'd lost all his family and there was no one to whom he could go. He begged me to take him with me and I saw no reason to refuse. I didn't realise what a good friend I had made at that moment. Just as I was about to leave, having collected all the food supplies I could, a fire tender arrived and asked if they could tag along behind my lorry. It seemed a good idea as we needed all the vehicles we could get, and the lorry didn't look as if it would last the journey anyway. We looked an odd assembly when we set out.

We travelled the prearranged distance and then set up camp. With the meal prepared we awaited the arrival of the column. When it eventually appeared the cadets seemed amazed to see me 'standing over the cooking pot'. Apparently I was supposed to have been killed! Just before they left, German bombers – who had been looking for any such large groups or columns of troops – had discovered the forest encampment and attacked it. The cookhouse had received a direct hit and an officer had been killed. Not knowing I had already left they had assumed the officer had been me.

I got a shock too. The majority of the officers turned up in their private cars, which were useful to have for emergency, but there were also the wives plus as much personal luggage as they could carry. Brzezina, on the other hand, who journeyed with our column, had left his wife and family behind and travelled light. After the first day the private cars kept up with me and no one was particularly anxious or interested in assisting in setting up camp for the column. The occasion arose when it was necessary to use a private car for me to find and collect food supplies. I asked to use one of them and I might just as well have been asking for the moon! When Brzezina arrived and heard what had happened he called the officers together and proceeded to wipe the floor with them, threatening that either they co-operated with me when I needed a vehicle or firstly their wives would be left behind and then their cars commandeered under the articles of war. From then on there were no more objections. Not concerned with their finer feelings, my responsibility was in finding food for the cadets. My duty towards my officer colleagues was only to feed them when the column halted, as instructed. As far as it went they were quite capable of fending for themselves; as much could not be said about the cadets.

Food was extremely scarce as thousands of civilians were fleeing ahead of us towards the Rumanian border. Fortunately I had the names and locations of military supply stores where food may possibly be obtained. With money I had been allocated I purchased perishable foods daily. On one occasion I bought a cow, which we killed and produced a veritable feast for the boys who were delighted after a long tramp. I couldn't have done without the services of my companion, the elderly chef; he was superb. Towards me, personally, he was a guardian angel one moment and a mother hen the next. There was nothing he would not have done for me and little enough I could do for him but allow him to remain with us. I was often too tired to want to eat. On such occasions he would surprise me with a special dish of chicken, where it came from I never did learn. But he sat until I wiped the plate clean then retired happy. (At this juncture I was still having a great deal of trouble with my stomach wound, which was even now open and continually weeping, and this no doubt contributed to my fatigue.)

In Rumania one of the things we heard was that some of the temporary catering officers in charge of cadets merely handed the allotted money over to the cadets themselves for them to purchase their own food en route. The result was that those at the head of the columns were able to acquire and buy all the food villages could spare. The remainder of the cadets virtually starved to death. Our way at least was practical and worked admirably. Everyone had a share and sufficient food to eat.

Fortunately we had good weather, without rain, and slept in comfort under cover of woods during the day. Some five days later we reached Luck, where I first learned to fly as a civilian pilot, so I knew the area extremely well. I looked first for the emergency food store, as the town consisted of a few army and cavalry regiments besides the small aerodrome. Taking one of the officer's cars I intended to bring back as much as I could from the store. While I drove along, German bombers appeared; I passed by a nearby church and heard the sound of praying and singing during the Mass. I reached the storehouse and the bombers were already preparing an attack; I realised they were aiming at the marshalling yard close by. I was too preoccupied with my own mission to worry much about them. They had already started bombing when I reached the depot. I was dressed in the air force long black leather overcoat, my revolver tucked into the thick belt, and wore the black beret. The whole outfit closely resembled the German uniform. Our own military personnel of the army and cavalry were not altogether familiar with our new air force uniform, particularly the working one that I was wearing, any more than they were of other aspects appertaining to the air force, which had become evident during the September campaign. In the circumstances my reception at the supply depot was irritating and dangerous, although I hadn't considered it when I arrived there.

The German bombers were busily engaged destroying the marshalling yards. I had finally located the depot I required only to be confronted by the army officer-in-charge, a major, in a terrified state. No doubt the bombing going on around us had severely shaken him, but even as I spoke to him as he stared at me in amazement, I realised he thought I was the enemy! In the midst of a raid I had suddenly appeared – I had paid no attention to the bombing (although I didn't like being in the middle of it any more than he did) and I was demanding food supplies from him for a large number of men. He looked as if he believed I had dropped out of the sky! I thrust my identity card into his hand and stated who I was and who the men were, 100 or so cadets and officers of the PAF, and stated my requirements. He didn't believe a word of it. He'd now pulled himself together and become aggressive and threatening. I could have 'acquired' the identity papers from anyone, he said. How did he know who I was? There was no alternative but to behave as he expected me to. He was in no mood to listen and had practically convinced himself I was a German. 'This is my identity' – my revolver was aimed at his chest – 'I've come for supplies and I intend to have them.'

When the cadets caught up with us and saw the food we had for them they were delighted, and by way of thanks intended to throw me in the air – but calmed down when I threatened to use my revolver. They were highly amused when I explained how I'd come by the supplies. It made a good laugh, although I couldn't blame the army officer. Fortunately he had soon calmed down and I had been able to take what food we required – an adequate carload.

On the afternoon of the 17th, while we rested in preparation for the night march, we heard the roar of aircraft in the direction of the east. To our amazement we saw a formation of five fighter planes bearing the Russian red star. It brought everyone to their feet in bewilderment at their presence over Poland. That same evening Brzezina called a few of the officers together and informed us that the Russians had now invaded Poland. It was the only information he had to give, or knew himself. The following day the Russian invasion was confirmed by radio, which brought about a fresh panic and additional confusion to the country and

Polish people. We were now faced with the question as to whether we would succeed in reaching Rumania. Brzezina received further instructions. This time he was urgently required to select the best pilots, navigators and mechanics from those travelling with him, and use whatever available transport there was to enable us to reach Rumania with all speed. Apparently the Polish Air Force – aircrew and mechanics – were being re-formed in Rumania.

Brzezina chose only single men (partly in preference to taking those who had brought along their wives). The cadets were put under the charge of a deputy. It all happened and was decided so swiftly that everything was still in confusion. The young cadets were stunned. It was impossible to assess the situation or know the position of the enemy. One could only hope to be able to make the border in time. This was as little as we knew and nothing more. Some of the columns of cadets did eventually reach Rumania safely. Others were captured by the Russians and taken to Russia where history repeated itself again.

Altogether Brzezina chose seven pilots: himself, Burstyn, Bielkiewicz, Kowalski, two third-year cadets, and myself; also one navigator and some of the mechanics. Most of the cadets in the column had been from the first and second years. The third year had been promoted just prior to the outbreak of war and to my recollection there were few of these in our column.

We requisitioned two Fiat vans from the local post office and took Brzezina's car and sped towards the Rumanian border, machine guns pointing out of the car windows in preparation for opposition.

We were now in the south-east section of Poland, her most fertile land. The populace were mainly Ukrainian and in some respects they were our greatest danger during the escape. Their language was practically Russian – the same alphabet – and they practised the same Orthodox religion. They were divided for and against Poles, similar to Eire with the British. During peace they had endeavoured to acquire their own separate state, especially in my home town of Lwow, where murders were committed out of hand by the extremists in an effort to obtain their objective. Some waged guerrilla warfare against the Poles, others realised the value of being with Poland. But on the whole they were left to conduct their own affairs and establish their own community, with schools and churches etc, and to use their own language and teach it in the schools without interference by the Polish authorities. Consequently the majority preferred to remain under the Polish Republic. The threat now came from those who had consistently fought against Polish rule and who now took up arms against the Poles – including their own neighbours with whom they had lived peacefully in comparative friendship until now, when Poland was invaded on two fronts.

So we drove steadily for one and a half days without incident. But late afternoon on the second day we came upon a column of refugees – thousands of them – a mixture of civilians and military personnel. From what we were able to see, military personnel predominated. All were moving slowly in the direction of the Rumanian border.

The road ahead dipped steadily towards a small valley. On either side were hills and we were unable to continue our drive at any speed as there was a bottleneck further on, so crammed with people that the rate of progress had dropped to a minimum. Suddenly, from the hills on either side of us shots rang out, bullets flying above the heads of the crowd. This was followed by piercing battle cries before the Russian cavalry charged down the hillside, riding their famous stallions. The whole column came to a startled and abrupt standstill. The cavalry were a ferocious-looking lot, fully armed with rifles slung across their backs, sabres hanging from their belts and each one flourishing a pistol, ready to shoot. We were surrounded almost instantly and ordered to leave the cars, which were immediately driven away. Inside was the food we had brought with us. We had managed to hold on to our few personal belongings.

Military personnel were then separated from civilians, officers from enlisted men. Our mechanics were taken away from our group, which left eight of us together. A fresh column was formed under the direction of the Russian soldiers and we were instructed to march towards the east and Russia. As military officers we knew what to expect and had no doubts about our fate. Instinctively we became a team waiting for the opportunity to make plans for an escape. As soon as we were able we began discussing our move. We agreed we must stick together and not allow ourselves to be split up; no one was to be permitted to slip away individually. If and when it was possible to separate ourselves from any group we were put with, we would share whatever food we each secured from the villages we passed through and would make sure we did not speak to anyone in the column at all. However, we saw no reason to try to escape at this stage for we were heading in the direction we wanted to go in any case. It was also safer to stay with the column than to march together as a separate group by ourselves. So we waited for the right moment to outwit and outmanoeuvre our captors.

One could sense the various reactions of those in the column: a woman's desperate efforts to protect and comfort her child against the ordeal ahead of them; a man's inability to face this new danger and surrendering himself to it without question. Complete resignation swept through the column. It seemed as if it was the collapse of the human spirit. The column stretched for miles, but along the distance we were able to see that there didn't seem to be a great number of Russian cavalry guarding us. As we moved along slowly there was no resistance to the capture. The logical explanation was that each had received one shock upon another, whereby an apathy followed that dulled their sense of survival. Physical action (it appeared to everyone) seemed useless. But there was no doubt at all that the cavalry guards would have opened fire at the first provocation.

On the first night we were ordered to lie down and warned that if any person stood up they would be shot. Drunken cavalry guards did in fact open fire that night further down the column, believing someone had moved, and they were feeling trigger happy anyway. The best thing was to lie quiet and hope!

Later during the night two from our group decided to decamp by themselves, ignoring the arrangement we had made. They succeeded in crawling away unnoticed but the next day they returned to us, having found themselves lost and very lonely without the security of the group.

Constant raids were made to take possession of our personal belongings and valuables. We found it easy to bypass the raiding party while other officers in the column gave willingly or were made to give up their property. The Russians were so busy collecting they didn't have time to notice what we were up to. Each of us slid surreptitiously behind the Russians and joined those already searched. Consequently we were able to keep all that we had on us, which proved most valuable later on.

On the second day, much to our surprise, the Russians handed the column over to the Ukrainian militia. This was even worse and we knew the time had come to make our escape. From the opposite direction soldiers dressed partly in civilian clothes came towards us, and we stopped them to ask where they were going. Apparently further along the line was a checkpoint where the Ukraine militia and the Russians were separating the intelligentsia. The soldiers were being told they were permitted to return to their homes but not so their officers.

We immediately began hanging back, allowing the column to overtake us gradually until finally we were at the very rear and the last little group walking in line. There were no guards at all, so when the next rest period came, which was very soon, we stayed sitting where we were when everyone else got up to move off again. After watching the end of the column until it disappeared from view, we knew it was now safe to move. Our first requirement was to rid ourselves of the clothes we wore and secure peasant working clothes. We still had money between us and valuable assets of our uniform, i.e. our silver wings, goggles, helmets. etc. We decided that none of us would retain any items of uniform that would give us away, apart from our leather overcoats. We could always say we had taken these from 'the officers' if we were stopped. Two of us, Burstyn and Bielkiewicz, spoke Ukrainian or Russian so that was a help to us; they could do the talking and the rest keep silent. In this way we might all pass as Ukrainian peasants.

We continued along the road in the direction of the column and after a short distance arrived at a village. After much bargaining and by exchanging items of clothing we secured the peasant clothes we required. The villagers were very hospitable and friendly, giving us food that was very nice and wholesome, and we were able to rest awhile. We all enjoyed a good shave as we didn't consider it necessary to keep our growth of beard, which could have been conspicuous if we all had one. The problem was our hands. The Russians were very quick on this point. They looked at your hands to discover your status, immaterial to your physical appearance or what you professed to be under questioning. We did our best to simulate the wear and tear of peasant working hands by cutting or tearing our finger nails and imbedding them with dirt and into the hands themselves. We knew we would get dirty very quickly en route so we

didn't exactly roll around on the ground, but we did dirty ourselves up
a bit.

We headed south towards the Rumanian border, walking in pairs at
a visual distance from each couple to enable us to remain in contact – a
safety precaution should anything happen to one pair in the group.

Our disguises appeared adequate – in fact, we looked more like bandits than peasants by this time. The tragic situation we shared ousted
rank; we were a team with one aim: to reach Rumania. Unfortunately,
the younger ones were apt to forget that as the oldest of the group,
Brzezina was finding it difficult to keep up with the rest. I noticed him
dropping behind, unused to walking for so long. The distance between
him and the group was lengthening unnecessarily so we slowed the
pace down to suit everyone.

Burstyn and Bielkiewicz were able to talk with the Ukrainian villagers
without arousing their suspicions. From the Polish villages we passed
through we were able to discover which communities were safe to enter
and which were potentially dangerous to us. Some guessed we were escaping and what our objective was and did their utmost to assist us, stipu-
lating which house was safe to spend the night in and so on. Without such
help we undoubtedly would not have survived to the following morning.
We carried maps and they made the essential indications for us. In
some cases it was necessary to pass through a village under cover of night
in order that we would go unnoticed. With such information gathered
in this way it was most useful in achieving this.

Eventually we reached a region where the land was now reasonably
flat and stretched as far as the eye could see. One could look across acres
and acres of land without anything specific to obscure the view. The grass
grew very high and in places it was possible to walk through it waist deep,
which provided excellent cover when it was needed most.

We spoke very little to each other as we covered mile after mile. Each
of our thoughts were concentrated upon reaching Rumania with all
speed, hoping to evade capture again. We walked as much as possible
along tracks, keeping away from the highway. But this was not always
possible and in these instances we had to take our chances. Abandoned
cars with empty petrol tanks littered the main roads. Tanks, also, which
had been used for escape purposes. We passed by freshly made graves

with plain little wooden crosses held together with string. Along the way-side or lying just inside a field were bodies of murdered peasants bat-tered to death – evidence of where Ukrainians and Poles had turned on each other after the invasion. But the sight that affected us most was to see horses and cattle that had been hacked to death for apparently no justifiable reason. It was horrific and sickening to see how they had been cruelly slain. The reason, if there had to be one, was plainly caused by misguided beliefs. We walked on in silence for the most part of our journey, for we had no desire or heart to speak. Our morale was affect-ed, knowing that our position was as dangerous as the area was unsafe. When we sought out a place to rest for the night we could never be wholly sure that we would live to see the dawn of the next day. Mostly we were so tired we even gave up taking it in turns to keep watch. If anything we slept like babes trusting in God's mercy.

We had neared the large River Dniester, which we had to cross to reach Horodenka, close to the Rumanian frontier. But first we came to a village and before we could avoid notice we had stepped into view of a guard standing in the centre of the main road. He wore on his arm the red band of the militia. We had no choice but to continue to walk towards him and naturally he stopped us for questioning. He was Ukrainian (he may also have spoken Polish – or understood it) and insisted we accompany him to the village hall where the authorities could further interrogate us. There we found ourselves before a better-dressed Ukrainian, in a sheepskin jacket, undoubtedly an educated man and we assumed a teacher from the local Ukrainian school.

Bogdan Bielkiewicz (from Wilno near the Lithuanian border) spoke Russian fluently and automatically became our spokesman. He said we were ordinary soldiers going to our homes in the south. Our interroga-tor listened quietly to the explanation but we sensed he wasn't convinced it was true, although he certainly didn't show it in his replies. Also pres-ent at the town 'count' during our questioning were various local villagers, forming a committee of sorts. When we had entered the settlement there had been no one in sight (apart from the guard) and the atmosphere had been one of shocked silence. It was a strange assembly gathered in the village hall. Whoever was left of the population (and presumably many of the men had been called up to fight), those of a responsible position were endeavouring to organise the affairs of the village and maintain justice. As in a western film we were 'strangers in their town' and therefore suspect. The objective was to discover our reasons for being there and to determine our fate. According to their beliefs and sympathies (collectively or individually) we were either fugitives to be handed over to the militia (or Russians who were expected to arrive at any moment) or patriots of Poland in need of assistance to escape the advancing enemy. Obviously some of the Ukrainian villagers were ready to welcome the arrival of the Russians. Others had no choice in the matter. Unhappily the Ukrainians found to their cost their belief in the Russians was not justified and they suffered as all nationalities did under Russian domination.

Although he quite plainly had no love for Poles, their spokesman preferred – for reasons of his own – not to disclose our true status (which undoubtedly he guessed) or arouse the animosity of the villagers. One can only imagine he was not convinced that Russian rule was best for the Ukraine. Instead he 'suggested' to send us, under the same guard who had brought us to the village hall, onwards to the next community 'across the Dniester in the direction of the south-west'. (In the direction we wished to go, as he well knew.) Pleased though we were we refrained from showing it, merely stating we understood perfectly his 'apparent predicament' concerning us.

So we crossed the river by cable ferry and continued on foot, escorted by our guard (who was nothing more than protection for our little group), towards the designated village. We hadn't eaten for about two days and were hoping for somewhere to find food. We came across a house set back off the road. It was quite a large farmhouse with outhouses. Enquiring of the guard if he considered it safe that we should go there to ask for food, he thought there should be no danger. Although four of the party were not convinced, with the guard accompanying us it was hoped there would be no difficulty. So finally Brzezina, Burstyn and Bielkiewicz came with me.

A young, pretty Ukrainian girl opened the door and listened politely to our request and invited us inside to a large room. There were other women present – the men were away working the fields. The mother invited us to seat ourselves at the long farmhouse table and soon we were

enjoying a wonderful Polish dish of eggs with bread and plenty of milk
to drink. They watched in great amusement as we ate hungrily, the young
girl talking to us meanwhile. She was educated and had been studying
at university to become a teacher. Inevitably the conversation came around
to the war and politics. Burstyn surprised us all by firing the direct
question at her as to whether she preferred to be under Polish or Russian
rule. Apparently she and her family saw nothing against living under
Polish rule and they were all horrified at the present position and
dreaded any change to come. We thanked them for their hospitality and
returned to our companions.

Having escorted us to the next village the guard told us we were now
safe to continue on without him. We managed to hire a horse-drawn cart
from a Ukrainian farmer to take us to the next settlement. Nowhere on
our route did we arouse further suspicion. We saw no Russian soldiers,
only peasants working in the fields. This part of the country was quiet,
but they must have heard the news of soldiers returning home over the
radio and took us for what we appeared to be. We were in the area
where they grew grapes for wine on the high banks of the River Dniester
and the countryside was very pretty. We were now approaching Horodenka,
the last village in Poland before Rumania, a small village approximately
10 miles from the frontier.

A barn in a field was our accommodation for the night and by sheer
chance we discovered the navigator had retained his flying helmet and
goggles. We were amazed he had managed to hide them from us as by
now we really had few belongings between us. However, we were furious he had endangered us all and immediately took them and buried
them in a ditch. As an added precaution we checked each other's belongings, but nothing further was found other than the identity documents
we had each retained. From these we tore off the front page giving our
name, photograph and official stamp, rolled the sheet very thinly and
stitched it into the lining of our clothes. The remainder of the papers
were torn into minute pieces and buried with the goggles and helmet.

We made an early start at dawn the next day. As we neared Horodenka
our spirits rose, for on the other side of the town it was just a short distance to walk to the frontier bridge and we would have made it to
Rumania. The main border post was 20 miles south at Sniatyn, with a

railway and main road going through to Cernauti, Rumania. We had to avoid any main roads, cities or towns to bypass these organised checkpoints.

Passing through beet fields, we helped ourselves to satisfy the hunger pangs. Then we came upon the sugar beet factory, complete with Ukrainian militia guard wearing the red armlet. Bielkiewicz went forward to talk, hoping for information; and to evaluate just how safe was Horodenka. Fortunately the guard was friendly and the rest of us joined them. He admitted his 'armlet' came in useful to him and to help others. He worked at the factory. On the instructions of the Russians, the Ukraine militia were catching all refugees passing through Horodenka to reach Rumania, so we should bypass the town.

On leaving him we decided to split up into two groups of four after skirting the town from the north. One party was to go east, the other south. Brzezina took the eastern route with Burstyn, Kowalski and one cadet. I went southwards with Bielkiewicz and two cadets. By travelling south, should it prove impossible to get to Rumania we would then be in a position to go through the Karpaty mountains into Hungary, and I was used to the mountain region.

But first, while travelling north round Horodenka, we came across a small aerodrome. On it was a crashed passenger airliner of the Polish Air Lines (a Lockheed Hudson). Possibly because we had been unable to join in the air battle against the enemy, and were on the run like fugitives from our own country, affected us to the extent that we threw caution to the wind and all climbed aboard the aircraft. And there we spent a mad five minutes shooting down every imaginary Jerry that attacked us! We were sitting ducks to any militia who might have been observing us. Or, perhaps, it was the last goodbye to a Polish aircraft.

Eventually we bid the others farewell, hoping to meet again soon, and each small group set off on its respective way.

We crossed cabbage fields and trekked down to a little village, then forded a small river; beyond were one or two village houses dotting the area. Although we would have welcomed something to eat and drink, both Bogdan Bielkiewicz and I preferred not to take any further risks so near to reaching the border. But the cadets insisted they could not go on further without either water or milk to quench their thirst. They were determined to seek refreshment from one of the houses. I told them we would wait for them further on under cover of the hill.

Bogdan and I continued onwards over a corn field on the hill; the corn had been cut and manure heaps every 20 yards were ready for spreading. Reaching the top of the slope we felt safe enough to stop and wait, hiding behind a particularly large heap of manure. Half an hour passed, by which time we felt convinced that something had gone wrong. Standing up and looking back down the hill towards the village we noticed a peasant driving a horse and cart that was loaded with manure. Crouching behind the cart as they moved were two young lads about fifteen or sixteen, each carrying a rifle and both wearing the militia red armband. Seeing us they left their cover and shouted an order to raise our hands and sprinted the short distance to where we stood. Obviously the cadets had been caught and revealed our whereabouts. We made no attempt to move, but Bogdan spoke sharply to them in Russian, demanding to know what they thought they were doing. We had been 'instructed' to return to our homes in Sniatyn by the Russians as we were only soldiers. What right had they to stop us! And gradually we lowered our arms as doubt showed in their faces and we made the most of it by pressing home the argument. As the old peasant in his cart had already continued on his way, the boys had begun to look frightened so we turned and walked on over the hill and they let us go, without objecting or using their rifles. Presumably they thought we would be caught in Sniatyn if there was still a doubt as to who we were.

Once out of their sight we breathed again and stopped to locate our position. Beside us was a track to the south; our map showed us that the Rumanian frontier was approximately 2 miles away, parallel to the track, but towards the east. Taking the track we crossed a single railway line and immediately ahead located a small village called Jasienow Polny. We decided to go through it and was again confronted by a one-man militia guard. We greeted him – as cheerfully as possible – and as he seemed disinterested we carried on straight past him. As the village looked deserted we thought it safe to try to get food, and at a church we knocked on the vestry door. We felt sure the priest was inside – we could almost sense him standing the other side of the entrance – but he refused to open.

Some 2 or 3 miles further on was a little forest on a hillock, ideal in

which to rest and hide and observe the road. We even hoped we'd been
wrong about the cadets and if they had escaped capture and taken the
same road we would still meet them at this point. We watched and waited
till early evening and time seemed to stand still. The silence was dis-
rupted by the sound of transport as five heavy lorries, each crammed full
with Russian soldiers singing their heads off, rolled past our hideout
travelling south. We just looked at each other with the same thought:
obviously the Russians had sent new troops to close the frontiers to
Rumania and Hungary. It had been puzzling us why we hadn't seen any
Russian soldiers after they had left the column we had been captured
with and turned it over to the Ukrainian militia. We realised later that
the first wave of Russian military had swept by as fast as possible to the
agreed line negotiated under the Ribbentropp–Molotov pact. As they
passed they handed instructions and the responsibility to carry them
out, on behalf of the Russians, over to the Ukraine militia. What we
now witnessed was part of the second wave moving forward to close
the frontiers. As both Germany and Russia sought to occupy the largest
portion of Poland, neither trusted the other. But as we had no knowledge
of the Ribbentropp–Molotov agreement as we escaped from Poland,
their strategy confused us. Not so their intentions to close the borders.
The one into Rumania was only 2 miles away, the nearest point to cross,
and we anxiously waited until it became very dark. We couldn't afford
to waste time and headed in the direction we hoped was the east, hurry-
ing across fields and streams – getting soaked in the process – and through
little forests. Somewhere around midnight it began to rain, the first since
war began. As we had covered quite a distance we felt we could afford to
rest awhile and looked for shelter in a field of sweet corn where the stalks
had been stacked together to resemble narrow 'wigwams'. We crawled
inside one of these and fell asleep almost immediately, but were on our
way again before dawn broke. At sunrise we found ourselves in the centre
of a pasture field. On the horizon was a crane-like zoraw (a small drinking well), and this gave us the clue that we had, it seemed, crossed over
into Rumania. The structure of the well was typical of Rumanian eastern design, as opposed to Polish. We didn't know when or at what point
during the night we had crossed the border but we felt certain we had.
The date was 23 September. Carrying on eastwards, now with a more

relaxed feeling, we came to the nearest village. It was easy to see that the peasants and their property were poorer than our own peasants. We had reached Rumania!

When we finally arrived at a village with a police station we 'gave ourselves up'. I suppose we had it in our minds that we would be direct- ed to where we could join up with our own forces – or, at least, find some assistance. We were exhausted, famished and indescribably dirty. With some distaste we were motioned to speak with the police sergeant. He didn't take kindly to our appearance either! For standing before him were two despicable-looking beggars and he took us for what we appeared to be. On the other hand we faced an immaculately dressed gentleman in a light blue uniform, a thick white leather belt and white shoulder straps plus pistol etc. The disgust he felt was written in every feature of his face and in his attitude.

We now had to rely on sign language. With some effort we tried to indicate who and what we were – military personnel, Polish Air Force pilot officers. Either he just didn't understand our feeble attempts or couldn't believe it. I made the very grave mistake of resting my hands on his beautifully shining desk, to take the weight of my body. We were both weary from lack of rest and food and drink, and also emotionally relieved at reaching our destination. The sergeant screamed at me in indignation for presuming to rest in his presence and defile his desk, and all but knocked me off my feet! This action broke whatever tension Bogdan and I had been feeling and we burst out laughing, which had the effect of confusing the good sergeant. So we took off our jackets and proceeded to rip open the seams, to his consternation, and took out the minute rolls of paper that were our identities, and these we offered to him, which he took very gingerly. Once he had scrutinised their contents his whole manner changed instantly. He was now 'greatly concerned' about our appearance and obvious fatigue. Two chairs were pulled for- ward and we were made to sit and relax. We needed no second bidding! Then tea was brought in and it tasted the finest cup I have ever had. Our host then said he would provide us with 'transport' (a horse and cart) to take us to the next village, where we would be put in contact with the frontier guard, to advise us and arrange further details.

Like all other Rumanian officers we were to meet later, we found the frontier guard also spoke Ukrainian and French. Subsequently we were able to discuss our entry across the border more fully and acquire information from him. Indicating the vicinity on our map where we had crossed over the previous night, he told us that there were very few frontier guards and none on duty in that particular area, which explained the reason why we had not been challenged. He stipulated we must proceed to Cernauti (using the same horse and cart) and report to the Red Cross and the organisation dealing with all Polish refugees. Cernauti was the nearest main town to the Rumanian border.

The Red Cross installed us in a building allocated to house Polish refugees. We found straw covering the floor on which to sleep and various other facilities including food, main washroom, hairdresser, etc, for which there was no charge. Before anything else we wanted a good wash and shave and the services of the hairdresser. In the main washroom we were delighted to find Brzezina, Burstyn, Kowalski and the cadet. Naturally we were enormously pleased to meet each other again, safe and sound, and had much to discuss. We needed to explain what had happened to the two cadets accompanying us. It was only fortunate that we hadn't decided to approach the village houses also. One of the two cadets eventually arrived in England in 1941 from Russia where he had been taken but, unfortunately, he was killed later on in the war. The other cadet had just disappeared and we never heard of him again. A fate that befell many others who were captured. That evening we enjoyed our first meal in a comparatively relaxed and carefree atmosphere of freedom. Or so we believed it would be.

Next day we were sent to Romano. There was a small aerodrome in the vicinity and when we arrived we found other Polish pilots there; the majority had escaped by air from Poland and had landed their aircraft on the nearby airfield.

This was the first opportunity we had had to deliberate on the war in Poland with some of those who had done what they could with the equipment and machines we had to fight the German Luftwaffe with, in the brief war before our country was finally overrun by both Germans and Russians – who had now divided Poland between them. We learned from our colleagues that our pilots had accounted for some successes in the air, which did something to cheer our morale and downcast spirits. With each new arrival or batch of personnel to join us, we discussed the situation. Gradually a picture was already forming, and what it revealed showed gross mismanagement of Poland's forces – especially the air force – which had led to her betrayal and downfall.

For Poland it was already the end and this was uppermost in our minds, but it strengthened our resolve to get somewhere to fight back, and steadily our intention to prove our ability in the air grew, and we were determined not to fail. We had long been idealists but this was now beginning to be governed by a cold determination.

There were thousands of Polish refugees arriving in Rumania and the Rumanians were doing what they could, as our money was swiftly dwindling. We waited to learn the next stage planned for us. While we waited we used what money we had to purchase new clothes, but before doing so we took ourselves off to the nearest photographer to have a reminder taken of our group in the clothes we had arrived in.

Then it was on to Galati, their next largest city, very close to the extensive oil fields and on the River Danube, which itself was very near the entry to the Black Sea. On the Danube one could observe the huge destroyers of the navy in the port. The River Danube was very dirty, white from the mud.

On the west side of the Danube stood a regimental camp that we were taken to partly under 'house' arrest. We heard they had already begun building refugee camps for internment. At the regiment army camp we were separated into two or three small rooms; there were also three Polish Army officers but we were not put in with them. The cavalry and army had fought magnificently during the short war, but we could not understand the resignation these officers displayed at the thought of being interned. We had no intention of allowing ourselves to be, so we kept strictly to ourselves, giving no hint that we were military personnel. If they wanted to, let them discover this for themselves, particularly the Rumanian commanding officers.

The camp was situated at the top of a high slope on a bank of 200 or 300 feet on the mouth of the Danube; from this slope we realised very soon that it was possible to negotiate it to get into the town without permission. This would not have been granted anyway, had we asked, because they had specified we should not leave the camp, and a Rumanian liaison officer was detailed to be our interpreter and guard under whose surveillance we were put, and only in his company could we go into Galati. We deemed it necessary, therefore, to search for any Polish authorities that may be in Galati, to assist us. One person we found advised us to go to Tulcea refugee camp, where he could then issue us with passports and arrange our release. Then he could help us further. So we took it upon ourselves to leave the camp one night and board the ferry to Tulcea. On the boat we were observed for about twenty minutes, while the boys played cards, by a man who later came to us and began speaking Polish. He asked if we were going to Tulcea and that if we were we should change our plans immediately. He seemed so convincing that we decided it was reasonably safe to talk with him and learn what he meant so we said that was our intention. He was dismayed and urged us not to continue to Tulcea, and that what we had been told in Galati was not entirely true – we could jeopardise our position completely. He suggested that as we were now free we should make our way to Bucharest and contact the Polish embassy there for help, and gave us the tram number in Bucharest that would take us there from the main station. We took his advice and left the ferry at the first stop – and ran straight into the police on duty. They guessed where we had come from and insisted upon taking us back to the regiment camp in Galati.

The colonel wasn't exactly pleased at our attempted escape and called us to his office to determine whether we were civilian or military. Their suspicions about us were now more or less confirmed by our behaviour, even though we refused to admit we were military personnel and insist-ed we were civilians. The liaison officer was convinced that, out of all of us, I was a pilot, and would not accept any other statement. He spoke perfect Russian and was very pro-Russian. He came from the northern part of Rumania, Bessarabia, and had had his suspicions about us ever since we had arrived. But no one could tell him I was not a pilot; he was most emphatic on this point. The colonel informed us he would let us know his final decision. In due course it came – he intended to send us, the next day, by express train to an internment camp halfway between Galati and Bucharest. It was as well for us that he did not decide to send us to Tulcea, for we learned from some Polish soldiers who had arrived from there that the refugee camp was plagued with malaria, which was rife in that area. There wasn't one person in the camp who was not suf-fering and shaking from its effects. We considered ourselves very lucky to have escaped that fate.

With the liaison officer as our guard we were put on to the express train, with the Polish soldiers. Already wondering how we could escape again, there seemed little we could do now, but we noticed that the train seemed to stop for only two minutes to pick up passengers and everyone had to board or alight very quickly before the train pulled out. We saw our chance – it was a slim one but it may just work. We waited as patiently as we could, saying little until the train pulled up at the destin-ation meant for us. We had minimal luggage but dawdled behind to give the impression of giving assistance to our army compatriots, who had rather a lot of baggage and boxes containing food and such like with them. Confusion reigned while we juggled with their luggage, handing it from one to the other, until it got thoroughly mixed up and the Rumanian officer equally confused as he stood hustling everyone around and trying to sort out the mess we were creating. Meantime, we made quite sure we did not leave the train while passing out the luggage. Then suddenly the whistle gave a shrill blast and without further warn-ing the train began to pull away and gather speed almost immediately. We crowded to the windows and gaily waved to those standing on the platform, and the last sight was of the liaison officer hopping from one foot to the other, furious at our deception.

We were all in a very spirited mood until realising that, although we were on the train bound for Bucharest, what we did not possess were tickets for the journey. When the ticket collector arrived we offered money to placate him and was relieved at his response. He, too, was not immune to accepting money any more than any other Rumanian official it seemed. Then it dawned on us that, even so, we still had the barrier guard to contend with at Bucharest station. We emptied our pockets once more to see how much money we had left between us. There was some paper money, which we decided to try and retain for the fare to the Polish embassy, and rather a lot of small change. We handed that over to one of our number and worked out what we could try to do in this instance. The plan we came up with seemed rather childish but because of this it might just work.

The train pulled in to Bucharest and we mingled ourselves with the flood of passengers heading for the barrier. Once there our friend pushed himself forward, displaying the coins he held in his cupped hands. We waved the paper money meaningfully at the now beaming guard, but our 'clumsy' friend missed his outstretched hand, scattering coins at his feet. The uproar was immediate as the guard, and everyone near him, bent down to retrieve the coins. Everyone but us, of course – this was our cue to run and we took off straight out of the main entrance.

The tram number we wanted stood outside, appearing to be waiting just for us. But which way to go? I suggested we took a taxi, which the others didn't agree with for the moment, believing it to be unsafe. But I pointed out it could be no more dangerous than to wander around, or stand where we were wondering which way to go, or by riding in a tram probably in the wrong direction anyway. If anyone would know where to find the Polish embassy a taxi driver would, and promptly called a taxi without more ado. As we clambered in I asked in French: 'Polonaise embassy?' He didn't hesitate, 'Oui, Polonaise embassy', slammed the door shut and off we went. He duly delivered us there and we gave him the remainder of our money, which satisfied him quite sufficiently.

Outside stood about 100 Poles talking between themselves; from the chimney we saw black smoking pouring as the officials burned papers and documents inside. Brzezina, being the oldest in rank, went inside to see what could be done for us. What we did not know then was that the air force were being given priority to get them to France or England, by arrangement with those two countries. We were told that we must get passports, and then after some time – during which they would make the preparations – they would arrange for us to be shipped out from a port on the Black Sea, a location we would have to reach ourselves. This was the only help they could give – nothing financial, and we must secure our own accommodation and fend for ourselves until we heard from them.

But we had no more money, and the only things of value left were our black leather overcoats. These we sold and procured an adequate amount of money in exchange. Then it was off in search of a hotel, and there I discovered some of my civilian sports friends from skiing, swimming and athletics. They urged me to stay in Rumania with them as they had already arranged for themselves to play for the Rumanian sports clubs and seemed to have settled in quite nicely. I listened to them and it struck me that they were of the belief that war would not come to Rumania. I wasn't sure myself, but I was a military man and was determined to press on in the hope of getting somewhere where we could reform ourselves and begin our fight, just as my friends wanted with whom I had escaped from Poland. I had no intention of sitting around waiting to see what happened in Bucharest. Upon finding a German school right next door, and seeing the influence they were exerting over the immediate populace, didn't help to qualm any of our fears.

While biding our time in the hotel waiting for news, I became seriously ill with an infection in my throat and tonsils. I ran a high fever for a few days and on the second day a Polish Air Force doctor came to visit me and thought I should be in hospital as I ran the risk of choking if my tonsils enlarged any further. I knew I would be discovered and interned if I received hospital treatment and refused to consider it. Somehow the fever abated without my tonsils growing any worse, and I was out of danger although extremely weak. Then came news that our passports were ready and awaiting our signatures. The others secured mine even though they felt I wouldn't be using it under the circumstances, for they were told to leave immediately for the Black Sea port of Balchik (now in Bulgaria) in order to leave Rumania. I begged them not to leave me behind and they agreed to take me. They bought tickets for the night train, then came back to half-carry me to the taxi waiting to take us to the station. I was utterly exhausted by all this and must have fallen asleep for most of the journey. Come morning when I awoke I found my tonsils had burst, covering the front of my clothes with blood but, surprisingly, I felt like a new-born babe, perfectly all right. Relief flooded over me when I found I could walk normally, unassisted, and refreshed myself in the washroom.

Balchik looked very like a holiday resort. The Rumanian King and Queen's palace stood on the private pier; there were sloping terraces to the Black Sea from picturesque villas; palm trees; and tropical fish, including orange-winged flying fish that leapt a good 10 yards from the water. We swam and lazed on the beach waiting for the boat – which did not arrive within the expected week, or the next. We ate at restaurants and were billeted out in some of the private houses. About 1,500 of us were waiting to be shipped out. I believe a boat from Constanca had taken about 800 Poles just three weeks before.

It was very depressing waiting for the boat; we were never sure if it would come or not. When it finally arrived it dropped anchor about half a mile from the beach and we had to reach it in smaller boats. Rumanian officers were given the responsibility of selecting who would or would not go aboard. In which case you either needed to bribe them, even though they had been paid to choose a certain number, or you invented or displayed your war wounds and other injuries to secure being selected. Having a rather ugly-looking scar to show off, I was fortunate to go aboard. A friend of mine, an excellent swimmer and very fit, swam to the boat after being rejected by the officers.

On the *Patrice*, fit to carry only about 200 passengers and a small cargo, some 1,200 men were crammed tightly into it, sleeping anywhere they could; not a single foot of space was free. There were a few small cabins, which they allocated to the officers. I shared one, having a top bunk with four others; it had one very small porthole. We were destined to go through the Dardanelles, a narrow strait in north-western Turkey, to the city of Marseilles on the southern coast of France. The Black Sea was quiet and calm and we stopped for five hours at Istanbul. Then a storm broke as we moved into the Aegean Sea between Greece and Turkey. The boat, being overloaded on top, with next to no weight in the bottom, rolled alarmingly. To get from one side to the other had to be done on all fours. I soon discovered the list to be 40 degrees. During the night the boat tilted on her side for a full minute and a half before righting herself. When we reached Malta the captain said he had never experienced such a frightening trip in his twenty years on the water, and refused to put to sea again for Marseilles until at least half went ashore to wait for another boat – British – to take them to France.

At one point during the journey to Malta, while we played bridge in the cabin (in the storm), I was on porthole duty to let in the fresh air and keep out the sea. I got so immersed in watching the rather interesting game I forgot all about closing the porthole as the ship rolled over and, within seconds, we were swimming in the cabin. We opened the door and out shot the water on the other side. But I was in disgrace for ruining the game.

There was only one way of remaining in your bunks at night in the gale, which was to tie yourself down with a belt as I did. There was almost no food to be had until we reached Malta and then the British Navy sent us over some fresh white bread – it was marvellous.

We sailed for Marseilles on a beautifully calm sea in bright sunshine, as if it were summer. We had left Balchik on 2 November and departed from Malta on the 7th. Only about 600 or 700 passengers were now aboard and we were able to enjoy this part of the journey in comparative peace. We arrived in Marseilles on 12 November 1939.

Chapter 7

France

There was friction during the whole of the trip. We had all been told we could not take personal luggage in a great quantity but we soon discovered some of the high-ranking officers had brought at least seven or eight cases or trunks. This was the start of the trouble. Many felt that they were already beginning to deceive us, as they had done in Poland. So inevitably grievances began to be aired by one or another – especially between the lower and upper ranks – until they grew out of proportion.

In Marseilles we were met by the French gendarmerie and the customs officers and immediately taken to the suburb of Bron in the city of Lyon. Bron was the central base of the Polish Air Force; the main headquarters was already established in Paris.

At Bron we found the cadets, NCOs and airmen billeted out near the airfield. We were told we were at liberty to find ourselves private accommodation outside the camp. I found a small room on the fifth floor of a house owned by a very nice old couple, which cost me 400 francs. I then found a small restaurant around the corner where I arranged to eat daily and pay monthly for my meals.

Many of the Poles at the camp felt Lyon wasn't the safest place to be, but one often saw displayed plaques proclaiming its security due to the Maginot Line, in which the local French apparently had complete trust. We did not share the same feelings.

With nothing to do at Bron and no aircraft to fly we felt a sense of dislocation. This didn't help matters and soon the situation began to get heated. We had already noticed the similarity of various factors between what we now found in France and those that had been obvious to us in Rumania and, previous to that, in Poland.

Those at Headquarters had arranged things for themselves very nicely. Their salary – and consequently the lower officers' salaries – were already determined and paid equivalent to the French standard. They were also supplied with uniforms, displaying Polish rank etc.

On the other hand, the NCOs, airmen and cadets, particularly the poor cadets, were as usual being brushed aside and ignored. Little provisions were being made or set aside for them. There could be only one outcome to these circumstances and they began to rebel. We couldn't blame them for feeling as they did for their situation was much worse than ours and was being allowed to remain so. They soon refused to obey orders and, consequently, a 'message' soon came through requesting us to 'calm them down'. We did what we could but felt great sympathy for them. It was then that we began to determine among ourselves that some stand must be taken to ensure against those procedures that had taken place in the past in the air force and were beginning all over again in France. Moreover, many orders, demands and decisions were coming to us from Paris that bore little relation or specific assistance to our present peculiar position.

General Rayski, our former commander of the air force, was in Paris and already his enemies at high command had started a campaign against him, and were using the reasons given for his dismissal in Poland as an excuse for not engaging him at Headquarters. A pamphlet was also circulated to his discredit.

As in pre-war days, the Polish Air Force was under the command of the Polish Army. The army made it abundantly clear they wanted an army general in complete command of the air force – and got their way. All the dissension at the top created similar suspicion and unrest among the personnel. If matters progressed as they appeared to be doing, with treatment the same as we had experienced in Poland, an eruption was bound to take place. And more so, as we were no longer in our native country.

History seemed to be repeating itself in France, as – yet again – this older command of men, greatly responsible for the mess being created, had no idea of the form of flying and aerial combat now in demand. This comprehension and implementation was vital to the war situation. Instead of placing us under the command of the one air force general who did understand our requirements and could direct us appropriately, we were put under the control of the army generals. We felt it to be the last straw and reacted accordingly.

Going straight through the ranks we formed a secret underground movement, based on a system of five. I belonged to the leading five members. They included Captain Stanislaw Michowski, former teacher of bombing in Deblin College, who was soon to become a great friend of mine. One of each group knew another five members and so on down the line. If there was to be a revolt – and we had sufficient cause to feel that way, as well as the ranks – we decided it was imperative to keep some control rather than allow it to run riot.

We didn't want bloodshed if it could be at all avoided. But as far as I could see the only way to achieve this, and have our demands met, was to take our manifesto to General Sikorski personally and carry small arms (pistols) to show our determination. If he agreed, it would be necessary to stay there and ensure our requirements were carried out to the letter. If the couriers were arrested – as well they might be – we would arrange for this eventuality by a prearranged signal or timing and the coup would be put into action promptly.

In our testimonial and statement we gave the reasons for insisting that various officers be replaced with others we considered – by their experience – more competent to govern. The list covered every point and the exact remedy in each instance, with replacement names of those who were open to the changes that had come with the times. In no way did we try to oust experienced men for younger inexperienced ones, or use personal grudges to cloud the issue. What we wanted was a modern and up-to-date air force.

Recalling the issues since, we had given the following grounds for our unrest:

1. December 1939. Found no flying and no work to occupy ourselves soon after arriving at Bron in Lyon.
2. Those of us who felt deeply about our state and what had caused us to be where we were, upon reflection found little we could be proud of and much to feel ashamed about – and very much more to anger us.

3. By discussions and talks between ourselves, some form of picture emerged concerning what had happened in Poland, although it was impossible for us to know the whole story. We could only base our findings upon what we had experienced and seen to be the case.
4. With regard to the dismissal of General Rayski in March 1939, and immaterial to what had been put out about him, we did not believe the truth had been allowed to be stated.
5. There was a complete lack of preparation for the war.
6. There was a lack of tactics that needed to be applied in the war by our leaders.
7. The fact that practically all the air force, especially our leaders, should find itself a little too quickly in Rumania before hostilities ceased in Poland, meant the ground forces were fighting completely without air force support.
8. Chief commanding general, Smigly-Rydz, was in Rumania before us. Most high-ranking officers plus their wives and all their baggage were there also. We were lucky to find ourselves in the clothes we stood up in.
9. By our own resources we found out what was expected of us. But in the main we were left to our own devices and tricks to get by – even on to the boat to France, for example, at Balchik. (Yet much has been said of the official organisation for the escape!)
10. On arriving in France, the first thing we experienced, as before, was that our high commanders had preceded us, complete with wives and baggage. (But not so in General Rayski's case, who left his wife in Poland.)
11. We found we had a new C-in-C of all Polish forces, General Sikorski. What did we know of him? Actually very little.
    a) He'd been living in France since before the war.
    b) He'd left Poland due to a disagreement between him and Marshal Pilsudski.
12. As all ranks were now thrown together the younger officers soon discovered a mutual understanding and equal footing with the NCOs, airmen and cadets.
13. In almost every instance their grievances and sufferings were far worse than ours, especially when all the promises they were given

did not materialise.

14. Who, in fact, held the administrative positions in the PAF Headquarters? The exact same officers who had occupied the roles in Poland. Who were also largely responsible for not allowing the air force the natural function of developing, as it inevitably must. Besides this, among them were those responsible for abuses in other administration matters in the air force, i.e. balance payments etc on graduation day at Deblin.

15. We received a further shock when we heard the chief commanding officer of the air force was another army man, General Zajac.

16. The distance between the high-ranking officers and us widened considerably.

    a)   The discipline started to fall rapidly.

    b)   There was complete lack of trust in most of the commanding officers.

    c)   The NCOs, airmen and cadets were rebelling and refusing to obey the orders of their commanders.

    d)   We, the younger officers, were being urgently asked to control the other personnel, as the situation was rapidly becoming dangerous.

    e)   They, who were responsible for the condition, would not so much as appear before the personnel, let alone talk to them.

17. Obviously something had to be organised by us to stop an impending open revolt, which could only mean bloodshed, and be uncontrolled.

These are some of the points that forced us into this action:

a)   In France the Polish Air Force was the predominant force. It was the largest in personnel of the three (army, air force and navy). It was also highly trained. Therefore, the main concern of Sikorski was with the air force as such, even though the position he held governed and commanded the entire Polish armed forces.

b)   General Sikorski resigned his military position in Poland in 1926, according to what little we had heard, based mainly upon air force advancements he apparently had wanted to secure. His disagreement

had been between him and Marshal Pilsudski; thereafter,
Sikorski retired to France to live.

c) We were naturally surprised to find him in command of us upon
   arriving in France and consequently began considering our entire
   position. For as the air force was so important – as it proved to be
   in the entire war – all the more reason why the reorganisation
   should take place immediately, with few objections. Especially in
   France, as the French Air Force were in a much worse mess than
   we were.

d) As we saw it, as chief of the Polish armed forces Sikorski had two
   alternatives to our ultimatum:

   1)   to arrest both our representatives and those of us in Bron, as
        the leading members of the coup, and deal ruthlessly with
        the matter;

   2)   agree with it – better still if he believed a reorganisation was
        necessary and dealt forcefully with the matter personally,
        seeing it put into effect and functioning correctly.

Point one he would not have found easy to apply as he would have
required the assistance of the personnel (other than his advisers – and
they stood with us), and the revolt would have already begun.

Point two was not hard for him to administer. Virtually his main
concern was the air force as his biggest and most important fighting
force, on which his attention was focused – or should have been.

Michowski, as the oldest among us, and the initial organiser, chose a lieutenant from the 1936 intake of students to accompany him to Paris and
present our manifesto to Sikorski. They arrived at the Hotel Regina where
Sikorski had made his headquarters and saw him without difficulty. They
presented him with our case, producing the manifesto and statement.
They had gone along expecting some kind of opposition from him –
even an initial amount would have been natural. Instead, to their utter
amazement, upon reading the papers through, without hesitation he
expressed his absolute full approval of the whole idea and reorganisation. Enthusing over it he stated it was exactly what he had had in mind
and thought to do. If they now wished they could safely leave it to him

to effect the necessary changes without delay.

With such a reception, Michowski and the lieutenant did what many others undoubtedly would have done in the circumstances – they left Paris feeling confident that they could trust his promises, and returned to Bron to report upon their reception. Personally, I was extremely sceptical and not at all happy they had left it solely in Sikorski's hands to arrange. But the others did not share my feelings and I was unable to persuade them otherwise in their present euphoric frame of mind. So I simply hoped we actually would shortly witness the reorganisation on the lines we had detailed.

But nothing happened.

Soon we became only too aware of the silent wrath of the high-ranking officers at Headquarters, who were now aware of our actions and intentions to oust some of them. Their fury was intensified by the fact that we had dared even to contemplate any disturbances or voice grievances, let alone initiate a full-scale revolt. We discovered that Sikorski had handed the statement and listing over to his adjutants, and thereby all the higher command had been informed.

Even from the little we knew of Sikorski, some, if not all, of the officers were prepared to accept that he was without doubt the right man for us. Therefore it could not be envisaged what had caused him to act in such a way. My friends were of the opinion that he had trusted his adjutants to carry out his instructions and had been deceived. I had my doubts, even though I was prepared to believe he had agreed with the plan. Looking back, I still believe he probably had good intentions – for had he not, he would have had to order our arrests and put Michowski and the lieutenant under house arrest, as well as having a revolt on his hands, which he couldn't afford to happen on foreign soil. But instead of going through with it he behaved stupidly, and recently I learned he was a man who could be swayed by the emotion of the moment, one minute agreeing with something, and the next either doing the complete opposite or taking no action at all upon his recent decision. Equally, it is possible that Sikorski's action was made for political reasons more than military.

Either way our enemies were now in full possession of all the details, including our names. From then on we were marked men. This was proved later when first myself, and later Michowski in 1943, were made to feel the full force of the hatred from those in command at Headquarters – simply for the attempt of all for us to establish reform. Their tactic was to wait for any one of us to make some kind of mistake, when they felt they could justifiably act to bring about a forceful reprisal. The true reason for the punishment exacted was, of course, never once admitted, or even hinted at in the case of myself and Michowski, but it was an open 'secret', known by all as time passed. No indication of the potential revolt was ever recorded in any official document.

Exactly how much of the unrest within the Polish Air Force was known to the French military authorities is difficult to say. In the main they appeared to be satisfied to permit the Polish military authorities to settle their own internal affairs without interference. They must have had some idea, however, when General Rayski left the Polish Air Force to join them, being content to hold the rank of captain. Later, in England, he did the same thing with the Royal Air Force and held the rank of squadron leader, forming the Ferry Unit on the African Gold Coast and then in Cairo. Much later he received air commodore rank.

As a final note on this matter, in France it was possible to revolt against the antiquated organisation of the PAF for we were all very much in the same boat; furthermore the whole of the PAF was in one place at the same time. On the other hand, in England this was not possible. Instead we held meetings, formed and published a monthly magazine, and talked as much as we could to those who were interested in the welfare of the personnel. In this way we did our best to show the cadets etc, that we still had their interests at heart and hadn't forsaken them.

Before the war really began in France and we waited for aircraft, two British officers came to Lyon to recruit Polish airmen for the Royal Air Force.

We were all a bit sceptical at the offer they made as we had heard the continental view that the British said one thing and did another. In this frame of mind we listened. When it was my turn for interview I decided I wanted as clear an answer as I could get first time, otherwise I wasn't committing myself. I had no intention of going to England and finding myself grounded and unable to fly at all. I asked for a 100 per cent guarantee on those lines. After some deliberation they offered 99 per cent. This wasn't good enough for me and I dropped my application. I was pleased I had later. When we finally arrived in England we heard all those who had come earlier were put to defending the coast on the ground. They hadn't got a sniff of an aircraft.

In the spring we received flying training on two-seater Caudron aircraft and the single-seater Moran 406. The commanding officer of the Flying Training School in the Bron area of Lyon was Major Marmier. He was a famous fighter ace from the First World War. According to an article I have on his life, for him the position he was given was a much diminished one than he should have received – it was almost a disgrace to be teaching us. But, in the event, he apparently thoroughly enjoyed his work with us and we got on well together. His deputy was Captain Rougevin, who was married to a Polish lady.

It was necessary to pass through the training course before we either received or were allowed to fly the aircraft meant for us. Also the French had no knowledge of how, or if, we could fly. But we acquitted ourselves successfully, proving our advanced fighter techniques, which surpassed their expectations of us as pilots. With the formation of the Finnish squadron we had hoped that Brzezina would be officially given wing commander position – it was through him that I was chosen as one of the pilots for this squadron – but, instead, the CO we were given was Commandant J. Kepinski. The squadron – later known as 1/145 Fighter Squadron – was based at Bron.

Kepinski was one of the officers we had wanted to get rid of, as he had originated from the cavalry, not the air force, and continued to think and act like them. He had little knowledge of operational flying and was incompatible with commanding an operational squadron. From his own manner and behaviour his fear of flying was overwhelmingly obvious to all. So again our anger was roused. What could be expected of an officer placed in a wing commander's position who intended only to direct operations from the safety of his desk? It was inevitable such a person would be disregarded by those he was seeking to lead. Our attitude towards Kepinski boiled down to a very simple fact: as a leader of a modern fighter squadron, which ours was, he was hopelessly out of place and out of touch with the requirements it demanded. None of us doubted his ability as a cavalry officer, but aircraft had to be flown, controlled and understood in every detail by its pilot, every moment in the air. Nevertheless, Kepinski remained our wing commander, although fully aware of the hostility towards him by his pilots, who found him lacking as a team member.

Immediately afterwards we started to fly the new Caudron 714 – part of the number delivered and promised to us. It was an interesting aircraft inasmuch as it was really meant as a racing plane, not a fighter; and was made almost entirely of wood – very fast but useless for climbing. Two machine guns had been put into the wings, which together with the ammunition added to the weight. It was entirely unsuitable for our purposes, apart from the fact it looked very like a Messerschmitt. It was so narrow in the cockpit my shoulders practically touched either side. A bigger man must have experienced great difficulty in flying it.

Typical of the difference in attitude between the Polish and French commanders was obvious on one occasion, when during one of my flights a fault occurred in my aircraft. The French reaction was that the pilot was the most important concern, aircraft being replaceable against that of a man's life. The undercarriage of the Caudron when it closed needed to shorten itself; there were two large clocks on the instrument panel showing the separate pressures required for that system. To close the undercarriage one manipulated a handle by pushing it forward and down. As I prepared to come in to land I went to release the undercarriage. I pushed the handle down but it became stuck halfway. Having no radio I could only draw attention to my aircraft by flying over the hangar and, as I hoped, crew came out to investigate.

They decided to send up another aircraft, a Moran piloted by my friend Glowczynski, with the important points of the cockpit drill written on its fuselage, as they thought I had forgotten what to do. He flew close to me so that I should read it. The third and final point of the drill was to use the emergency bottle, which contained liquid with high pressure. It was supposed to correct any fault and enable you to land. When the handle for the undercarriage was open the pressure in the bottle could be safely used; with it half open, as mine was, it was dangerous to utilise. Nevertheless, I decided to employ it and switched on. There was a tremendous explosion and the cockpit and I were covered in wooden wreckage and a violet substance that all came from behind me at the back of the aircraft. The handle went down but the lights went out. Now I had no idea what had happened to the undercarriage. So again I flew down for them to have a look.

Later on I learned that Marmier – upon seeing that one half of the undercarriage was down and the other only halfway – immediately issued orders for me to be told to bale out. Kepinski, on the other hand, was determined not to have it. I was his pilot and had to do what he said: I must land, for he was responsible and so on. All I could see from the air were great preparations and activities below, with fire engines and ambulances lining up. I knew something funny had happened and flew up and down waiting for them to show me what it was. They drew a sketch on Glowczynski's Moran and sent it up for me to look at. I decided to land by tipping the aircraft on to the left side with the undercarriage fully down, placing all the pressure on that side and expecting to spin around the aerodrome until I stopped – or at least I hoped to.

I had a full audience watching to see the result. As I came in heavily on my left wheel and touched down, the right wheel jumped into position and I rolled along beautifully, with no problem. The French were delighted that nothing serious had happened to me and carried me shoulder high, calling for a champagne party straight away. What had actually saved my life was the sheet of armour plating behind the cockpit seat. I could not have survived the explosion otherwise. There was nothing left behind the seat, the wreckage had smashed into the cockpit from either side of me, demolishing everything. All that was left at the back were the four bars going down to hold the tailplane. We all got a tremendous shock to see the state of the aircraft.

One of our pilots was actually killed in the Caudron on crash-landing when the armour plating came loose and fell forward, breaking his skull.

We received the initial delivery of Caudron 714s approximately 6 May – I believe the official records state a much later date – the final ones were received in Villacoublay, where we were later transferred.

We heard that Germany had invaded Belgium and Holland and we were prepared to defend Lyon. To do so we had only four Morans; the Caudron 714s were not yet fit for operations. The Germans attacked Bron a few times. The planes were distributed on small satellite fields off the aerodrome. Only petrol, oil and ammunition could we obtain from the main aerodrome and, we would fly there after a raid to refuel and then return to our fields on stand-by. I landed at 12.30 p.m. one day, taxied to the hangar and asked the French warrant officer to refuel my aircraft. He reminded me that it was their lunch hour. I was so furious I shot the ground at his feet three times with my revolver and cursed him in no uncertain terms. We had only a few aircraft with which to defend them and they dared to refuse to refuel us as it was lunchtime! Within five minutes my aircraft was filled and ready for take-off.

In the last week of May we were called to defend Paris, as we were the only available squadron left not operationally active on the front line. We were stationed at Villacoublay just outside Paris. The aerodrome was small and only had entry from the south-east or south-west; any other direction was obstructed by a factory and the hangars, which went the length of the airfield. As soon as we arrived the French were amazed we were flying the 714s (both the Morans and the Caudrons were obsolete when we received them); they told us they had lost five test pilots in them, the aircraft were no good and definitely should not be flown.

It has been stated officially that on 25 May the French Minister of Air inspected the squadron and suspended all flying because of structural defects in the aircraft – presumably the 714s as these were the main ones we had – and the balance was soon delivered to us at Villacoublay. However, although we were aware of the structural defects ourselves, if it was so that the aircraft were inspected and such an order was given, we were not aware of it. We certainly were not granted the opportunity of deciding for ourselves whether or not to carry on flying them. Not that we would have ceased operation of the 714s, only that we were not consulted. Frankly, we would have flown wheelbarrows with wings rather than nothing at all!

While we were at Villacoublay it was more noticeable by all in the squadron that Commandant Kepinski, our wing commander, was hardly flying at all and this had its effect on the atmosphere between him and us.

On 24 May an order came through for one member of the squadron to collect some special orders from the Hotel Regina in Paris – Head-quarters – and deliver them to Bron. I was detailed for this duty. I did as I was instructed and reached Bron rather early, about 7 or 8 in the morning, and waited in the duty officer's room until the commanding officers arrived from their personal lodgings in the town. They were expected at 9 a.m.

While I waited I chatted to the duty officer, who wished to know the position in Paris and whether there had been any attacks on the city. I told him that while there had been no real battles with the Germans so far, the biggest conflict for us was with our own CO, who didn't fly with us but just issued the orders. It was a common opinion expressed by the pilots of our squadron. I wasn't aware that when he went into the deputy commander's office to inform him of my mission, he also passed on my indiscretion regarding Kepinski.

Suspecting nothing, I delivered the orders to Deputy Commander Lusinski and went off to prepare myself for staying one night at Bron before returning to my squadron.

Apparently this was the opportunity the officers in higher authority had been waiting for. They wanted to exact punishment for our former 'near revolt'. As it happened, Lusinski had been on our blacklist for replacement. Much later I heard he had telephoned through to Kepinski in Villacoublay and reported what I had said, strongly 'suggesting' that he began flying immediately. He paid heed and asked for an aircraft the same day, and to everyone's amazement took it up for a flight. No one in the squadron knew why any more than I realised what had taken place. I returned to Villacoublay from Bron on the 26th or 27th. The day after I was summoned to report to Headquarters at the Hotel Regina to see Zajac. Before I went I casually asked Kepinski if he had any idea why. He obviously knew but brushed my question over without offering any pos-sible explanation. I arrived at Headquarters and, without being taken to see General Zajac at all, I was suddenly confronted with an army offi-cer who told me I was under arrest. No reason was offered; I was simply informed that I was now under his charge and he would be escorting me to Villacoublay to collect my personal belongings and then I would be taken to Lyon–Bron. When we arrived at Villacoublay my friends were astounded to learn of my arrest, and then for the first time the officer offered the reasons. I had complained that my commanding officer (Kepinski) had not been flying. This excuse made my friends furious, stating that what I had said was no more than the truth, which they could all guarantee as they had themselves expressed it. What they said did nothing to change my situation, of course, but they all refused to continue flying unless I was released immediately, and they wanted to see one of the higher authorities from Paris.

This was the situation at Villacoublay when I left with the army officer, for Lyon. It was very unpleasant for him, I could see, as he realised what I had said was in fact true. But he had his orders to carry out, however much he sympathised with my position. Yet it was obvious he wasn't in the least happy about it.

The Polish commanding officer at Lyon–Bron was Colonel W. Iwaszkiewicz, who had been the commanding officer at Deblin Cadet School when I first joined in 1935. He was an extremely nice man, typical of the better-class officer, and an excellent pilot. On the other hand, Lusinski, his deputy, was completely the reverse.

Arriving at Bron we went immediately to the CO's office where Lusinski was already waiting for me. He said little except to inform us we must wait until the CO, Iwaszkiewicz, arrived. As soon as he did we all went into his office where he listened while Lusinski formally told me that I was under arrest. When he finished speaking, Iwaszkiewicz quietly reminded him that he (Lusinski) was not the commanding officer at Bron. Then to me he said he would like us to have a private talk together. He had been glancing towards the other officers in the room when he had suggested this and, as they made no effort to move, he got up and directed me out of the door of his office and right away from the building altogether, with the remark: 'Let's get out of here where we can talk.'

Outside while we walked around he asked me to explain exactly what had happened. I did so and then he told me not to worry as he would arrange it all the next day when he would be able to see the French commanding officer in charge of Lyon–Bron, General Igor. He would place the whole matter before him and see to it that I was released immediately; I should meet him at 10 a.m. the following day.

Next morning I waited outside the office of General Igor while Colonel Iwaszkiewicz put my case before him. It was not so very long before the colonel came out of the office smiling at me. He said I mustn't worry any further, it was now all settled and I was released. He took my hand and shook it firmly, wishing me good luck and I could now return to my unit in Villacoublay.

The gist of General Igor's decision had actually been as follows:

a) Legally they had no right to arrest me in this way when there was a war in progress.
b) Had I really committed a serious offence I should be court-martialled.
c) He, personally, believed that what I had said was the truth. Therefore he considered the whole matter stupid and irrelevant, particularly as he knew I was one of the best pilots they had in the Polish Air Force; and a war was on that needed to be fought.
d) If, in fact, what I had said was not true, it was their duty by the rules that compelled them – in Paris – to court-martial me.
e) None of it should actually have transpired in Lyon–Bron as they had nothing to do with me or I with them. My squadron was now in Villacoublay (Paris) and it was therefore the responsibility of the Paris Headquarters.
f) Finally, as Paris had apparently disowned further responsibility of the matter by referring me to Lyon–Bron under his jurisdiction and the principal prosecution witness, Kepinski, had not presented himself to state the case as false against him, he, Igor, felt perfectly justified – considering all the facts placed before him – to release me forthwith.

Convinced I was now free to return to my unit, with the matter officially concluded, I went straight to the mess to collect my belongings. I was just on the point of leaving when Lusinski came to me and, again, placed me under arrest. I was more than surprised by his action and tried to explain to him that General Igor had authorised my release. It made not the slightest bit of difference; Lusinski was determined that I should not be freed. He refused to listen to anything that was said except to say that he, personally, would see to it that I was court-martialled. He marched me off to a cell-like office where I was to remain for the next two days. Frankly, I had no idea whether or not Colonel Iwaszkiewicz or General Igor knew what he had done and considered it hopeless to do anything more, or whether they were kept in complete ignorance of the fact that their orders had been countermanded. I never found out which; I only knew that Lusinski was determined to keep me under arrest. I couldn't see how his commanders could not come to know of my position, but that was the situation. While I was held in the cell, Lusinski sent Lieutenant Glebocki, a lawyer, to prepare my defence. Even he said there wasn't very much he could do for me.

After two days I was taken by closed car to a French prison. It was surrounded by two high walls, the inner 15 yards high, the outer 10 yards high. The prison was square in structure, with a large building in the centre and a smaller, adjoining, one for the officers. The whole place looked exactly like I imagined Sing Sing to be. My personal baggage, effects etc, were taken from me and I was given prison clothes and a number, 680, then taken to the small officers' building where I was to be kept.

There I found a Pole, a former Foreign Legion soldier. His stature was very formidable, strong and bearlike, and small eyes; apparently he could be very vicious when aroused. But he was also very intelligent and clever; he spoke German, French and Polish fluently. In the First World War he had been one of the first instructors teaching in the Polish Army. The Germans had placed a substantial bounty on his head, as he had been hugely responsible for the capture and deaths of many German personnel and agents. When he had escaped from Poland and arrived in France – as we had done – he joined the Polish Army, but being part French he also teamed up with the French Intelligence Service. Upon discovering his criminality, the Poles had arrested him and sent him to prison. The French did not interfere, possibly having no wish to clash with the Polish military authorities.

We had a batman who was quite a character and with whom I got along very well. He was a Corsican, badly crippled; the front part of both his feet had been affected by frostbite in the First World War. He was a batman in service life but had been accused of stealing and imprisoned; and just like my own case, there had been no inquiry. I discovered there were approximately twenty other Polish servicemen in the main building, all incarcerated for minor misdemeanours; in each case no inquiry to prove their guilt or innocence had been undertaken. There was also a Polish Air Force lieutenant with us in the officers' quarters who had experienced exactly the same treatment. We had all been accused of gross insubordination.

The rest of the inmates of the prison were former Foreign Legion soldiers, Spanish and Germans mostly. Those who had fought with Franco in the Spanish Civil War, after which they had run away and joined the Legion. As soon as the Second World War was declared they had been automatically interned under the rules of the Legion for not having completed one full year's service, which would qualify them to serve the French in the fight against the Germans.

I spent most days taking advantage of the warm summer weather of June in the small exercise yard. After about ten days of being there we heard over the radio that the Germans had reached Paris and that France had collapsed. Almost immediately after, I received a visitor, a personal friend of mine from my year at Deblin, Jurek Godlewski. When Paris fell and the Polish forces were again on the move to escape the Germans, he had flown his aircraft south but it had been damaged and he was forced to land. He reached Bron and enquired where I had been taken and what had happened to me. He came straight to the prison to bring the news.

From him I learned that after I had left Villacoublay, and the pilots were refusing to fly, he had first begged them not to do anything silly on my behalf, which may not be of help to me. Then he went to see the uncle of his wife who was Foreign Minister Zalewski to General Sikorski. While the pilots had been discussing my case it had suddenly dawned upon them the reason for the surprising action of Kepinski in asking for an aircraft to fly on the day I was at Bron; now they knew the reason, this had incensed them further against him.

Meanwhile, Godlewski had met with Zalewski and explained to him what had happened. Zalewski had immediately gone to Sikorski and informed him of all that had taken place. Sikorski promised to issue orders for my immediate release. Godlewski returned to Villacoublay and told the pilots of the result, and they all naturally expected that I would be freed almost instantly.

As it could be seen, the orders never reached me. What happened in regard to them was a matter for conjecture. It all took place about the time the Germans were very near to Paris. When the air force were told to move out from Villacoublay and there still had been no sign or word from me, Godlewski resolved to find out if there was still anything amiss. Unfortunately he had no proof, in the form of signed documents or a warrant, to show of General Sikorski's order, only the fact that he had been there in Paris and informed of the result by Foreign Minister Zalewski. Therefore, at Bron he had learned where I was and could only come to tell me what he had done on my behalf.

My friend also told me before he left that the northern coast was now occupied by the enemy and all were making their way south. Some were flying across the Mediterranean to Africa, hoping to reach England that way; others were trying to go by boat. We discussed the fact that, once again, we were running, something we had anticipated on arrival in France and were able to sum up the situation from what we could see and learn. We all felt it was only a matter of time before we would have to move again.

Jurek gave me 400 francs from the small amount of money he had with him, wished me luck and hoped we would meet again in the very near future at our next stop, probably England.

There was quite a commotion to be felt in the prison and we were soon informed of the intention to evacuate us to Marseilles, to another institution, and all our clothes and belongings were given back to us. But what happened next I will never forget because it did not make sense, was grossly unnecessary, yet without doubt the intent blatantly obvious.

With an escort of approximately 120 gendarmes with guns and bayonets – one guard every 5 yards – we were marched to the station where a special train was waiting to convey us to Marseilles. The officers tramped at the rear of the column and the atmosphere was ghastly. The poor women in the town openly wept as we passed through, which wasn't surprising because of the spectacle they witnessed. As we marched I noticed huge oil tanks alight, that had been specially blown up before the Germans arrived.

All the Poles had been put together in one carriage, and I sat in a compartment that also contained some of the Spanish and Germans. As we travelled to Marseilles plans for escape were being discussed quite freely.

This was possible without fear of the guards as there was hardly one to be seen. They had all been left behind at the station as it was not considered necessary to put them on the train itself. One minute we were being treated as desperate criminals and the next almost left to our own devices. The Germans and Spanish were determined to flee at the first possible opportunity. There was nothing wrong with the idea, except for where it was done.

I reasoned with the Poles that as we were going in the right direction, for us, what was the point in leaving the train in the middle of wild country where there was little hope of acquiring help and more chance of recapture. At least, in Marseilles, we wouldn't have to travel further, being already at our destination. It would be more opportune to bide our time and see what happened next. We took a vote on it and agreed to wait.

At Marseilles station we were immediately put under heavy guard again, exactly as we had left the former prison. But we were not allowed to leave the train. There seemed to be some confusion. Apparently there was no room for us in the local prison and they decided we must be transferred to Aix en Provence. There we were taken to a former Foreign Legion regimental barracks, now unoccupied except for us. There were no beds, only straw. The Poles were all put together in one large room. A Dutchman joined us there who was a Foreign Legion man, and a French prince whose wife was a Polish princess. I never did quite understand why he had been arrested – he wasn't sure himself – but he believed the French authorities were of the opinion that he did not want to fight. It was all rather strange, as he was very badly crippled in any case.

We had our little Corsican batman with us and although now we were not so heavily guarded as in the former prison, we were not allowed out of the camp. However, the barracks were not so enclosed as we had experienced before – everything was much freer – and our Corsican friend had permission to go to the town, where he would buy various little things for us that we needed and could pay for with the small amount of money we had.

On 17 June the French war was over. We could hear jubilation and cheering coming from the outside, in the town. I was terribly depressed and thought to myself what a ghastly mess it all was. I had to get to England somehow, as quickly as possible.

As soon as I could I had word with the batman and asked him to venture out on the pretext of shopping and find out the position, especially how to get to Marseilles; what and where were the checkpoints; and also to bring me a map.

Some of the Legionnaires had already fled from the prison upon hearing the war in France had ended. But some had been caught crossing the bridge over the river en route to Marseilles. It was not difficult to escape from the regimental camp, as our window overlooked a fruit orchard behind the 10-foot wall enclosing the barracks. Our personal baggage had again been taken from us; all I had left was my French uniform that I wore, my military identity and a little money.

With the help of the map and what the batman was able to tell us we set about making plans for an early escape. The bridges were the most dangerous to try to cross unless we had some sort of pass or papers. We managed to turn out some quite official-looking documents that the French prince wrote on to say that we were Polish soldiers rejoining our units. We produced a stamp mark with the aid of an egg engraved then rolled on to the paper. It was agreed that just four of us should make the first attempt to reach Marseilles, the little group consisting of two other Poles – a corporal and a sergeant – the Dutchman and myself. I promised the others that as soon as I learned of the situation in Marseilles, I would come back to Aix en Provence and give all the details to the batman, arranging to meet him in the small café opposite the barracks; they could then plan their own escapes accordingly.

At 10 p.m. that night the four of us left the camp by way of the wall and through the orchard, beyond which we met the main road. It was raining slightly as we followed the road for some time, but we began to doubt that we were heading for Marseilles as the road climbed higher into the hills. We saw a small farmhouse and knocked to enquire our position. We frightened the only occupant inside, an elderly woman, on finding four men on her doorstep late in the night. But we were able to ascertain that we were on the road to Grenoble not Marseilles. She gave us the right direction, whereby it was necessary to retrace part of the way we had just come, but we found the highway to Marseilles and then came to a bridge that was heavily guarded. We were stopped and produced our forged papers, which satisfied the guard; he saluted and we crossed the bridge with no difficulty.

The other three began to tire, as they were not so used to walking as I had been trained to do. We found a bigger farmhouse that had a large chicken house in which we installed ourselves for a short rest. The chickens were livid at being invaded, but fortunately the occupants of the house remained undisturbed and we slept for about $1^1/_2$ hours. Marseilles was about 31 kilometres from the barracks and in the early dawn we reached the outskirts. We caught the first tram into the centre and sought out a café for a little food and drink.

It would have been too conspicuous to wander around Marseilles as we were so knew we should find a room. The safest place to hide was where the brothels were. Who knew Marseilles? The Dutchman as a Legionnaire had spent some time in the city and suggested the old port. On the west side of the basin square were the Italian quarters and, although they looked thoroughly disreputable, we chose one of the houses and confided to the French madam there. I was a Polish officer escaping with my friends – would she hide us? There was no question that she would not; we were taken immediately upstairs to a large double room with two large beds. I told the boys to sleep while I scouted around for information and see what could be arranged. I tried to look least like a military man by putting my short-sleeved dark blue shirt outside my air force trousers, and with dark glasses I looked reasonably like the city folk.

I went first to the French military garrison headquarters and talked with the officer in charge, a major. I showed him my official air force identity papers. He told me that on the east side, and near to the church with the statue of the Golden Madonna, there was a camp for Polish personnel; in his opinion I should report there. I said I would, thanked him for his information and left without the slightest intention of actually doing so. I did not propose to run the risk of being imprisoned again, once they discovered who I was, as they were bound to sooner or later.

A civilian identity was the most important to obtain, should I not be able to escape from France, and from the civilian identity office I would receive an identity paper providing I supplied them with a photograph; I did so and was told to collect the paper the following day. While there I enquired if there was any train going anywhere beyond France. They seemed to think there was one due for Spain taking refugees. At the station I was told the last one had already gone the day before. There was little else I could think to try at that moment as it was getting late, so I returned to the room and gave what news I had to the boys. I offered Madam money for food but she refused to take it from me.

It was as well to try any of the consulates for help – and it took time seeking out their locations – although in each case I found them closed; everyone had already left France. But at least I had obtained the civilian identity, which enabled me to move around more freely. Finally I tried the American Consulate which, I learned, was also acting on behalf of the British. At least the staff had not left, presumably because the USA was not yet at war with Germany.

I stood behind two gentlemen, waiting to see the secretary. From their conversation together, which I could not help but overhear, I realised they were also Polish, and aircraft designers. I did not attempt to talk with them, thinking it better to see what kind of reception they would receive as specialists. We were all invited into the secretary's office and in no time at all it was obvious he wasn't interested in giving any assistance. He was most abrupt and very rude; his message was clear – he wanted nothing whatsoever to do with any of us. The fact that his nation was not in the war showed very prominently in his attitude. It was foolish of me to attempt to seek help from him if he wouldn't even contemplate assisting these two other men, who would be immensely valuable.

Without having spoken a word I turned and walked out of the room and downstairs to the main entrance. I felt terribly disheartened and depressed at what had just taken place. I noticed the doorman watching me as I went to pass through the main entrance of the building; he leaned forward and spoke to me in Polish. This was a pleasant surprise for me and answered his query why I looked so dejected. He suggested I first go back to the station and make further enquiries about the train, which they knew definitely had not yet left for Spain. But should all else fail there was one last slight possibility. At 3 p.m. I would have the opportunity to speak with the captain of a ship and he, the commissionaire, would act as interpreter for me. My spirits rose again and I did what he suggested by going back to the station to make enquiries. Yet now I had set my heart on getting to England by way of this ship, if at all feasible.

I hurried back to the room in the Italian quarters to explain this new possibility to my friends, who were as anxious as I to get away to England. At 3 p.m. on the dot I stood on the steps of the American Consulate desperately hoping for the captain's assistance. He came down the stairs towards me from the secretary's room and I approached him with the commissionaire. But it was not necessary for the latter to interpret for me as the captain invited me to speak French slowly to him and he would understand. He was very pleasant and listened kindly to my request: there were four of us who wanted to get to England, could he please help us? I explained who I was and that I was a fighter pilot. He acquiesced. Come to berth G before the customs officers arrive and he would hide us in the coal bunkers. Be there at 3 p.m. sharp the following day, as they would sail at 6 o'clock in the evening.

I told the boys of the arrangement and that they must decide for themselves about going. I would have to travel to Aix en Provence the following morning – 27 June – to give the batman all the information I had gathered, as I had promised. If I failed to be back by the time they had to leave, they should go on ahead without me.

Very early the next day I caught the bus to Aix en Provence and luckily the batman came into the café where I was sitting anxiously watching for him. I wrote down all the news I had to give him, then finally left to catch the bus back to Marseilles. It had gone 3 o'clock before I returned to the room to collect my few belongings and pay for the room. The boys had already left and Madame shed a few tears at our going. But there were two French Foreign Legion officers, and was asked if I could take them with me. I was forced to explain to them how impossible it was for me under the circumstances. I had no power to get them on to the boat, or if I could even manage to get there myself as it was late already. I felt sorry for them as they were awfully upset, with tears in their eyes. At least they had a country of their own upon whose soil they could fight, I told them, whereas I was without a country, just running from one to the other with the Germans following me and my countrymen wherever we went.

I arrived at berth G and saw the ship being loaded by crane with cars, and the English people going aboard. On deck at the top of the gangway sat the captain at a table, with customs officers and gendarmes standing behind him. Now was the moment to take the bull by the horns. I walked straight up the gangplank and came to a halt in front of the captain's table. 'Hello Captain,' I said; he was observing me with a very amused twinkle in his eye, obviously waiting to see what I did next. I turned to the customs officer and handed him my military identity. As he examined it he suddenly smiled and recollected that I had arrived in Marseilles on 12 November last year. 'Yes, Sir, I also remember you.' 'Very good luck to you. I wish I could go with you,' he said and passed back my identity papers. The captain looked very pleased and relieved, and called to ask a small group of English passengers if there was a spare berth in one of their cabins for Lieutenant Lanowski. A young Englishman came forward and offered me the other berth in his cabin. Within seconds the first thing asked of me was if I played bridge.

At 6 p.m. we sailed en route for Port Said to collect a Czech division that the captain had been instructed to take aboard; the crew of the ship were already busily preparing it to accommodate the 1,300 men. A roster was soon made and adhered to by the passengers. Each had a job to do to keep the vessel running smoothly and in perfect order. The women washed and cleaned, the male passengers stoked the boilers with coal. That was the first and only time I became a ship's stoker! The captain informed me soon after we sailed that the boys were hidden aboard safely. After we sailed they were allowed to come out of hiding and join in the daily duties. There was not one complaint from anybody concerning the jobs they undertook and the system worked beautifully.

We arrived in Port Said on the 28th and picked up the Czechs. I made friends with a small family of three: a French-born mother and her two children, who spoke perfect French and English. There was also a French officer aboard and it was soon arranged by the French lady for us four to have an hour's English lesson with him daily as his English was fluent. Later on there was a little trouble with him when I was told he was speaking against us to the captain. My friends were all for disposing of him over the side, but I first I spoke to him and warned him to be quiet for the sake of his own safety. Fortunately, he realised the danger he had put himself in and there was no further talk about us. He had no grounds to speak of anyway as we were only too grateful to have been allowed to sail to England.

In Gibraltar we saw a great number of the British Fleet, such as the *Hood* – battleships, cruisers, destroyers, etc. We sailed around Spain and reached Liverpool on 12 July.

Chapter 8

England

As we entered the docks the chimneys of sunken ships and boats could be seen protruding from the water.

From Liverpool my friends and I were accompanied to Scotland with a British officer, to the encampment of the Polish Army, situated in the hills under hundreds of tents. My first question to the Polish warrant officer was where was the Polish Air Force? The main headquarters were installed in the Rubens Hotel, Victoria, opposite Buckingham Palace. The majority of the air force personnel and some higher officers were in Blackpool. As this army company received air force members in England, they sent a telegram of the various names to both the Blackpool and London Polish military authorities, who would then authorise the transfer of the personnel. This took about three or four days. I knew what this could mean in respect of myself and I was not proved wrong. I informed the warrant officer that having included my name in his next telegram, should the transfer for me not come through after four days he needn't look for me or concern himself about me any further as I would be gone anyway. He was rather taken aback by my statement, not understanding the reason I was so sure my name would not be called for, and I did not bother to go into details.

The fourth day arrived and so did the reply telegram with my name omitted; consequently I left the camp and caught the first bus to Glasgow. I had a little money that had been given to me, but no fare was demanded from me by the bus conductor and very soon I learned from my friends that various public transport and entertainments were offered free to us, which was very nice.

Somehow I managed to acquire the address of where to find the other members of the Polish Air Force, who were lodged in Glasgow in a large church hall near to the docks. There I met again many of my friends; General Rayski was also there, with his deputy, General Deborain. The accommodation was rather primitive, with straw on the floor to sleep upon.

I was very pleased to see General Rayski again, as were my friends, his thought for us was shown when he refused to be placed in a hotel, according to his status – he wished to share whatever accommodation and facilities his men were given.

Once we were deposited in the church hall no further notice was taken of us and we were left by the authorities to make contact ourselves with our military headquarters. We could have passed quite some time in Glasgow doing nothing had we not done something about it. The first thing we thought to do was to move to more respectable accommodation. The answer was the YMCA building. It cost 1 shilling a day and those of us who had money paid for those who did not; we felt more comfortable then and it helped our morale.

The next item was to forward all our names to Blackpool and London for transfer to the main base in the northern seaside town. Again I knew what this would mean, but my name was included with all the rest when the telegram was made. The reply cablegram came for the transfer to Blackpool. Every name was included in the list – with the exception of mine. This did not deter me but rather helped to prepare me against what to expect in the future. I ignored the rebuff and set off with the others to Blackpool.

When I arrived, the astonishment on the faces of the superior officers was unmistakable, particularly that of Lusinski. I was registered along with the rest by the British and given an identity as Second Lieutenant Lanowski, No. P-0711. Oddly enough I was billeted by myself in a hotel where only the previous week all the Poles had been taken out and quartered elsewhere. This suited me admirably. I had my French uniform still and the short leather jacket that was part of it. Very soon we began to receive pay of £18 per month.

Michowski was in Blackpool, one of those who had delivered our statement to General Sikorski in Paris. Slowly we began to organise ourselves once more. What faced us were the same old problems. Firstly, the cadets, who were quartered in Preston. Completely secluded, no one was bothering about them, or doing much to help or encourage them. Although we knew that here in England we should not attempt any kind of revolutionary activities, we intended to live up to standard in our behaviour and guide this younger generation by example. We would do what we could not to let them down, or feel that they were drifting without proper guidance and support from their own military superiors. They felt very much left out of the great fight about to come.

Secondly, came our feelings and morale. Looking back to the beginning of the war – in Poland – and the dreadful shock at the cruel and bloody speed of the occupation, the double-cross served on us by the Russians, and the hopelessness we felt in France, convinced us that we must soon run again. Arriving in this small British island, for those of us who were not lucky enough to be posted to the front line immediately, it was very important not only to keep up the morale of the airmen and NCOs, but to do so for our own sake too. We had yet to be convinced of, or fully understand, the spirit of the country and whether it could stand against the bulldozer of the Third Reich. Also, we had yet to be accepted as fully trained military men, which did not happen until the Battle of Britain.

Thirdly, the meetings and discussions we held were of vital importance, together with the preparation and co-operation of all ranks. Both mental resilience and moral discipline must be effected for the forthcoming battle of the life of the free world. To this end we started printing a small magazine for Polish personnel called *Walka I Praca* (The Flight and Organisation).

Before I arrived in Blackpool two bomber and two fighter squadrons had already been formed, just prior to the Battle of Britain: 300 and 301 Bomber Squadrons; and 302 Fighter Squadron – Posnanski – 13 July 1940 and 303 Fighter Squadron – 2 August 1940. At this stage of the The Battle of Britain 302 and 303 Fighter Squadrons were led by British officers; approximately fifty Polish pilots were in these RAF squadrons.

As experienced combat-trained fighter pilots, one thing we couldn't understand was why it had taken so long for the British high command to make the Polish squadrons operational. We had much more flying and gunnery training than any other RAF pilots at the time. There were air,

air-to-air and ground gunnery competitions between the RAF squadrons and the top three places were always occupied by the Poles. Our opinion was that Air Chief Marshal Dowding was being either bloody-minded or ignorant of his requirements and the trained resources available to him. My personal view was that Dowding was responsible for the deaths of many of the young untrained British fighter pilots, some with only half an hour's training on Spitfires.

During the Battle of Britain the Poles who were taken into the British squadrons proved their worth, as shown in historical records. With the formation of further Polish Air Force squadrons, some of the Polish pilots were transferred from these British squadrons practically in the middle of the Battle of Britain. As a result, many of the British squadron leaders sent cables to the Air Ministry threatening to resign if the Poles were removed, as they considered them crucial to their squadrons. Nevertheless, the Polish pilots were withdrawn to assist the rapid formation of Polish squadrons.

With the introduction of additional fighter squadrons, each squadron commander was instructed to choose the fighter pilots he wanted in his squadron. On each occasion that my name was submitted it was discarded by Polish Headquarters: 306 Squadron – rejected; 308 – rejected; 317 – rejected.

At first my friends refused to believe they would exclude me when I forecast that it would happen, and told them not to waste their time submitting my name. From the point of view of those at Polish Headquarters it was dangerous for them to accept me in any one of the squadrons, immaterial to the fact that the Battle of Britain was in progress and every conceivable pilot was desperately required. My experience and qualifications as a fighter pilot – and equally as a sportsman – made for the best possible combination (which I was fortunate to have) for fighting and specifically for surviving in battle. However, their instinct told them to obstruct and restrain my career on its natural progress whereby they would not be compelled to acknowledge either my battle achievements or future promotions – a source of danger to them.

Possibly it was hoped that I would get so angered and despondent at not being chosen or detailed to a squadron that I would eventually transfer to the Royal Air Force. Even had I wanted to – and the thought did come to my mind on several occasions – it would not have been possible. Based on their own rules, and due to the agreement they had with the Poles, the British air force would not have been able to accept me as a member. They also allowed the Poles to exercise their own disciplinary action, upon which my case would have undoubtedly been based by Polish Headquarters. But had I attempted to approach the RAF, the Polish high command could easily have denounced me as a deserter. Therefore any such action by me in this respect was impeded and had me caught either way.

One day, as I sat in my hotel room, I received a visit from a young Polish airman from Rubens Hotel. His position there was as a clerk, which I gathered he had also been for the headquarters in France. He had been chosen among his friends to inform me of a matter involving me that caused them some concern, for, as he explained, they were all aware of what both I and the other members of the 'underground movement' had endeavoured to do on their behalf in France and what had happened to me as a result. In their position at Headquarters – before and now – they naturally were in possession of details connected with the various orders that necessarily passed through their hands in transit from one department to the other. Recently information given to the Royal Air Force Intelligence indicated that I was a dangerous Communist. I assured my young friend that this time it would not be so easy for those who obviously intended to get rid of me – not in England.

At the same period I had obsessed that I was constantly being watched wherever I went by a Polish officer and this brought about a second matter. Actually it was rather a stupid order to have detailed to this man, for had I anything to hide or was involved in anything that could warrant this observation, my behaviour would have been vastly different to what it was and he had already been shadowing me for quite some while. I decided it was time to put an end to his routine and to his surprise I startled him by walking up to him one day and asking him if he had anything to communicate to me and suggested we talked in my room. Apparently he had been instructed to approach me but was reluctant to do so as he was afraid of both me and the 'organisation' to which I belonged. This, of course, was a ridiculous reason, yet obviously he had been given the impression that we were capable of ruthless behaviour, which had terrified him. Nothing could have been further from the truth, but as he had never been one of us or held our opinions, this must have accounted for the fear of his personal safety.

He had been instructed to inform me that if my attitude changed completely and I agreed that what the superior officers did was correct in all respects, my promotions and decorations would be assured forthwith. Naturally, this state of affairs was unbearable to endure, and it required great effort on my part to maintain a semblance of patience until such time that the right opportunity would come to counteract this implacable attitude, and I could get back into the war and participate with my comrades.

While I was forced to wait in this manner a couple of things happened to prove the extent of the efforts to obstruct me, should I attempt an approach into the Royal Air Force, and, on the other hand, persuade me into their line of thinking and acceptance of their ruling.

It wasn't in my nature to be moulded in this way, which was the very reason they had failed to accomplish this in the first instance. I held my own opinions and beliefs and told the lieutenant to convey to those at Rubens Hotel my reply, that I had no intention of bartering my beliefs or principles solely to ensure promotions or decorations, and to assure them I would never change.

Very few of us Poles spoke English, some a smattering perhaps, but fewer still good English. Therefore lessons appeared essential; to the British at least, for we were of the opinion then that it was totally unimportant and did not relish becoming schoolboys taking class lessons again. As far as we were concerned the necessary English words that would suffice were 'Bandits', 'Break', and 'Okay', plus a few descriptive technical words of the aircraft, all of which we felt could be mastered in a short space of time. Whatever else was spoken could be done in our native tongue, especially as the Polish Air Force organisation was more or less established and Polish squadrons were forming. In fact, later we did actually speak Polish in the air as Polish controllers were operating on the ground.

It was depressing and infuriating as each day passed and the Battle of Britain had come and gone. All the pilots who had been previously taken into the squadrons were now coming to rest and were able to give those of us left behind a fuller picture of the situation but, naturally enough, not the whole extent of it. We had heard only of the fate of some of our friends by word of mouth or from letters, but now we knew more. The number of Polish pilots killed in the Battle of Britain was 26, with Polish victories (enemy aircraft shot down) standing at 203.

Upon the return of our friends I learned of the death of one of my greatest friends, Alosza, killed just after the Battle of Britain. He lost his life with two others (another Pole and one British) in bad weather, the three of them crashing into the hills of Redhill in Surrey. With the exception of Alosza, who even so had not been killed in action, none of my personal friends of my training year who took part in the Battle of Britain lost their lives at this time.

But 1941 proved the hardest year during the 1939 to 1945 period, as now, for the first time, we were the attackers over enemy territory (France), albeit in much smaller numbers than the Germans with their large waves of aircraft. In 1941 we went as fighter cover for the bombers whose numbers were equally small; for example, 12 bombers (Blenheims) able to carry only a very small bomb load. The cover required for them was 6 to 7 squadrons (12 to a squadron) and we could meet up to 300 German fighters.

According to my personal records I lost six friends in that year from our promotion year of 1938: J. Czerniak; M. Samolinski; J. Godlewski; J. Grzech; J. Kosmowski; and T. Nowak – all good pilots. In the beginning of 1942 we lost another three excellent pilots, one shot down and two accidents: J. Daszewski (shot down); Feric (Ox); and F. Szyszka, who had finished as number one cadet of our year and also, more importantly, he was the first pilot in the Second World War to experience being shot down by a German Messerschmitt pilot while descending on a parachute over Warsaw during the war in Poland in 1939. He received approximately thirty bullet wounds in his body, miraculously not one of them serious. He was cared for and nursed back to health secretly in a Krakow hospital, and as soon as he was able, helped to escape to France where we were all gathered.

The news of the Germans' despicable act spread like wildfire in Poland itself, and among us, and was met with a deadly hatred that changed our whole attitude of an honourable fight; it now contained no mercy, either expected or given. In England we sensed the shock our British counterparts felt at our attitude; our only reply to this was that time would give the proof. The greatest fear of captured German airmen was to be told that unless they co-operated with information required by the British Intelligence Service they would be handed over to the Polish Intelligence Service 'for questioning'. Later, we saw that British opinion did change towards this dirty war game. Through the honourable outlook held by the Allies the average German ace could claim to have survived being shot down five or six times, baling out as they were ordered to do if finding themselves in an impossible fighting position, so as not to risk being killed.

Meanwhile, forced to wait and hope for an opportunity to resolve the situation holding me, Kepinski, my former CO of 1/145 Polish Fighter Squadron in France, and over whom my arrest had supposedly occurred in Paris and Lyon, arrived in England having been helped to escape from France where he had been shot down not long after I was arrested. My friends and former pilots of 145 Squadron had already told me how he came to be shot down. It would appear he had flown in formation with a Messerschmitt in the belief it was a Caudron 714, which he was flying at the time, both aircraft being very similar. The German pilot, seeing the French aircraft, went immediately into attack and shot Kepinski down. To my knowledge there is no official account of what truly occurred. However, Kepinski was later awarded the Polish Virtuti Militari. When he arrived in Blackpool he was in a very poor state. Within a short while I learned that he had changed his opinions on the subject of flying techniques, and had realised that we had been right all along. Moreover, he upset himself with his thoughts, stating that I never spoke to him or would shake his hand. Michowski came to me and suggested I pacify Kepinski by shaking hands with him. Although Kepinski was one of those who had caused me to suffer a good deal, I admitted to Michowski that while I bore no particular grudge against Kepinski, to meet him again meant little to me. Even though he now understood how wrong he had been, the situation for me would remain, but I agreed to a handshake all the same. Michowski was present when I met Kepinski socially, shook his hand, and talked with him for a short while; it was obvious as a pilot he was now finished and, unfortunately, he had suffered indirectly because of his views and former behaviour.

It was during the time that my friends were again dispersing to different squadron units, that through Michowski I heard of the possible formation of a Polish council whose object would be to safeguard various aspects concerning Polish nationals and keep a watchful eye on military matters, investigating any such problems that warranted their specific attention, on Polish military or governmental procedures.

Meantime, on 21 January 1941 I decided to send a letter through authorised channels to the commander-in-chief of the Polish Air Force, Major General Ujejski, requesting an official inquiry, having outlined my situation of inactivity. I received no reply whatsoever and this I rather expected. But early in March a tentative posting came through for me. It was to attend a training unit to undertake the beginners' course for inexperienced pilots!

Before this posting was confirmed and I left for the unit, the Polish council actually came into being and some of the Polish parliamentary members came to Blackpool to learn various details for themselves regarding the Polish Air Force. The air force was the focus of much of their attention due to its rise in popularity in Poland just before the war; also they held the idealistic view to which we all subscribed during the war years – that of returning to Poland after the war had ended. Therefore, our affairs during the war years must be constantly watched to adhere to the standard required of us from Poland.

There was one particular lady member, a Mrs Zalweska, who devoted herself to this course and ideal, and it was to her that I decided to write and send my complaint regarding my position. I did not have long to wait to know if it was accepted for it was taken up immediately. Mrs Zalweska, with two other members, Mr Fohierski and Mr Bielecki, undertook the investigation.

On 21 March I forwarded once more a letter of request for an inquiry to Major General Ujejski, again through official channels, and waited for the result.

From Mrs Zalweska I was told that when my case was presented by her and her two colleagues it caused quite a considerable disturbance in the meeting. The discussion became very heated, with explanations being demanded, and the request being put forward for General Sikorski to attend personally to give the reason for not placing me in an active squadron. But – after the meeting and tempers had calmed a little – it was considered that probably the commander-in-chief of the air force should be the one to answer the question why I was not allowed to fly and fight in a squadron and, consequently, Major General Ujejski was called to appear before them to give these answers.

While all this had been going on my posting was confirmed and I had already left for Old Sarum and was supposedly being trained to fly. Ujejski obviously received a shock at the summons to appear before the committee, for not long after I received a telegram from his headquarters at the Rubens Hotel granting me an interview on 22 April. From the training unit in Salisbury I went to London to attend the interview. As soon as I entered his office I realised the shock he had received, for the look upon his face was pure fright. He stood up immediately I entered and offered me a seat. Even so, he tried to place me in the position of accusing them on totally unjustifiable grounds. He did not understand and saw no reason why what I had stated could be so. He was so typical and representative of his kind holding the responsible positions at Headquarters, it was pathetic. Not only that but a comedy to have to witness and partake in, especially at such a time.

The only satisfaction I took from this 'interview' was the knowledge that they had not had it all their own way. Even so, I apparently needed to go through the various training units for flying instruction – I must understand this – it was the requirement made upon them. The fact that I was already trained and available to be placed in a squadron – as all my other colleagues had been, months before – was brushed aside as a minor detail whenever pointed out. The interview concluded with a warning against any further hindrance to keep me from a front-line squadron. I would attend the training units, after which I could expect a proper posting to a fighter squadron, and a time period was agreed upon that he 'gave his word' would be kept. I left him with the intention that I would make sure of it.

Chapter 9

Operational training unit

On 29 April I was posted to Penrhos, North Wales, to the Air Observers' School.

Within a short while of training I was instructing on bombing techniques and air-to-air gunnery shooting. There were about seven or eight other Poles at the camp. We were billeted in a wooden hut, with one batman to so many rooms; most of the batmen were elderly Welshmen who were very nice and kept our accommodation spotless. My batman ensured I had fresh flowers in my room each day, which was a pleasant surprise. We flew Fairey Battles – one of the first light bombers – and used it to train the boys on air-to-air shooting. Two aircraft, each towing a target, took it in turns for the boys in either plane to fire at the opposite target. I asked each pupil if it was his first attempt and, if so, I'd fly very close on to the target, whereby his shooting resulted in looking like one bullet hole. When his confidence of hitting the target was established, I would then gradually move further away on each successive shoot, seeing the aim and firing improving each time. The students found this method encouraging and helpful.

One Polish pilot with us was considered too old to send to the front line for aerial combat, but as he wanted to carry on as a pilot this job was suitable for him. Being younger and mischievous we played tricks on him in the air. After the shoot ended, whichever Pole flew with him in the other aircraft would manoeuvre very close to him until his rope (holding the target) was over their wing, then would fly forward, lifting the rope higher, with the consequence that his plane's tail would come up and the nose down, forcing him into a dive. When he realised that we were the cause of this he complained to the CO that those young devils were trying to kill him. It was very unfair to him but irresistible to us. Fortunately, he understood we really meant him no harm and friendship prevailed.

I was converted to the Blenheim light bomber. Bombing practice for the boys was allocated for approximately 1 hour 20 minutes. I often arranged with those who flew with me to leave it to me entirely to get them exactly over the target site on the right direction, speed and height. They could then drop their bombs as soon as the target came into their bomb sight. We could complete the runs in about twenty minutes to half an hour and then go and enjoy a flight in the high mountains of North Wales. The group captain got to hear of these trips, although he had no idea who was making them. I warned the cadets about careless talk and who they spoke to. But as they enjoyed themselves they kept our secret, although there was always a battle between them as to who was to fly with me. Generally two or three would pile into my aircraft in anticipation.

As the course neared its end there was a feeling that the group captain wanted to keep some of us there as instructors for as long as possible. I went to him to ensure my posting to an active squadron, under the agreement I had with Ujejski. He didn't seemed concerned by this and insisted I must wait until the Air Ministry made such a decision to transfer me elsewhere. I dropped the hint that I would assist in making sure that decision was made.

It meant waiting for the right opportunity and day to fly in such a way he wouldn't want to keep me. On the west side of the aerodrome was a small mountain, with aircraft hangars at the foot of it. The wind invariably came from the west and after take-off we flew up over the hangars, above the mountain and turned immediately into the circuit. Behind the mountain was a small river that circled the airfield and flowed into the sea on the east side. On one normal bombing practice day, with the cadets as my passengers, I decided the time was right. I taxied, opening full the throttle on both engines to get my speed, and headed straight for the hangars while at the same time switching the engine ignition on and off; this caused a violent bang each time I switched on. Pulling up straight past the hangars, still manipulating the ignition, over the mountain we went and disappeared the other side. The terrific racket of the series of explosions I made had brought everyone out to see what was wrong and, as we dropped out of sight behind the mountain, they all waited for the explosion to come as we crashed. They were still standing there listening, wondering what was happening, as I descended upon them from the east in full dive. I'd flown on the deck along the river – hopping up and down like a frog – out towards the sea, then back vertically over the aerodrome, scattering them as I pulled out to climb back up for aerobatics – then stalling and another dive, I beat up the aerodrome before disappearing over the mountain to start all over again. I obeyed the group captain's call to his office after we landed and reminded him that in light of what he had said about the Air Ministry issuing a transfer, I had arranged one myself. He didn't want pilots like me, now did he? 'Certainly not,' he agreed glaringly. My new posting came within the week.

On 9 September I went to Ashworth to join 55 Operational Training Unit. The station was situated between Newcastle and Sunderland, a few miles from the Tyne docks that were dotted with barrage balloons. You had to be careful on take-off, for two minutes after brought you upon the first balloon. Stringent care was vital to avoid accidents, especially during the bad weather of the autumn. Again, I was supposed to be trained – a formality – this time as a fighter pilot; the aircraft we flew in were Hurricanes. Each day that passed was a wasted day, for I should have been in the front line.

The Hurricanes had come from the Battle of Britain and were in shocking condition, but the British mechanics worked miracles on them to make them fit for flying. The pilot instructors were also Battle of Britain pilots and their nerves were in a very poor state. When we wanted to fly in close formation with the instructor the poor chap couldn't stand to see another's wing so near to his face; it had a very bad effect upon them. The course was to last six weeks and then I would finally be assigned to a squadron, so as patiently as I could I endured those long weeks.

Just as the course was ending I was called to the wing commander's office. His request for me to stay on as an instructor was unthinkable; I didn't hesitate in my reply – I just refused outright, as if I hadn't heard what he said, and didn't want to listen. Fortunately he realised how I felt for he overlooked my blunt, aggressive refusal to be waylaid like this. If he tried to keep me I'd create such hell that he'd wish he hadn't done so. But after this barrage it was my turn to listen. As he explained his position quietly I understood that he too had a problem. He was desperate to retain a few good pilots, which was important to keep the school to a standard as the next course students were to be Canadians and some Australians. He promised he would not try and keep me longer than the next six-week course. Would I now reconsider? It wasn't an easy decision to take but I didn't feel fully justified in refusing, and I appreciated his open frankness to me. I wanted him to understand, though, that I would stay for him personally because of it. As I left I added – only half jokingly – that anything more than six weeks would result in a court martial for both of us; he smiled but took the point.

The Canadians arrived; they were inexperienced and it showed. This war appeared to be a game to them, but they made use of the shelters and their tin hats when the Jerries came over at night to shoot down the barrage balloons. They were far away from knowing aerial combat. They had just six weeks to learn, so they had to learn fast and learn well if they were to survive. From my personal viewpoint, what I saw was pathetic and a tragedy because I knew and understood exactly what they were about to face in the leading squadrons. I also knew it was a human impossibility to train and instil in them in the time available the extent of what was vitally necessary. My main problem was dealing with their attitude, which was exactly as it should be – spirited young men unaffected by fear and not having experienced the 'dirty' cruelty that it now was. Given time they could be moulded into excellent pilots. But going into the realities of war with this naïve frame of mind could cost them their lives. Although I realised my job was hopeless before it began, nevertheless I tried various means to antagonise them into appreciating their inexperience. And this I did by playing the game of cat and mouse with them in the clouds. This produced the effect I desired, with excellent results, but it almost cost me my life in the process.

The trainees liked their fun and spent evenings drinking in the nearby pubs, often missing the last bus home and having to walk. Consequently they were so tired in the morning that I often arrived to start the morning's practice flight to find no one – or very few – up and around. I'd have to give the order for them to be assembled in ten minutes, which wasn't taken kindly. In addition, they couldn't understand why – as a Polish pilot and obviously very good – I wasn't in the thick of the fighting.

Why should I be in this job, particularly when I was young and healthy, when they would be going off to the front? Their attitude to me was rather unpleasant but understandable. There was only one way for me to gain their respect and attention and that was to prove to them, in the air, that I could impart the knowledge of aerial combat, which they lacked. There was no point in going into any other details as to why I was there instructing them. It wasn't long before we really began concentrating on the little game of hide and seek, or cat and mouse, in the clouds. The fact that they were unable to keep on my tail constantly was a source of intense irritation to them and this culminated in the day they decided to try a trick or two of their own.

There were basic rules it was imperative to observe as for safety, necessary even in real battle. The ultimate aim of this activity was manoeuvrability and the art of understanding the turn – or corner, as in a vehicle. As a practice game the rules were such that I – the mouse – was allowed only half power; my pupil – the cat – had the use of full power. The point a student was required to learn was knowing when not to use full power to get on my tail and stay there as we weaved from cloud to cloud. I would fly as close to the cloud as possible, but never through it, for he could lose me easily and that wasn't fair.

Usually the trainees were quite anxious to be the one to have the dogfight with me when the weather was just right, each determined to be the one to hold me this time. But one day when I saw the weather was good and suggested straight away that we should have a dogfight, one jumped immediately at my offer while the others just stood silently by. When I had entered the room, the flight had been conspicuously quiet and his eagerness belied their manner. I sensed immediately they were extra earnest this time not to fail and I knew I would have to be on guard what this particular pupil may do. We did various manoeuvres and although he did quite well, he kept losing my tail. Then as I successfully evaded him for another cloud, turning to go round it on the right side, his excitement and irritation caused him to break the basic rule – he turned left and approached from the opposite side. We found ourselves hurtling towards each other in a likely head-on collision. As I pulled with all my force on my stick, he had thought to do the exact same thing and we both flew vertically upwards, with a hair's breadth between the undercarriages of both aircraft.

I continued up for a further 5,000 feet, levelled out, closing the throttle slightly, then called him over the radio to join me and waved my wings for him to come. When he didn't do so I then heard him speaking to the control tower; I couldn't hear exactly what was being said but something was obviously wrong. So I asked him what it was and he told me that he couldn't fly very well as something was wrong with his arm. The control operator told us she would call the ambulance and fire tender right away.

Meanwhile, I told him that I would get him safely down but he must do everything that I did. 'You fly on my wing and I will bring you in to land on the aerodrome, and I'll touch down soon after you. Don't do anything else, only exactly what I do.' Fortunately, he did just as I told him, flying with me all the way. I brought him on to the approach, we lowered our undercarriages and flaps and I took him right to the ground and he made his landing. As I pulled away to re-circle the airfield I saw the ambulance, which took him to the sick quarters as soon as he stopped and switched off the engine. I went straight away to see him as soon as I landed to find out what was wrong with his arm. When he pulled on the stick to climb, as I had done, the force and speed had dislocated his arm from his shoulder. The doctor soon put it back for him.

My pupil had done very well to land, as the Hurricane had one rather bad arrangement in the cockpit. The mechanism for the undercarriage was on the right, and to release or close the undercarriage required you to take the control stick in your left hand. How he manipulated the landing gear with his right arm wholly out of action is unclear – perhaps by holding the control stick with his knees and using his left arm to operate the undercarriage gate formation.

The student didn't say how he had come to dislocate his arm, and I didn't give the reason why I thought it had happened either, as he had learned his lesson the hard way. But from then on there was no more 'funny business' from any of them and they stuck to the rules without deviating; as a result, our relationship also improved.

As autumn proceeded the weather worsened, with clouds, rain and fog reaching to ground level. I had warned the trainees of the bad weather they would sooner or later come across while flying, and impressed upon them that they must apply essential rules, particularly until they became

more experienced. I advised them of the possibility that during a formation flight they may lose me if the weather was poor, and if they did
not know where they were they should hope for a cloud break and use
it to come down and land.

At that time there wasn't radar to assist the aircraft. When flying in
the clouds they should use their instruments, and for a blind landing the
flaps must be down and speed at the minimum while descending slowly.
In this way if they hit something, on the ground, they had a very good
chance for a crash-landing without fatal incident. But they must keep
their nerve and follow the rules exactly. If fortunate enough to descend
into clearer weather, they could then fly close to the ground, but if not,
a crash-landing in the nearest field, even if their aircraft suffered,
would hopefully keep them safe.

On a day that the weather seemed to be reasonable for flying, I took
off with two of the Canadian pupils, an officer and a sergeant. We did a
few exercise manoeuvres and then came back for landing. Very poor weather conditions met us as we descended through the clouds. I instructed
both of them over the radio to keep as close to me as they possibly could
and not lose me. But both of them did eventually, and I found myself
completely on my own. I hoped they would remember all I had taught
them and follow it in detail, but I had the feeling that at least one of them
may not make it. I just hoped the feeling I had would be proved wrong.
One of the boys – the officer – did exactly what I told him and successfully crash-landed, emerging without a scratch, even though his aircraft was a complete write-off. The other, it would seem, must have lost
his nerve and was killed outright as he hit the ground. I had an idea of
approximately where I was – I saw a hole in the cloud and dived straight
in and within the next 5 to 10 miles there was the aerodrome quite clearly
for my landing.

A court of inquiry was held and I was required to go to the town; it
was the first time I had attended a British inquiry. I had been terribly
upset at the death of the young boy, but the counsellor holding the inquiry
did his utmost to console my feelings – I had done my job and it was
just one of those things that could happen. What he said was perfectly
true, of course, but all the same I was terribly depressed the boy hadn't
made it back safely.

At the end of the six weeks Wing Commander David kept his promise to me. I was posted to 308 Polish Flight Squadron (Krakow), which actually was the same fighter squadron – albeit given a new number – that I had been with in Poland before the war had started and just before I was sent to Deblin. It was then 121 Fighter Squadron. We still had the same badge – a lightning arrow with a feathered wing in flight. I was converted straight away to Spitfire Mark IIs and to my amazement two weeks later I received a further posting to 317 Fighter Squadron in Exeter. This had been arranged for me by my friend Brzezina without me knowing. Therefore I was only able to complete five practice flights after conversion before leaving for the Devon town.

Chapter 10

Operational fighter squadron

When I arrived at 317 Fighter Squadron, I found that Brzezina had received a posting to Polish Headquarters for a desk job, and later became Chief of Staff. We seemed fated not to team up again in the same squadron. The squadron leader now was H. Szczesny. The aircraft were Spitfire Mark vs, which had 2 x 20 mm cannons and 4 x .303 machine guns. A British squadron was also stationed on the aerodrome, as was a squadron of Polish night fighters, No 307; they had Beaufighter Mark iis. We experienced a very unpleasant atmosphere because of the unreliability of the Rolls-Royce engines on the Beaufighters – there were many fatal accidents, often with damage to our Spitfires. Rumours circulated fast and furious that the engines had been sabotaged at the York factory. We felt as bad about the accidents as our friends, for as a result of them their morale suffered badly.

Air Chief Marshal Dowding paid a visit to Exeter aerodrome. The purpose of his visit was to improve the relationships between Fighter and Bomber Commands, for apparently there was reason to establish better relationships. He had come to give a talk on the subject; a disguised order would probably be a more apt description. His speech came as somewhat of a surprise to the Poles, who failed to understand the necessity for having to seek such co-operation. Then, at least, it was considered by us our greatest duty to defend them and, naturally, even more so the Polish bombers – our own countrymen. We remarked upon this to Air Chief Marshal Dowding and it was a relief to us to be assured by him that his words were not intended at Polish fighter pilots.

As time and the battles progressed, individualism grew in the air, in the Polish Air Force as much as any other air force, and strict observance to one's duty as fighter cover for bombers had to be adhered to over and above one's ambition to seek out the enemy for oneself, even if it meant forgoing the desire of a battle engagement. Therefore, the Air Chief Marshal's words, even at a later date, applied to all forces in the air.

A Junkers 88 shot down by 307 crashed 2 miles off the aerodrome and some of us went to look at it. It was the first time that I had seen a German airman, even though they were all dead on this occasion, and the first occurence I had viewed a Ju88 up close too. The German armament amazed me with the precision with which it was made in comparison to ours (British). As no one else was there, we were able to examine the airmen's identities and the decorations they wore; one even had the Iron Cross. Upon satisfying our curiosity we left them exactly as we had found them for the proper authorities to deal with.

Before the squadron was posted to the front we had a rather memorable visit from a British flight lieutenant who called at the aerodrome for a specific purpose, one of many stations he visited for the same reason. He had previously escaped from a German prisoner of war camp, and back in England wanted to prove the complacency of the attitude on British air force stations in reference to their security, by establishing the ease with which an unauthorised person could enter any one of them. For this mission he gained the full authority of the Air Ministry. To prove his point he entered each station past the main guard on duty dressed in full German air force uniform, complete with all-German decorations including the Iron Cross, speaking only German and behaving quite conspicuously in every way.

When he came to Exeter – which was mixed British and Poles – he marched through the main gate unchallenged by the sentry on duty, rapping out some remark in fluent German to the guard; in return he received a very smart salute and passed without opposition until he finally arrived at the headquarters. Here he confronted a Polish adjutant on duty, who was stunned by the audacity of the 'German' airman and surprised at being confronted by one on an Allied airfield apparently completely free. He suddenly realised this was a very clever deception and then endeavoured to persuade the British flight lieutenant not to continue to risk his life with this subterfuge – where Poles were concerned, they were more likely to act violently first and ask questions after!

By all accounts he did the same thing in London, walking through Piccadilly with no one taking the slightest notice of him except for one dear old lady who when she saw him said in a vexed voice: 'Oh dear, oh dear, the invasion has started already.' Presumably the whole intention was to improve the security arrangements of the air force bases.

On 30 March 1942, 317 Fighter Squadron was ordered to move to Northolt to replace one of the Polish squadrons going for rest up north. I was very pleased as since I had been with this squadron, apart from one operation and a few convoy duties and scrambles, nothing much had happened. I knew that once in Northolt we would be really busy under 11 Group, stationed around London, the south and east; everyone was pleased at the move. It was as we hoped and we were soon operational. We were equipped with Spitfire vbs and could fly operationally up to 33,000 feet, having a one-stage supercharger, but the range was rather poor. For instance, we were unable to fly to Paris; our farthest safe range was only as far as Lille.

This was the year that we termed 'propaganda year' for morale, the war year of nerves, the test being on both sides against each other. We noticed that although the Germans took off, they did so more as a formality against us as they hardly ever came for a fight. Especially seeing, as they did, well trained and organised squadrons.

At this time the system had already reverted to team fighting instead of the individual combat that had become necessary in the Battle of Britain. It was both useless either to chase the enemy to force a fight or involve ourselves in a prolonged battle, due to the shortage of range of our aircraft and the orders we were under not to attempt it. Nevertheless, there were times when we were irritated by the enemy's unwillingness to approach us and occasionally we disregarded orders and sought to provoke them into retaliation. But invariably they evaded furiously or dived to lower levels where they were safe. If by coincidence we met Germans at, say, 25,000 feet, both sides would immediately climb to secure the advantage of height and make use of the sun. Spitfires had the upper hand in climbing over the Messerschmitt, and as soon as they saw we had gained the height over them they descended straight away, diving to the deck. They were safer still in this respect as the Spitfire was not adequate for prolonged diving. Our maximum safe speed was 460 mph;

to exceed this would put her out of control.

The armament on our craft was not as good as the Messerschmitt's. All the guns were situated in the wings, bypassing the propeller. The cannons had only sixty rounds each, even though our vital weapon, as some of the ammunition carried explosive heads. Only with the cannon ammunition could you see the immediate result of your firing and where you scored your hit, enabling you to correct your deflection if necessary. This was the most important part in air-to-air or air-to-ground battles for the success of the operation. With the rounds we had it was necessary to be experienced to be able to use our armament to the fullest advantage when the ammunition of the cannon lasted only nine seconds in all. It required a very accomplished pilot capable of controlling his excitement to achieve three, three-second bursts to attain the objective. Later, the number of rounds was increased to more than 120.

The noise of your cannon was a psychological reassurance, for once they were silent the pilot felt bereft of ammunition, even though he still had the use of his four machine guns. These each had 300 rounds and, due to their placing in the wings, the best firing range was between 300 and 500 yards, which was another reason to be experienced enough to use them effectively. As the machine gun did not possess the advantages of the cannon – unless you succeeded in killing the pilot of the enemy aircraft or striking a vital part of the plane, shooting it down – you could well finish up losing all your ammunition and the enemy aircraft would still get home to fight another day.

With the introduction of the Focke Wulf 190 by the Germans we received a shock for, apart from it being an excellent fighter aircraft, it carried three cannons of 20 mm, firing through the prop in a synchronised manner – which according to our scientists, mechanical synchronisation of heavy machine guns and especially cannons was impossible. Not until after the war did I learn that the whole system was electrical. The only thing wrong with the Fw 190, as one of the best fighters of the war, was the expected lifespan of its engine before overhaul of only 100 hours. However, the Germans could afford this due to their system of production.

An unpleasantness we had to contend with was the effect of the cold air – especially in winter – as we climbed during a flight to 30,000 or 33,000 feet, and 39,000 feet in Spitfire Mark ixs. The heating system was entirely inadequate in supplying warmth to the pilot due to the unsealed cockpit, therefore he well nigh froze at this height at minus 20 degrees. On landing our hands, clenched in one position, were sprayed with oxygen by our mechanics, who each carried his own bottle with him to his allotted aircraft for this purpose. Our hands then slowly unfurled but remained ice cold for hours after, and so did our feet. Yet in battle the excitement and concentration would counteract this condition until you relaxed on the way back home and it would become noticeable.

After the war ended I was given some German flying boots and gloves by American personnel – they were beautifully made, the boots like ski boots and the gloves made from angora fur and grey chamois leather, both items electrically heated. Pilots here, during the war, were always given the impression that German equipment was rubbish. At the close of hostilities, when capturing supplies in Germany, the Allies were astonished at the excellence of German equipment and tools, which needed to be seen to be believed.

The squadron consisted of between twenty-four and twenty-six pilots. It was therefore possible to make two sweeps of the sky in one day, dependent upon the weather, with a complete change of pilots for each operation. The situation that was found over enemy territory determined your personal battle achievements in an encounter. For instance, during the test landing at Dieppe by Canadian ground forces on 19 August, 317 Squadron took off four times (two flights for each pilot) – on the second and fourth sweeps the enemy was engaged and a battle took place. On both the first and third sweeps – in which I took part – there wasn't even a sniff of enemy aircraft, and all our group could do was watch the boys on the ground below while we kept cover for them.

We made many flights over France, on occasion as escort cover for bombers when the fighter squadrons could expect a more definite encounter with the enemy fighters. But usually we made sweeps without the bombers, from 25,000 to 33,000 feet, but on those occasions there were hardly any engagements with the Germans. Therefore we all anxiously waited for the time when we could fly deeper into enemy territory and extend our range, with the aid of extra tanks for our aircraft – urgently needed – and so force them to fight us.

If contact was made with Jerries when escorting bombers, it depended upon what position you held at that time – i.e. top or bottom cover or front position – as to what your action could be. When flying as top cover you could only look on at the battle raging below between your friends (holding bottom fighter cover) and the enemy, and provide cover protection for them from additional attacking aircraft. And all the while waiting and secretly hoping they would call for your assistance. On these occasions many of us, myself included, were unlucky enough never to receive the opportunity to have a go. And as this situation persisted, it had a very demoralising effect upon the pilots concerned. Consequently, we waited impatiently for the Allied invasion to take place, to give us an opportunity to make our mark. My morale was one of those to hit rock bottom and desperately needed a boost. It could easily have you believing there was a jinx on you.

Fighter Command were obviously aware of the weakening morale. Operations, code-named Rhubarb, were arranged, which meant four aircraft only would fly at low level all the way to the French coast, attack any enemy concentration of guns or military transport effectively, then clear out back to base. For safety purposes there were rules to be followed, namely that cloud cover should be complete, i.e. ten-tenths and low, 1,000 to 2,000 feet.

On 24 July 1942 I led one section of four Spitfires on a Rhubarb operation. We arrived at the French coast near Le Touquet and found ourselves in perfect sunshine. According to the rules I should have ordered an immediate return to base. There was a quick discussion between myself, Lieutenant Mencel, Lieutenant Kratke and Flight Sergeant Lewczynski, and without hesitation we all agreed to press on and continue the op. On reaching the coast we could see we had taken the enemy by surprise – they were running to their guns, but we had already passed overhead before they reached them. Inland we saw a platoon of German soldiers scattering and throwing themselves to the ground as we opened fire in all directions, sweeping along and causing havoc among them. I then instructed our return, hoping that we would have a clear exit without casualties. Unfortunately it wasn't quite so.

We raced along just above the ground, the dark shadows of our aircraft moving beneath us. In sight of the coast, with the sea stretching ahead of us, all hell was let loose from every gun in sight and from all directions, as the enemy had waited for our return. Their view of us was perfect as we sped low over the water, which seemed to boil beneath us as bullets and shells skimmed the surface – as a boy throws pebbles – whipping the waves angrily in pursuit of us. A thump caused my aircraft to shudder violently, but she didn't falter and kept her speed together with the other three aircraft until we were at a safe distance. I guessed I'd been hit, the only question was where? I glanced in both directions checking on my friends as we flew in finger-four formation; they were all okay. Within a few minutes I got the answer when I discovered that my rudder control had gone. The boys followed me as I flew up to a safer height of 300 feet and then we climbed to the cloud ceiling, approximately 2,000 feet. With the reasonably good, quiet weather I was in no danger as the use of my rudder was unimportant in these conditions. Back at base I told my friends to land first, just in case my Spitfire crashed, but she took me down safely. We could then see that a 40 mm shell had smashed into the rudder. Luckily, I wasn't reprimanded for continuing the operation against the rules, and after a couple of days with the mechanics my aircraft showed no signs of having been damaged.

By this time Northolt was a completely Polish station and we had begun to make it more representative of us. Apart from the headquarters run by British personnel, plus the cooks, WAAFs and the op room – which was actually 5 miles away directed by the British but with Polish controllers constantly in attendance – everything else was Polish; the doctors, dentist, priests, engineering department etc.

While sitting around at dispersal or relaxing in the sun on our 'quieter' moments, we had some distractions in the way of our adopted 'pets'. The squadron had a little dog as a mascot called Pygmy. He was a funny-looking little thing, which was the reason the boys had adopted him, and was a faithful friend to them like many of the animal mascots adopted by various squadrons. But Pygmy got into rather bad habits – with a bit of encouragement from the boys. When I visited the station once I walked to the dispersal area where I knew I would find my friends on stand-by. As I went to enter the hut Pygmy was sitting outside on the steps

As an Officer cadet at Deblin officer cadet school, taken 1937, the year before graduation

(Above) As refugees fleeing the German invasion
before boarding the ship to Marseilles 1939.
Witold back, row 3rd from left.

(Inset) At Deblin officer cadet school 1938,
pictured with Jan Zumbach who later became
one of 303 Squadrons top scoring pilots.

(Above and below) Pilots of 317 Squadron taken at Northolt 1943.

Seated in his spitfire Mk Vb (JH-Y) taken at Northolt 1943.

Publicity shot taken seated on the wing of a Spitfire Mk Vb.

Seated on Spitfire Mk Vb 'Bazyli Kwiek' (JH-V) originally flown by Stanislaw Brzeski, Witold often flew this Spitfire.

Pilots seated at dispersal Northolt 1942. Witold seated, second from left.

Pilots of 302 Squadron Northolt 1943. Witold 4th from right. The airfield was located very close to the local houses which can be seen in the background.

Witold receiving his second 'Cross of Valour' 1943.

Publicity shot of the pilots of 302 Squadron taken at Northolt 1943 in front of a Spitfire Mk IXc.

Witold flying his Spitfire Mk IXc. This is a still shot taken from an army co-operation flight where his spitfire was filmed for the purpose of aircraft recognition for the allied troops on D-Day. He was filmed doing various close passes and take-off and landing at Northolt 12th February 1944.

Francis "Gabby" Gabreski seated in his Spitfire when he flew with 315 (Polish) Squadron before the USAAF came over to the UK. Gabby asked to be able to fly with a front line Polish combat squadron. This is what initiated the transfer of several Polish pilots to the 56th FG.

Witold playing with Pygmej (pygmy) which was one of the several Northolt mascots. Witold was Pygmej's favourite and was often seen with him when Witold was not flying.

(Above, left) Boxted March 1944, as Intelligence Officer with the 355th Fighter Squadron, 354th Fighter Group taken with Gus Allen and Clayton Gross in front of a P–51 B Mustang. (Above, right) Boxted March 1944, as Intelligence Officer with the 355th Fighter Squadron, 354th Fighter Group taken with Robert Goodnight.

(Above, left) Colonel Hubert 'Hub' Zemke commanding officer of the 56th Fighter Group when Lanny joined the 61st Fighter Squadron. (Above, right) Boxted March 1944, inspecting the ammunition belts in the wing that feed the 0.5 inch machine guns of a P–51 B Mustang.

Lt Colonel Francis 'Gabby' Gabreski (born Franciszek Gabryszewski). Gabby was CO of the 61st Fighter Squadron when Lanny joined the 56th Fighter Group. Picture taken whilst seated in his P–47-D (HV-A) clearly showing his 'kill markings'. All of Gabby's Thunderbolts assigned to him were unnamed.

Group shot of the pilots of the 61st Fighter Squadron taken June 1944. Lanny is on the back row 5th from the right. The Polish pilots who were transferred temporarily to the 56th are all central on the back row surrounding Gabby Gabreski. The picture was taken in front of the P–47 Thunderbolt 'Silver Lady' (HV-Z) which became assigned as Lanny's main Thunderbolt before he received his Mk 'M' Thunderbolt.

The group of Polish pilots transferred to the 56th Fighter Group taken with Gabby Gabreski in front of 'Silver Lady'. Left to right Boleslaw 'Mike' Gladych, Sawicz, Gabreski, Rutkowski, Anderz and Lanny (note, Janicki and Gabszewicz were also seconded to the 56th but are absent from this photograph).

Lanny pictured with Gladych (centre) and his wingman Eugene Barnum (killed 1944) in front of Gladych's Thunderbolt.

Gladych and Lanny pictured in front of one of the huts on Boxted airfield.

Lanny in full flying gear Boxted 1944. Possibly taken in front of HV-C 'Slugger' as flown by Joel Popplewell.

Lanny, Boxted 1944 pictured in front of Gladych's P–47D (HV-M) with left to right, Kolepeda, Gladych, Moffat and Barnum.

(Above) 'Silver Lady' shown with her ground crew and distinctive crown on the engine cowling. This Thunderbolt was flown by Leslie Smith, Gabreski and then was assigned to Lanny as his own Thunderbolt. Shown here fitted with the clear 'Malcolm' hood. 'Silver lady' was later given to the 9th Air Force.

(Above, left) Lanny receiving his DFC at Boxted November 1944, from Gen Jesse Auton, wearing his Polish dress uniform showing his 3 star Polish rank of Kapitan (RAF equivalent of Flt Lieutenant). (Above, right) Lanny's P–47 Mk `M' pictured with his mechanics in front of his distinctive personal emblem.

Lanny's personal P–47 Mk 'M' (HV-Z). This particular Mk M was the first production M given to 56th FG and shows Lanny's personal insignia on the cowling. Lanny first flew this Thunderbolt on January 23rd 1945.

The 'Terrible twins' as they came to be known, nicknamed by Gabreski. Lanny pictured with Gladych Boxted 1945 beside Gladych's Mk 'M'.

Press cutting highlighting Polish fighter pilots over Berlin, the heartland of the Reich.

(Above) Witold's Polish dress uniform jacket with his distinctive personal badges highlighting his flying career for the four air forces he flew for during WW2. On the lapels are his Polish rank of kapitan, top left above the pocket is the Polish pilot wings, immediately below is the American 'Senior pilot wings', Left jacket pocket shows the squadron badges of 302 and 317 (Polish) Squadrons, Right jacket pocket shows the French 'Armee de L'Air' pilot wings. Above the right pocket are the RAF pilots wings.

(Left) Lanny's A2 flying jacket showing his personal emblem replicated. Also on this jacket are the bars of his 'temporary' rank of captain given to him whilst he served with the 56th FG.

appearing most odd, like a statue and just as immobile. Not a muscle moved or a whisker; he looked stupefied. I called to him softly, rather afraid he'd fall over with shock if I spoke his name too loudly. It made no difference so I went inside to my friends. I asked, 'What's wrong with the dog? He's sitting frozen stiff outside and glassy eyed.' 'He's been drinking too much beer again,' I was told, 'so we've put him outside to sober up.' I just stared, then burst out laughing. It fitted – no wonder he hadn't answered me when I talked to him, and probably didn't know which one of me had spoken!

Pygmy's drinking habits continued while he stayed with the boys, moving around with them when the squadron was posted. He was still with the squadron when I joined them later. We knew of his fondness for ale so took care where we placed our glasses. But any unsuspecting guest who visited the mess usually put their drinks down on the floor next to their armchair, and it was an open invitation to Pygmy to come and sup. Usually it was British officers who didn't know about him and we stood by to see the reaction of those Pygmy had deprived of beer. The result was always highly amusing to watch as they accused each other of drinking each other's ale. We said nothing at all, and Pygmy just sat with what looked like a stupid grin on his face.

There were various mascots in each squadron – a duck, pigeons, a monkey and dogs by the score – who would not only attach themselves to the squadron but to the pilots in particular. They probably sensed that we wandered from place to place, always on the move, just as their basic instinct called upon them to do. Often civilians would come to us, sadly or hopefully, asking if their dog was with us and could they have it back. We would take them where the dogs were and perhaps theirs would be among them: if so they were delighted to have found their pet. But within a day or two the dog would be back at the station and nothing would keep it out. We took them with us most times when we moved about the country replacing squadrons.

At one time when we transferred to an aerodrome to take over from another unit, the mechanics decided to load the dogs on to the aircraft that carried our equipment – they considered it the easiest way to transport the dogs. When the aircraft landed at the new station, by chance the British group captain happened to place himself near to it as it stopped for unloading. When the door was opened it was absolute bedlam as dogs of all shapes and sizes, colours and breeds – yapping and barking furiously – tumbled from the plane, clearing a good 5 or 6 feet to reach the ground. The group captain didn't know what had hit him. Very soon an order went out all over England that no dogs or pets were allowed in the aircraft. We still took the dogs with us wherever we moved, though, regardless of the new rule – and presume that others did the same.

Our station commander was British, Group Captain T.N. McAvoy, but had a Polish deputy. He took over on 17 March 1941 from Group Captain Stanley Vincent, who had grounded the Poles for speaking insufficient English – which he considered dangerous in the air – just prior to the Battle of Britain. Neither was he convinced that the Poles really could fly until the absolute proof in the battle changed his view, but the Polish pilots never quite forgave him for it.

With the arrival of McAvoy it was rather a shock for the Poles, as his physical appearance belied his tremendous spirit and capabilities as a superb leader. He met the challenge of these young, spirited and ambitious 'daredevil' pilots – who saw in turn a man who had obviously suffered enormously. McAvoy had broken his back but he met his condition with a force of courage and determination, proving that as a pilot he could still fly and refusing to wear the steel support that would have prevented him from doing so. He asked the engineer to arrange special mirrors in certain positions to enable him to watch the tail of his aircraft, as we were able to do with the usual type. He proved to be one of the greatest friends we had and our admiration and loyalty were his. It was with sadness that the Poles saw him leave the station on 20 October 1941 for a new post.

Group Captain Adnams took his place. He obviously realised he had quite a formidable task to fill his predecessor's shoes and gain our confidence. Two ways were open to him: to adopt as closely as possible McAvoy's manner and attitude towards us; or the obvious alternative, in which case he might just as well have asked for a posting straight away. What he did was to establish respect and confidence very quickly. He was a younger man than McAvoy – and extremely light-hearted, which eased the tension and helped gain contact with everyone at Northolt, who could now relax and not have to prove themselves all over again.

With the arrival of 317 Fighter Squadron and for some reason known only to himself, Group Captain Adnams took a personal liking to our squadron. Squadron Leader Skalski, my friend and former colleague from the same student intake year of 1938 in Deblin, was our squadron commander. Due to his particular interest I found myself involved in a serious discussion with the group captain in the mess. Putting it very politely, but very much to the point, he asked me why I was only a flying officer when most of my friends were already flight commanders or squadron leaders. It was a fair question even if it took me by surprise. I explained in one short sentence. 'It's a result of "dirty politics", Sir,' I replied and it was his turn to look nonplussed. 'But, if you will excuse me, Sir,' I continued, 'it's not exactly considered an honour for you to be our station commander is it?' 'Touché!' he said and held out his hand to shake mine with a broad grin on his face. From that moment a personal friendship developed between us and, because of this, as a Pole I was able later to prevent an unpleasant occurrence by the Polish station commander that neither he nor I agreed with, making Adnams very cross. He quickly became aware of who was my worst enemy and, choosing the right opportunity, took it upon himself to clarify one situation at least, to his intense enjoyment.

I was sitting in the mess reading quietly, as the wing had gone on an op and those of us not in this sweep were relaxing or enjoying ourselves in our own various ways, and the station itself was very quiet. A car drew up sharply outside the mess causing me to look up as Adnams appeared in the doorway. 'Lanowski, your arch enemy Pawlikowski is here at dispersal. Come on, I want you to come with me, I'll introduce you to him.' As he started up the car he added, 'He can't say any more that he had nothing against you, as he's never met you. That should scotch that excuse. Let's see what he'll do.'

We pulled up in front of dispersal and Pawlikowski was standing on the tarmac outside talking with Wing Commander Janus and another friend of mine, Squadron Leader Rutkowski. We got out of the car and Adnams walked up to Pawlikowski while I followed a few steps behind. They greeted each other and chatted for a moment or two, Pawlikowski glancing towards me several times, wondering what I was doing with

Group Captain Adnams but not knowing who I was. Then Adnams said quietly, beckoning me forward: 'By the way, Pawlikowski, I don't think you have ever met Flying Officer Lanowski, have you?' Realisation came into Pawlikowski's face, hardening his features, but he had no option but to shake hands with me and talk politely for a while. From the others gathered there only the three of us, Pawlikowski, Adnams and I, knew the significance of this seemingly coincidental meeting. From the look in Adnams's eyes while he watched as I conversed with Pawlikowski, I knew he was enjoying this moment. Then we excused ourselves from their company as Adnams wished to go to the ops room to see how the boys on the sweep were making out. 'Come with me,' he suggested as we got back into his car.

By way of an explanation, Group Captain Stefan Pawlikowski was the commanding officer of the Polish Fighter Command. He was one of the oldest pilots, his skill originating from the First World War when he had trained with the French Air Force and flew with them in the latter part of this conflict while a cadet (as an adjutant – a French rank).

I had no knowledge of Pawlikowski, like many others, until I was in France. When he began holding a major position in France his actions and attitude – especially towards the younger officers and men and, of course, the cadets – aggravated an already explosive situation. What happened in France concerning Commandant Kepinski, myself and my arrest and imprisonment, involved Pawlikowski directly, inasmuch as he chose Kepinski to command 1/145 Polish Fighter Squadron. What increased the antagonism towards me was my point of being proved correct beyond doubt regarding the type of flying squadron commander any fighter squadron should have, as well as my approach to, and the action taken, by the Polish Civilian Council in London. So, although it was perfectly true that we had never met before, Pawlikowski was very much aware of who I was, and his influence contributed much to circumstances affecting me. But I learned from various friends, that when my name was referred to he insisted that he had 'nothing against me, as he had never met me', the kind of reasoning that tended to irritate the listener and confuse conversation, either intentionally or as a personal safeguard. While Adnams had chosen to try and remedy the situation, indeed it served its purpose, it made little difference to the attitude that continued to prevail.

It was the first time I had visited the operations room while a big op sweep was in progress, this one over Lille, and the atmosphere was heavy. The table held the map of southern England and northern France, with position markings indicating our wings and the Germans. I was surprised to see so many Jerries in the air. I looked at it in horror, imagining the most deadly of battles in progress and was relieved when Adnams decided we should leave. He had been told that for the moment no battles were taking place, but he was as concerned as me, and we both wanted to get back to the station as the boys wouldn't be very long before returning to base. I was ten times more nervous in that op room than I ever was in the air. To our amazement when the boys landed they behaved most unconcernedly. When we asked for their report on the Jerries they just stared at us. 'What Jerries?' They hadn't seen a single one! I never wanted to be taken to the operations room again – I had suffered agonies for that lot!

In one of the two large hangars on Northolt, Winston Churchill's York aircraft was kept for his personal use; it was based on the station constantly and serviced there. Churchill paid the greatest compliment to the Poles during the severest time of the war years. He said when he felt at a very low ebb, the spirit and fierce determination of the Polish fighter pilots boosted his morale when he visited Northolt. This was a tremendous honour for us, especially so when he invited two Polish pilots to be escorts and accompany his daughters, Sarah and Mary, out for an evening's entertainment. When the chosen two returned, everyone was immensely interested how the evening had gone and plied questions at them, as we had imagined how we would have felt. 'The Old Boy was marvellous,' we were told. Apparently the ladies had not been quite ready when they arrived at the appointed time and Churchill apologised for keeping them waiting. 'You know what ladies are, let's go and have a drink,' he said, pointing the way to an adjoining room from the hall. 'Or shall we have it here and sit and wait for them?', indicating the stairway. 'And he would have done, too,' laughed the boys. 'We felt much at ease with him and from then on the evening was perfect.'

Churchill understood and appreciated very much our feelings and our attitude towards the fight; if he gathered strength from our resolve it was as much a privilege to us as the compliment he paid by seeking it from us.

Approximately at the end of a six-month tour every squadron from the line was required to rest. However, it was optional and wasn't always essential for that purpose. But there were eight day-fighter squadrons in the Polish Air Force and obviously a rotation was necessary. When extra fighter squadron strength was required, Heston aerodrome to the south of Northolt was used to facilitate the Polish squadrons, being close to one another.

Due for resting in September, 317 moved to Woodvale, near Southport in Lancashire, to 12th Group. There we practised air-to-air and air-to-ground gunnery, formation flying – high and low – aerobatics, army co-operation and night flying, in order to keep up the standard, as it was always possible to deteriorate in these skills unless they were kept up. Apart from this it was nice to relax – even if we did not want to admit it – and it revived us for an unusual outing at rather a late hour during the night of 31 October/1 November 1942.

Squadron Leader Skalski told me to organise night flying for about six or seven pilots. In the afternoon I made preparations, informing those concerned: the chief engineer, the mess, transport, the Meteorological office for special briefing and the pilots themselves. Normally flying started at dusk and continued on through until about midnight. Just before tea I phoned the Met office for a weather report and was told that reasonably good weather was expected. But half an hour later they rang me back to say the weather was deteriorating from the west over the Welsh mountains and had caused a Lancaster bomber to crash in that vicinity, suggesting I cancel night flying, which I immediately did.

That night everyone retired for the night quite happily thinking no more about it. At about 10 p.m. I was suddenly woken up by our batman telling me the group captain was on the telephone asking for me. The first thing he wanted to know from me was why we were not flying, and I told him what the Met office had informed me. 'But the weather's perfect,' he replied sharply. 'You mean you want us to fly, Sir – now?' 'Of course, why not?' he snapped. The first thing I had to do now was to waken and contact everybody concerned and their language when I did so was most expressive. Then I made my way to dispersal. On the way I noted grudgingly that the weather was indeed perfect, which didn't help matters or lighten my spirits. The air was so peaceful I could even hear the waves lapping the shore half a mile away, and noted a clear sky with a full moon beaming down at me, and twinkling stars!

Already waiting for me when I arrived at dispersal was the group captain. He surveyed me grimly and questioned: 'Have you sufficient night-flying experience?' Reading his mind I'm sure he was wondering why a lieutenant flying officer should be in charge of night flying. To make matters worse he asked: 'How many night flying hours have you?' 'Five or ten, Sir,' I said, and stood very stiffly to attention. 'But none in this country,' I added. That should set him off, I thought, and I could see that it had. In growing fury he stormed straight out of the hut without saying another word.

The boys had been arriving during this exchange and had watched with great amusement. As soon as the last one arrived I held the briefing, which went very much as follows: 'Gentlemen, the group captain appears to think I am not fit to be in charge of night flying. Possibly he thinks the weather was used as an excuse because we don't like night flying. So perhaps we should convince him otherwise? ... All right, we have perfect weather so we fly aerobatics, no one on the station sleeps tonight, or from here to Blackpool. We fly at low level and Blackpool Tower, I think, is ideal for a dogfight, don't you agree? Good. ... Anyhow, gentlemen, you know exactly what I mean, and I have the fullest confidence in you. Do your utmost best – and, please, no collisions. Okay, scramble.'

The aerobatics were quite an experience; I'd never done them in the night before. As there was no horizon we constantly looked for the moon, which popped up in the most unusual positions – grinning at you – and you were pleased to find him again. The Polish controller in the operations room must have enjoyed himself at the conversations taking place, but the poor WAAFs had no idea what we were saying, although apparently the atmosphere of the 'exercise' infected them: 'What the hell's happened to the moon? I've lost the thing. D'you see it?' 'Got it,' came the reply.

'Gentlemen, it's time for the station to wake up – we dive.' One by one we turned and dived straight at the airfield, roaring over the buildings to climb and then come in to refuel before taking off once more. Now for our visit to Blackpool (which we had got to know all too well in 1940). Our wing lights, red and green, reflected on the water as we flew at low level over the sea.

'Ah! Three lovely piers for leapfrog. Then on to the tower for a dogfight,'

I ordered. We cleared the piers one at a time then circled Blackpool Tower in a furious chase, snapping at each other's tail. From there we made a mock attack on Blackpool aerodrome at Squires Gate, then climbed to 5,000 feet, by which time the searchlight boys on the ground had decided to join in the fun, sweeping the sky to try and catch us in their beams. We promptly doused our lights and dived straight at them and as we passed over their heads each searchlight in turn was switched off, causing total darkness, while they waited to spot our lights as we flicked them on again. It was a rather dangerous game to indulge in, for had they caught and held one of us in their powerful beams, blinding the pilot, he could very easily have hit the ground. As soon as lights were put on afresh, the searchlights once more swung towards us, by which time we had turned ours off another time. After a while we dived towards them, bidding them goodnight, before flying back to Woodvale for a final landing. On the following day Squires Gate threatened to open fire at us if we attacked them again.

We all slept for the remainder of the night, thoroughly satisfied we had proved – even to ourselves – that we were capable of night flying, but anticipating, also, the outcome of our performance when facing the group captain next day. Apparently he was overloaded with complaints by telephone and Skalski was called to give an explanation. I had already taken the precaution to inform Skalski of all that had taken place the previous evening to prepare him.

The first complaint came from the group captain himself, informing Skalski that he considered I did not have enough experience to take charge of night-flying practices, to which Skalski answered heatedly that he knew exactly what he was doing and that he had always maintained that I was a better pilot than he was from our days in Poland. As for the rest of the complaints placed before him, he concluded that the group captain had given me no other option and, in any case, he would have done the same himself under the circumstances.

Skalski was the type of person who wouldn't hesitate to speak his mind and offend if necessary when he knew he was right, regardless of rank. Especially when the matter concerned him directly, as now, by ordering me to arrange and lead the exercise. As the fighter ace of the Polish Air Force he was in the position to make himself heard and, if the group captain had not been aware of it before, he knew now he'd met his match.

Brzezina's post as Chief of Staff at Polish Headquarters did not exclude the prospect of us remaining in contact with each other, and often he sought my personal opinion in respect of various postings, mostly on the placement of Polish squadron commanders. In March 1943 he let me know that I would soon be transferred to another squadron as a flight commander. So prior to this posting I was detailed to the Fighter Leader School, for a period of four weeks, which had recently been opened by the Air Ministry near Bath.

Chapter 11
─────────────

Fighter Leaders' School

On 1 April I reported to the wing commander (flying) at the school. He looked at my name before him and then at me. 'Pole,' he said. 'Yes Sir,' I confirmed. 'In that case you needn't remain here. You're free to return to your squadron.' To my added surprise he continued: 'You Poles already know all the answers. So you can go, young man. There's no point in wasting time unnecessarily, yours or ours.'

I was naturally taken aback at first, but he was quite serious and he really meant that I should leave. 'If you don't mind, Sir,' I ventured, 'I'd be pleased if you would allow me to stay, there's still a lot to learn and I'm sure the school has much to offer. And if I may, when I've finished the course perhaps I could let you know what I think.' 'Fair enough,' he said and gave me permission to remain with them. I was very pleased I'd stayed and upon looking back it could easily have represented the beginning of NATO – all nationalities flying in the air forces in England were there, including the Fleet Air Arm.

The school consisted of two sections: flying and planning, and timing of the exercises; and lectures and discussions with high-ranking experts from the Air Ministry and the air force industry. There were two flights, each with squadron status and fully equipped, with squadron leaders in charge. I was detailed to 'A' Flight under Squadron Leader 'Laddie' Lucas, famous fighter pilot from the defence of Malta, a well-known golfer (and after the war a Conservative MP in 1950). He was one of the most charming Englishmen I ever met and knowing him – even for that short period – I understood the personal magnetism and drive that drew the support of his men in Malta to stand successfully against the impossible odds facing them.

Other friends I made included three Fleet Air Arm pilots, and a particular one who was a Norwegian squadron leader. Throughout the course the Fleet Air Arm pilots kept trying to persuade me to join their service. Actually I would have liked very much to have done so, due to the close friendship within the confinement of the aircraft carrier, as your survival depended upon each other. But the obsolete aircraft they had, prevented me from giving it any kind of serious thought. My friendship with the Norwegian lasted until I heard that he had lost his life a few weeks before the war ended.

The basic principle of the course at the school was to learn to lead and plan for a squadron and wing. Each took turn as acting squadron leader or wing commander in the air. The most interesting and exciting feature of the exercises centred on the meeting point of the three squadrons coming from various directions to join up and proceed to the target area, all timed to the last second before returning to base. Each of us were constantly amazed at the detailed success of every such exercise, which today is a formality rather than a necessary feat as it was then.

The lectures and discussions were of tremendous value between us – as future leaders – and those from the Air Ministry, as free opinions and basic facts could be aired by any one of us and listened to seriously by them (without fear of reprisals for us), to be conserved for future appraisal or review. I had quite a heated discussion with 'Sailor' Malan concerning finger-four formation, which the Poles flew – and was now widely accepted as the best fighter formation – as against the old British formation of line astern. Some still advocated the use of the latter and, although he admitted the advantage of finger-four formation, he held that it required very experienced pilots. But, as I pointed out, it was not impossible to apply it immediately during training – even initial instruction – using as much practice as necessary to perfect it, thereby guaranteeing its benefit to the pilots who would then fly and fight as a team, which was vital. For the first time it was possible to meet and talk with industrial designers and production experts. They even went so far as to bring a prototype aircraft to us to examine and discuss.

When I went to say goodbye to Squadron Leader Lucas and the wing commander, I thanked the latter for having allowed me to stay and, in spite of the opinion he had expressed at our initial meeting, I assured

him I really had learned a great deal to my advantage and I considered
the school was exceptional; it was a pity it had not been opened that
much earlier. I thought that every flying fighter leader should be 'encouraged' to attend, especially if they considered they knew it all!

I then returned to 317 Fighter Squadron and we moved to RAF Martlesham
near Ipswich to begin operations there on 1 May 1943. We were involved
in the special defence of the East Coast as the German Fighter Command
retaliated with Rhubarb operations of their own, using Fw 190s, flying
longer distances from Belgium or Holland over the North Sea. It was safe
for them to attack the East Coast as there was no ground defence to speak
of, and our fighters were concentrated in the south of England to operate the northern French coast. It required very fast action indeed to get
into the air to intercept them, within the maximum of two or three
minutes, and immense co-operation was necessary between us and the
radar station 5 miles away. Enemy damage was actually negligible as they
made one swift attack, then ran. We invariably sighted only their tails as
they sped for safety. The danger they posed was mainly on the coastal
convoys and it was necessary for us to supply constant cover for the
convoy patrols.

  Scrambles were frequent. For instance, on 15 May it happened to me
six times, and on the sixth occasion I was in my best blue uniform. On that
occasion I and my friends, who did the same as me, had no business to
be in the air at that precise moment. As it happened there was a station
party in the mess – a monthly feature – and to cheer up our colleagues
in dispersal who were ready for immediate take-off, we decided to take
them a drink. All would have been well for us to enjoy our drink with
them had not the sirens gone off after we had been there only about fifteen minutes.

  No one really anticipated enemy activity as it was already dark, but –
instantly – we were all propelled into action. Those in readiness were in
the air within thirty seconds; the rest of us, dressed as we were, took
one look at each other and in unison grabbed the nearest parachute
and took off towards our aircraft, yelling at the mechanics to start the
engines. In that scramble the whole squadron was in the air within
1 minute 50 seconds. In the event, the entire squadron was not needed

– although a telephone call had been made to prepare for action – but we had already gone. After landing we carried on with the party, celebrating our record for the number of take-offs – which we had just broken, more by a fluke than design.

On this day I had earlier received a telephone call from a friend of mine who had some news for me. He suggested I should celebrate well that night as my greatest enemy had been shot down, and did I guess who it had been? Tentatively I enquired if it was Pawlikowski, and I had guessed correctly. Apparently Pawlikowski had chosen to go on an operational sweep with one of the squadrons from Northolt; unfortunately for him they were attacked while over France and he was shot down and killed. He had been the most vulnerable of the group, because the other pilots were in constant training to be equipped for such battle, and he was not. He had taken a gamble in going, especially on such an operation, and had lost.

Another such officer, a group captain who took over from him, attempted the same thing, but he, at least, was more fortunate. What possibly inspired this behaviour from these higher officers could well have been initiated by General Sikorski – he had stated that he would decorate only those who faced the enemy. It was the opinion of many pilots, though, that ill-equipped as these officers were, they would have been served better by simply hanging Hitler's portrait in their office to qualify for this distinction. Safer, too, for those pilots who may have been required to protect their more inexperienced flying commander.

Chapter 12

302 Squadron

On 17 May I received a posting to 302 Polish Fighter Squadron (Poznanski) as a flight commander and deputy squadron leader with the acting British rank of flight lieutenant, with equal pay to that rank. We received £24–25 depending how many days the month held. Nevertheless, my Polish rank remained as lieutenant (flying officer).

Our earnings were inadequate for our requirements as we had to pay for our uniform, mess bill and keep. As we had no homes of our own to go to and consequently could not claim additional expenses as the British could, both here and overseas, our income had also to cover expenses for a short-term pass and the five-day holiday a month essential to aircrew. To most of us either of these was unachievable. The position became very serious as pilots without money for this holiday had to remain on the station itself, where it was impossible to rest mentally, as was very necessary. It also led to a rather comical situation over the amount of remuneration we were given. Our own NCOs received equivalent to two-thirds of the officers' salary, but as they were not required to pay any expenses or buy their uniform etc as we were, the value of the money they pocketed exceeded ours. So when told they had been put up for promotion to officer rank they refused the 'honour' as it wasn't in their interests to accept.

After a few months the Air Ministry concluded that something must be done to remedy the situation as the system was being made to look foolish. They decided to pay the NCOs more – above the officers' income – when they received promotion to officer rank. But the officers' remuneration remained the same as before. It was given to balance the expenses they incurred as officers.

A generous gesture by Lord Nuffield – who gave all aircrew fighting under British command, both British and foreign, £1 a day for each day's holiday – enabled us to have some kind of respite. Although immensely grateful to Lord Nuffield, regarding our pay we had our own saying, paraphrasing Churchill's speech from the Battle of Britain: 'Never so many … pay so little … to so few.'

At Hutton Cranswick, near Hull, I joined 302 Fighter Squadron and very shortly from there we moved to Heston as fighter strength for the Northolt squadrons. Our CO was Squadron Leader Baranski. While not a dislikable person, as a squadron leader we found him out of date. I was 'A' Flight commander and Flight Lieutenant Boleslaw Gladych was 'B' Flight commander. Due to the modern methods of flying, it was essential that Gladych and I had an agreement between ourselves that when Baranski led the squadron, one of us made sure to be with him.

We did the usual sweeps to France and Holland, and the extra tanks the aircraft now carried under the fuselage enabled us to increase the range by forty minutes' flying time. We could now reach as far as Paris. In spite of these new airborne opportunities, I missed my former 317 Squadron. However, they too were at Heston and were posted with us to Perranporth in Cornwall, between Newquay and St Ives, and a friendly atmosphere flowed between the two squadrons.

There was an arrangement the Polish Air Force had with the Air Ministry, which was that whenever the squadron moved, our aircraft came too. We held this as vital, as our mechanics were excellent in their workmanship and knew our own planes well, devoting themselves to their maintenance. Because of this we never took over another squadron's aircraft. For some unknown reason, on one occasion this arrangement broke down, with the result that we found ourselves taking over approximately forty-five aircraft (two squadrons) from the Canadian squadron that had just left Perranporth. When we heard this the week before we moved, our engineers, with a stream of our mechanics, preceded us to Cornwall to check the aircraft over and prepare them for our arrival.

When they examined the aircraft – Spitfire Mark vbs – they were dumbfounded. The cooling system (a mixture of glycerine, alcohol and water) was so thickened, that in an effort to drain it they were lucky to get a trickle. So they put the substance in a bottle and forwarded it to the Air Ministry, together with the astonishing news that thirty-five engines (Rolls-Royce Merlins) required immediate replacement. The Air Ministry immediately sent a team of experts to investigate; in the meantime, our squadron was grounded until the matter was sorted out.

It was a heartbreaking job for our mechanics, who worked day and night to repair the extensive damage, having left our own beautifully kept and serviced aircraft behind for others to take over. But they worked instantly until they were satisfied with their efforts, and we again had aircraft to be proud of. Their standards of servicing were so high it was a privilege to fly the planes. As pilots, some of us were apt to take the work of the mechanics a little too much for granted, and so this experience came as a lesson to us all.

At the end of August/beginning of September 1943, 302 and 317 Fighter Squadrons were posted together to Fairlop, Essex. Our sweeps were now centred over Dunkirk, Boulogne and Calais, baiting the Germans into believing an invasion in this sector was imminent. At this period American day bombers, particularly Fortresses, were making continuous day raids over Germany, but their fighter-cover escorts, Thunderbolts, were not yet adequate as their range was too short to give efficient protection. These aircraft were also insufficient in numbers and their crews inadequately trained to keep constant cover for their bombers. It was thought as well that the numbers flying in such close formation, some 60 or 100 plus – each Fortress bristling with .50 inch heavy machine guns with approximately 1,000 rounds each (or more) – would be so powerful that no German fighters would be able to get through their defences, but this was proved to be drastically incorrect. The Germans threw themselves at the Fortresses and some well nigh wrote their names on the bombers with their ammunition. British Fighter Command was asked to give fighter cover to the Fortresses on their return journey and we did our utmost to protect them. But even our short range inhibited this aim and all we could manage was their last 50 miles over enemy territory. In many cases it was heartbreaking and humiliating to have to watch from a distance while deadly attacks by German guns tore into the bombers. Then as soon as we reached the vital meeting point with the Fortresses, the enemy aircraft would disappear.

It was at this time that I first became aware of how far into the distance I was able to see, for when I commented to the wing during our flight that the Germans were attacking the American bombers, none of my colleagues knew what I was talking about as they couldn't see the battle for themselves. My visual range was soon to become a joke among my friends, yet it proved to be extremely beneficial, not just to myself but to those who flew with me.

Late in September 302 Squadron moved to Northolt, with 317 again receiving the same posting. The commander of 302 changed from Baranski to Squadron Leader W. Krol; this was an advantage as Krol was more suited to us and also of our own generation. To our pleasure we received new Spitfire Mark ixs with twin superchargers for high-altitude flying; we could now fly up to 40,000 feet. We still operated the same areas that we had done from Northolt, but the difference now was that we could engage in battle higher and more successfully with our new planes and, of course, we were still covering for the American Fortresses.

In January 1944 I heard that Brzezina had enquired what was proposed for me, as I would soon be finishing my operational tour (my first). Was I being given a squadron? Apparently 'no' was the reply. What about promotion? Brzezina had asked. Again this was met with a refusal. My friend at Headquarters by this time was quite concerned on my behalf and signified that one or the other must be given to me at the end of my tour, and due only to his determined intervention my promotion was finally granted. The official order arrived at Northolt authorising my elevation to the rank of kapitan. Rightly or wrongly I refused to accept it or wear its insignia. Of course I was fully aware of Brzezina's effort to attain this for me, but the fact that Headquarters were so obviously against sanctioning this or a squadron to me made me equally disinterested in receiving the promotion.

This brought Brzezina on a trip to Northolt to know the reason for my action. I endeavoured to thank my friend for what he had tried to do for me and assured him I did appreciate greatly his support, but I could not do without a squadron. This was the next step to enable me to continue flying – which was my sole object – and it could not be attained unless given a squadron. As this was the procedure, what comfort or worth was there in being promoted – just to be behind a desk?

And this was obviously where I was headed. Brzezina, naturally, was cross; he understood my feelings very well, yet I had upset him so for the sake of my friend's thoughtfulness I could do no less than take my new rank and I became a kapitan (flight lieutenant). But if I was to become desk-bound, which was a depressing prospect, the outlook for my future now looked extremely bleak.

I felt my tour of operations to be wholly incomplete, which vexed and disappointed me. Even before the end of my tour came the full realisation that I would soon be leaving the squadron, with the apparent end of flying for me. The effect of knowing this showed itself in my manner and upon my features as each day passed. For months we had all been anxiously awaiting the impending invasion, and as time went on and nothing happened a great many of the pilots grew dissatisfied, eager that it should take place. It was now obvious to me that when it began, a strong possibility was that I would not be participating in the actual battle – as also denied during the Battle of Britain. Many of us felt, too, that the missions we were operating were of insignificant value or achieved very little. For me it was now a dead-end operation as my fighter flying time was coming to a close – unless Headquarters changed their minds and gave me a squadron.

Knowing this end was near I preferred it to be over and done with. Even to contemplate any prospect other than being operational I found unthinkably distressing. One certainty was that another fight was immi-nent with Polish Headquarters, for I had no intention of allowing myself to remain grounded one moment more than I could avoid. There was no justifiable reason for it while I was fit and able to continue as a fighter pilot and when every ounce of experience and competence was needed, particularly in the immediate future. How or in what way I could induce them to reconsider me for another operational tour I had no idea, except that I must do so.

The end of February 1944 saw the finish of my first tour: I had com-pleted 97 ops and 220 op hours; there was now only the forms requiring my signature and the certificate verifying the completion of my tour, and that would seem to be that. Squadron Leader Waclaw Krol called me to his office for this formality. Over the previous months we had become good friends and as such we now talked together. Twice, he said, he had put my name forward for the Virtuti Militari, a prominent decoration in the Polish Air Force. 'It was a waste of time, wasn't it?' he stated rather than asked me. I knew it had been and he had come to realise it too. I appreciated the fact that he wished I could have somehow remained in the squadron on flying duties, as I too would have liked, but under the procedure this was not possible. With the signing of the necessary forms, came the closure of this particular period in my career with the Polish Air Force.

Chapter 13

A short interlude

After completing my tour with the PAF, I was automatically entitled to one month's leave. I didn't particularly want it and didn't look forward to it. My morale was at its lowest. I had only two enemy claims to my credit and, on the couple of engagements with the Germans, nothing of any encouragement had happened as they had quickly run away from us within minutes. The rest of the time not a solitary enemy aircraft had been spotted to do battle with.

After the month's leave was up, liaison duties faced me as my next job – a purely nominal position with little to do. In anticipation of this, before I had actually left 302 Squadron I had made three trips to Halesworth (near Ipswich) for the purpose of scouting, due to a rumour that was circulating with regard to the American squadron there. We had heard that Lieutenant Colonel Gabreski – the American fighter ace, of Polish descent – had been tentatively probing for Polish pilots to fly with the American Air Force for a short while, but my visits on these occasions proved fruitless.

Immediately my leave began I called upon Brzezina at Polish Head-quarters to enquire what he knew on this subject. He had heard nothing but, very soon, thirty Polish officers would be detailed for liaison duties for a short period only with the American 9th Tactical Air Force. Fighter and bomber Polish officers were required for this scheme and he would put my name on this list. I thought, perhaps, there may yet be the oppor-tunity for flying, so waited to see what happened. Ten days later I was instructed to go to the headquarters of the US 9th Air Force to take up my post as liaison officer.

After primary lectures for the first few days we were then assigned to

our various American squadrons as intelligence officers. The posting I
received was a fortunate one as I was attached to 355 Fighter Squadron,
354 Fighter Group – later acknowledged as the famous squadron of the
US 9th Air Force. The squadron commander was Lieutenant Colonel
R.W. Stevens.

The friendly atmosphere of the group was welcoming and I took up
my position without any qualms. With all the thoughts I had in my mind
at the end of my period with the Polish Air Force fighter squadrons, it
took me a while to fully appreciate my exact position and responsibilities and what it really entailed in being a liaison officer. Uppermost in
my thoughts was still the possibility of resuming an active flying career
and, if it was to be, I could do worse than being attached to the American
Air Force. What did it matter providing this ambition was achieved! They
were equipped with brand new Mustang P-51Bs (with Rolls-Royce Merlin
engines); they carried 6 x 0.5 inch heavy machine guns; and extra fuel
tanks enabled them to fly as far as Berlin and back.

My hopes raced ahead of me, especially when I was allowed to carry
out my own conversion on to this aircraft. I had no sooner completed a
first familiarisation flight, than on landing I announced that I was all
ready to begin participating in operations over Berlin, and 'pronto'. I
must have looked very crestfallen when it was diligently explained to me,
as one would to an excited little boy in pursuit of dangerous adventure,
that this was not possible due to my position as intelligence officer –
having access to all the secret files etc, their American Headquarters
just would not sanction such a practice in case I was shot down. I was
deflated! It put me back to square one. All I knew at that moment was
that these boys were doing what I too should have been doing, and they
had a greater advantage than we ever had, apart from the Battle of Britain,
for now was beginning the greatest battle of all – against Germany
itself. I wanted to do my share and it seemed I couldn't.

This sent me back again to Brzezina at Polish Headquarters, hoping
for a lead to get back into flying. Perhaps someone had had second
thoughts and now a position was vacant – commanding a squadron for
instance! No such luck, of course, but apparently he had heard that the
US 8th Air Force, upon hearing that the 9th Air Force had Poles with
them, decided to do the same and Lieutenant Colonel Gabreski's plan

began to materialise to secure Polish fighter pilots from the Polish Air Force for flying liaison duties with the USAAF, indirectly under his command.

'Put my name on this list,' I asked Brzezina. With this new hope I returned to my American station – Boxted – intent that they should release me from my duties with them. After explaining the position to Lieutenant Colonel Stevens he agreed to let me go, regretting having been compelled to refuse me operational flying duties and fully appreciating how I felt. During the time I had spent with them and straight away after my conversion (one solo flight in the Mustang), I flew with a young American pilot to Northolt. His name was Gus Allen and he was excited about visiting Northolt, a British and Polish station. It was virtually deserted. All Polish aircraft had gone to Sussex and only a British skeleton staff remained. It stayed this way until after the war, when it was put to practical use as a future airfield. BOAC and BEA formed there.

On my next flight I went to Deanland near the Sussex coast to visit my former squadrons, which had set up a tactical wing in preparation for D-Day. Nos 302, 308 and 317 Squadrons were all squadrons I had formerly been attached to. They were pleased and interested to see for the first time an American Mustang on the ground, giving her a thorough going-over.

At the of April and I was discharged from the 9th. Famous as it was, it was no use to me. I went to the distribution centre of the Polish Air Force Headquarters at Blackpool to await further instructions from the Rubens Hotel in London. Within a very short while I was directed to report to a unit of the 8th American Air Force. Five other Polish pilots would be reporting for duty at the same time. I was amused to discover that my destination was the station I had just left – Boxted near Colchester – station number 150. The 8th had taken over there, replacing the 9th.

Chapter 14

The USAAF 8th Air Force

There is only one way that I can explain this important period of my career – I was a racing driver reaching for his goal on a professional racing track. My experience so far had not proved exactly satisfying for a variety of reasons. After the Battle of Britain – which had been denied to me as a fighter pilot – I was dissatisfied and felt convinced something bigger was needed than the type of flying we were doing. It was a personal feeling and had nothing to do with claiming I knew, or presumed to know, how we should or should not operate. I simply felt restrained and frustrated.

At Boxted station with the 56th Fighter Group I was soon to feel the difference in my position to that previously – I was now accepted for what and who I was: an experienced fighter pilot. As such, I was one of those the American Air Force desperately required and had freely admitted to. With no further constant opposition I felt it was now entirely my responsibility to prove whatever worth I was, and was free to get on with my job. I gladly accepted the challenge and eagerly looked forward to the day, very near now, when I would be in an aircraft's cockpit, flying with the others with one aim in view.

Before coming to join the American Air Force we had all heard the stories of the amazing victories publicised in the press and radio claimed or awarded to the American airmen, and the first job to be done was to clear one's mind of these notions so one could form an unbiased opinion from one's own experience. It was necessary in order to understand and appreciate our American counterparts and their efforts, and this I did not find difficult to do. There was so much to learn and understand that one needed an open mind to absorb it all.

First, each squadron consisted of 16 aircraft – 4 flights each with 4 aircraft. (The British was 12 aircraft, 2 flights of 6 aircraft each per squadron.) They had an immense amount of reserve aircraft totalling approximately 50 per squadron. Therefore on the station was 150 aircraft (the entire number of fighter planes that the PAF had had on 1 September 1939 to fight its war).

Boxted station contained three squadrons collectively called a group. A wing consisted of five groups (five separate stations in other words). In the RAF the naming was reversed.

The 56th Fighter Group, which I and my friends were now attached to, was already the top-scoring group of the American Air Corps in the European theatre, and belonged to the 65th Fighter Wing, 8th American Air Force. This latter also included the 4th Fighter Group, 361st Fighter Group, 355th Fighter Group and the 479th Fighter Group.

The entire American Air Force was gradually changing over from Thunderbolt P-47s (which they had used so far) to Mustang P-51s. But, upon it's own request, the 56th Fighter Group was allowed to continue flying Thunderbolts.

Mustangs were easily acceptable for the average pilots and had a longer range, but later (in 1945) Thunderbolt Marks N and M were improved in power and fuel carried, bypassing the range of the Mustangs and able to fly to Moscow and back. I gathered – and soon discovered for myself – that the Thunderbolts were rather special to the 'individuals' of the 56th Fighter Group.

Chapter 15

56th Fighter Group

The 8th American Air Force was used for long-range daylight bombing, with fighter cover. It included three bomb divisions – the 1st and 3rd flying the Fortress bomber and the 2nd flying Liberators. Each division produced approximately 500 operational bombers. In 1944 it was normal to have 1,000 aircraft on raids per day.

Fighter pilots had originally been under a separate command. As in other Allied forces, they were a law unto themselves. There was no exception here either, as bombers sometimes found themselves without their detailed escort, fighters having flown off to do battle elsewhere or seek out a target or the enemy somewhere other than where they should have been. The American authorities appeared to have found the answer to this problem by scrapping the separate command, instead allocating a fighter wing to a bomb division. The 65th Fighter Wing (which included the 56th Fighter Group) was assigned to the 2nd Bomb Division (Liberators). The situation now was that if fighters were found lacking in their cover duty they were liable for penalisation by their bomb division. The scheme worked perfectly from then on.

At the beginning, long-range bombing by Fortresses was not as successful as expected, in spite of their ability to defend themselves (each carried 10.5 mm machine guns). Even in large waves of bombers in groups of 100 to 150 plus per raid, the German fighters were still playing havoc among them. This was partly due to the inability of Thunderbolts to protect the aircraft over the entire range they had to fly. Mustangs, on the other hand, proved more effective at the time, with their longer range. It was not until later that modifications were made to Thunderbolts that extended their flying range.

The commanding general of 2nd Bomb Division – who subsequently became our own – was Major General W.E. Kepner. He often liked to come to the 56th to fly Thunderbolts. Being a fighter pilot himself he had affection for this aircraft and probably the comfort it provided in the cockpit layout had something to do with it. Its spaciousness suited his rank and heavy responsibility! He was delighted to receive a picture I sent him, made by a Polish pilot and friend W. Potocki (who became a well-known test pilot after the war for AVRO (Canada)). Kepner was highly regarded on the station. Occasionally he came on operations with us, especially on certain flights such as testing the radar used by the front line to prevent accidental bombing by their own air force. He later became the commanding officer of the 9th American Air Force in Germany.

Those of us who joined the 56th at Boxted were: Flight Lieutenant Sawicz; Squadron Leader K. Rutkowski; Flight Lieutenant B. Gladych; Flight Lieutenant T. Anderz; Flight Lieutenant Z. Janicki; and myself. We were attached to the 61st Fighter Squadron under the command of Lieutenant Colonel F. Gabreski. All of us were experienced fighter pilots, perhaps not aces in the sense of being able to claim top scoring rates, but each an individualist in his own right nevertheless. We had all been without jobs waiting to be given a Polish wing or squadrons to enable us to begin flying again (or a desk job in my case) and were available to be sent on loan to wherever was required. The USAAF were in need of a boost to their current situation. They were short of trained pilots and were expanding their force quickly, taking one of their own superior pilots out of each group to lead a new one – or to inspire a particular group that had not been doing so well. The USAAF's losses were increasing constantly, and the replacement with new fresh, young inexperienced pilots was not a complete asset as there was insufficient training and practice available to them, especially with the vagaries of the British weather.

The 56th decided to have a small Polish flight within their group. It was a combination of wanting to secure experienced pilots in its tip-top position within the 8th Air Force, and as a gesture towards the Polish Air Force.

The link with the American Air Force was already forged, warranting our attachment. It was also good for us – as regular Polish officers – to be able to participate in fighting the enemy over their own soil, which could not be done at that time in Spitfires flown by the PAF. Lieutenant Colonel Frances Gabreski and other Polish Americans had been trained by the Polish Air Force at Northolt from 1941. They had come from America to fight voluntarily with the Polish Air Force in England before the USA entered the war.

There were nine Poles in all in the 61st Fighter Squadron: Gabreski, the six of us from the PAF, and two other Poles of American descent who had transferred to the USAAF around the time we were attached to the 56th in 1944. They too had joined the PAF in 1941, as Gabreski had, but were happy to stay with the Polish Air Force until they finally decided they should transfer to their own country's forces.

The Polish air force officers – six of us – took it in turns to fly, leading our own 'flight', which we could only do four at a time. Later on when I flew as Gabreski's or Zemke's wingman, there were five from our Polish flight in the air. Ours was an uncommon situation for there were two squadron leaders and four flight lieutenants all together, representing one flight. Even the American airmen on the station settled down to this unusual state of affairs before long. Although there were no barriers between us and the boys of the 56th, it was natural that both sides would inevitably watch each other carefully.

We were soon to discover the freedom exercised in the missions demanded teamwork to an even greater extent than it had done in the RAF/PAF. Strict planning and control of every move in the air was employed. But we soon found that in the American Air Force air discipline could all too easily be forgotten or ignored in the hunt and ensuing heat of battle, by virtue of the particular type of operations undertaken. Both forces therefore had produced their aces and 'individuals' in the air, either due to, or in spite of, the various systems and methods of operations.

Low-level flying and team formation flying (battle and display) in squadrons within a wing had taken specific importance in our former practice and past training, so we had these advantages over our American counterparts and were demonstrated during our period with them. We were to establish our own small Polish group. Abiding by the principle of formation we maintained it, relying upon each other for cover and support throughout the operations. We were to suffer only one loss from our flight.

Chapter 16

Zemke

Being attached to the famous 56th we had the opportunity to witness the achievements that brought them fame. I considered this was due to their exceptional CO, Colonel Hubert Zemke. He was, without doubt, the best commanding officer I flew under. He was tough, not only towards the boys under his command, exercising strong discipline on the ground and in the air, but applied the same treatment to himself, which made for greatness. After one particular operation, for example, at post-briefing he publicly apologised to all for us – using some four-letter words against himself – for having 'spoilt the whole damn show' in his opinion, adding: 'Gentlemen, I fine myself £20.' Without exception he exerted on everyone a system of fines for errors committed in the air.

Zemke always listened attentively to any new ideas on tactics put forward by any pilot at various occasions throughout the day, and would retire to his own personal quarters for complete privacy to mull it over. At this point everyone knew he had his 'thinking cap' on and wouldn't dream of disturbing him. If the idea was thought to be workable it was accepted for trial at the next briefing and included in the operational plan for that mission, thereby testing its practical advantage. If successful it would then be adopted by the group and also forwarded to American Headquarters with a report for use in all other groups. This appeared to be normal procedure in the USAAF and the report and order would appear on each air force station in the daily orders from the high command.

In his off-duty hours he was a reserved man because of his personal discipline. But there was not one person on the station who was not aware of the fact that here was a sympathetic man whose desire was to help, understand and give assistance to any problems – personal or official.

It is understood that he studied the Russian Air Force system, having been sent to Russia by the American Air Force to do so. As a result he became rather pro-Russian. Later on he was to be liberated as a POW in Germany and what occurred at that time changed his mind. He found himself a prisoner on 30 October 1944, having baled out of his Mustang after it had its wing ripped off in bad weather conditions. He was a CO of 479th Group at that time, after leaving the 56th to reorganise the other group, which needed a boost. As CO of the POW camp, when the Russians liberated them he needed to deal with them directly to co-ordinate the return of all the Americans to England. He found that his idea of an immediate release was unacceptable by the Russians, which infuriated him to such an extent that he gathered a group of air crew together and with them left the camp and reached the Baltic Sea, where he acquired a boat. This brought them safely to England. Being without a unit at this time, due to his capture, he came immediately to the 56th at Boxted. Everyone was delighted at his safe return, but later on during a conversation with me he complained bitterly about the Russian attitude at the camp, which had altered his opinions of them, to my great amusement.

He had authorised our small Polish 'flight' into the 56th. The vast majority of American fighter pilots were very young, with a short service career and fighter experience in comparison to ours. It was obvious his intention was to bring a more specific European perspective to the war in general and an Allied point of view and behaviour by having us with them. By which means they could observe these points for themselves at close quarters in preference to learning the facts by less personal means. It worked both ways as it was an experience and lesson for us also.

Zemke's manner towards us as his 'guests' was extremely friendly. He treated our skill and knowledge with respect as an equal fighter force. He gradually got to know each of us personally – socially as well as in the air – although he was normally reserved.

There were many top-scoring American pilots in the 56th besides Zemke. Among them, of course, our commander Francis Gabreski, Dave Schilling, the celebrated 'Bob' Johnson who, when he returned to America from the European theatre in 1944, was the highest-scoring American ace of the war with twenty-eight confirmed kills against the fighter pilots of the Luftwaffe. Gabreski possessed a very quick reaction, the benefit of good eyesight and was an accomplished shot. He spoke excellent Polish which, he said, had improved during his short stay with the Polish Air Force at Northolt.

The structure of the entire group was centred very much on the group itself, and its aces, in contrast to the PAF and the RAF, who concentrated on the separate squadrons and their commanders.

The 56th's scoring record in the air – at the time we joined them – was almost equal to all the Polish squadrons in England. But the extensive range of their aircraft, the fights that mainly took place over Germany itself, the tools of the trade and the tactics, all helped to subscribe to their superior scoring results.

Thunderbolts of the 56th were specially painted red on the cowling, gaining them the name 'red-nosed' Thunderbolts. We heard from the 2nd Bomb Division that whenever the group took over fighter cover they (the bomber crews) left their action stations and enjoyed a much-needed cigarette. Such was their faith in us and it was very gratifying to know. Nevertheless it was irritating that the Germans would refuse to give us a fight.

The P-47 was heavy and rather fat, with a very powerful radial engine: water injection for emergency to give extra power through cooling of the cylinders. This gave approximately 600 extra horsepower, which was considerable. But it was damaging to the aircraft engine if used too often. It was for emergency use only, and I had the need of it once. The advantage of the radial engine was immense as it was possible to get back home even with one piston completely shot away. The supercharger was based on a turbine system, using exhaust gases, and was positioned at the tail end.

The cockpit was very well designed compared with other smaller fighters I had flown. It was the roomiest and most comfortable I had experienced and beautifully warm whenever required. The hood was electrically operated by pressing a button. Our mechanics even built storage units for cigarettes, matches and ashtray – which we had no right to use anyway!

Armament was this aircraft's greatest advantage. It carried 8 x 0.5 in heavy machine guns, each with 300 rounds – 2,400 in all. Oddly enough the 0.5-calibre machine gun was a replica of the Polish machine guns we had before the war. These were the safest I had experienced without any mechanical failure. The ammunition exploded on impact, approximately every second one, which was essential for a correct result and for the satisfaction of the pilot. After 240 rounds there came 10 tracers to warn the pilot he now had 50 rounds left on each gun for emergency use. Until the latter part of the war, 1945, it was extremely dangerous to exhaust your ammunition completely – after the tracers – over Germany. You always had the long trip back home. As leader of a squadron or group a safety margin must be retained. His duty was to safeguard any pilot under his command and see that his order was carried out with regard to the above. It was a well-known fact this safety was not observed strictly in the American fighter groups. The point has been debated often, but safety in your unit was top priority in comparison to the score attained. This could also be said for leaving the 'Big Friends' (bombers) to the mercy of enemy fighters when your duty was to protect them, however boring or frightening it was.

The Thunderbolt was very poor in a dogfight, especially at a low altitude (below 15,000 feet). But the plane had a terrific advantage when diving. She behaved just like a bullet; steady as a rock and deadly to the enemy. No German aircraft could escape this form of attack. At such speed one could easily sail right past the victim unless your reaction was quick and concentrated. Later, small dive brakes were installed. Many times I exceeded 600 mph when diving. The makers of this aircraft, Republic, had their own representatives on the station to discuss improvements, which were immediately forwarded to America, and our suggestions for them were forthcoming with amazing speed.

Chapter 17

Operations

After conversion to Thunderbolts, which took us a week, my first oper-ation was on 21 May – a short sweep over France. The following day we were ordered to Osnabrück and Bremen, Germany, and I shot down my first enemy aircraft with the 56th. The Poles were flying Red Flight and I flew Whippet Red Two. Red Flight was engaged as top cover when Colonel Gabreski sent another flight after a train near Rotenburg on the main railway line and he accompanied them.

A battle with Fw 190s took place below us and we dived in to assist. I saw one Focke Wulf fall out of the sky in flames and another dogfight in progress. Just at that moment I glanced up and saw another four Fws at 5,000 feet, climbing and turning; I called out their position for attack, turning sharply to follow them. I went for the last one, firing a short burst, but he turned too sharply for me. While engaged I kept watch around and below, suddenly spotting a P-47 firing in a dogfight below me. The pilot's eagerness and determination had engrossed him so entirely that he was unaware of the deadly circle he was in – machine-gunning one Focke Wulf and hitting him in the stern, with another 190 on his own tail, firing at him. I yelled at him through the radio to 'break' as I turned and dived immediately towards the circle to help him. I realised he wasn't part of Red Flight and sensed he was one of the young American boys. In the dive it was the first time I experienced the shock the Thunderbolt gives one in their first battle dive. At the speed she travelled it took a couple of seconds for me to give deflection and fire a short burst from about 400 to 500 yards distance, but with no result. With such speed I was within 150 yards and firing constantly at the enemy; in seconds I had turned on to his tail and could see I was hitting him along the length of the fuselage as I closed upon him. Then suddenly the Fw 190 exploded in front of me. Being so close, I was taken straight through the debris and involuntarily shut my eyes as the remains of the 190 whipped past my cockpit.

I don't recall experiencing any elation in that moment and continued searching quickly around me for the young boy in his P-47 who I had come to assist. I sighted him just ahead of me climbing, trailing very slight white smoke. He was endeavouring to join three other Thunderbolts just above us. I sensed our air battle was now over and flew to join him, knowing that he would definitely need assistance and I hoped fervently he would be able to fly with us back to base. I almost reached him when he suddenly turned slowly and sadly into a dive straight towards the ground. As I watched helplessly I felt that although I had taken the Jerry off his tail, it was seconds too late. Any feeling of success for me was impossible as his aircraft exploded.

I flew up to join Gabreski in the sky above me and very soon we sighted one lone Messerschmitt 5,000 feet below us, hastening towards the safety of the clouds. Gabreski dived immediately below the cloud while I kept cover above in case the Me 109 popped out at the top. He didn't, and as soon as Gabby rejoined me, we formed up with the others and set course for England. West of Lingen we sighted two Me 109s at 20,000 feet. One of them dived from this altitude, inviting us to chase him. Being low on fuel and suspecting a trap we spurned his offer and continued on course for home, leaving him for the next time around.

To show the power the P-47's armament possessed, I had attacked two enemy aircraft and had fired only 800 rounds (100 for each machine gun) leaving 1,200 rounds still for use!

After two and a half years of operational flying I had now found myself in a fighting circus beyond my dreams, where there was so much that could be given and would be accepted without quibble. The amount of personal flying and hard work brought with it a tremendous atmosphere of comradeship and eagerness. So much so that the civilian and political life that was going on outside the station ceased to exist for us. Our intense interest was occupied only with the activities of the group, and the constant intelligence reports that detailed our scoring position within the American Air Force for the European theatre. My physical condition was as healthy as it could be, in spite of the fact that the job was harder than I had ever anticipated it could be. It simply served to increase my energy. I felt as I had done when I entered the skiing Olympic Camp in Poland in 1938 and found I was able to exceed my own expectations when I trebled my previous distances, something I had thought impossible to do.

And now, here I was, with a similar opportunity to develop and better my unsatisfactory performance of the past. My ideas received equal consideration with any other pilot of the group, which was gratifying. We could anticipate more than one fight at a time because we were able to be in the air longer during a mission than we had been in the PAF. Naturally, we would have to adapt to new routines and methods. Our achievements and mistakes were more noticeable, owing to the reason we were there as representatives of the PAF. We were, after all, in the top-scoring American fighter group in Europe.

A typical day with the group was unlike anything we had been used to previously. Invariably it was fully occupied with an exhaustive programme. The basic differences were in the actual operational flying time – anything from three to five hours in the air – and the missions themselves, which included not only protection for bombers but freelancing in groups of squadrons, strafing military targets – aerodromes, trains, barges, transport convoys etc – after the cover duty was completed. This freelancing was not confined to any one American fighter group in particular, but executed by each of them.

The other distinction we noted was the lack of training or practice provided for new pilots. As often as not the operations themselves were relied upon for the gaining of necessary experience.

Between 5 and 6 a.m. – after D-Day even earlier – we were called for an 8 a.m. take-off. You could already hear the mechanics running the planes' engines. Then it was a quick breakfast, either the British favourite of bacon and eggs or American fare of maple syrup 'flapjacks', plus the usual steaming cups of coffee. Each squadron was provided with its own bar and restaurant (they liked their comfort!). After landing, even before the main intelligence briefing, the pilots ate a hearty meal and drank their constant coffee. American facilities for food were well known and lacked nothing on this station. It was well above what we had been used to and took time for us to become accustomed to such ample supplies. But we were not complaining! Then it was on to the briefing room, while Fortress and Liberator bombers already roared overhead forming into their various groups. Hundreds of them. Each leader fired a different-coloured flare to signal to his 'sheep' to join him.

The briefings were vital to all taking part in operations, particularly as one day's mission differed completely with that of the next. The weather, also, often determined the extent of the day's activities.

It didn't matter which way we Poles looked at it, everything was on a much larger scale. For us, at least, bombers and fighters were in complete co-operation on the mission and the separate briefings given to us were the same on the various stations. Our first speaker would be the intelligence officer, who gave the exact details of the coming operation, and a brief account of the results of the previous day's op if it had any relevance to the one in hand and contained certain information valuable to the present or future undertakings. Then came the fortune-teller – crystal ball in hand for our amusement – our dearly beloved Met officer who never believed in his own forecasts, which had all too often been proved wrong. He was always greeted with ribald remarks and catcalls of 'Go away – you fake.' This never deterred him from carefully putting down his 'ball' (a lamp globe set on a piece of wood, battery and bulb inside) and switching on, being 'all set for business'.

The group commander then detailed the orders for the entire structure of the group. At this point we would be asked for any suggestions or comments anyone had to offer, a common practice for points of view to be stated and taken into consideration by the commander. The atmosphere was always serious – other than when our funny man arrived (Met officer) – but nevertheless was still congenial and relaxed.

The Roman Catholic chaplain always attended the briefings no matter what time of day or night and, as soon as it was concluded, those who wished could stay behind in the briefing room after the rest had gone to take Holy Communion before take-off. As soon as the briefing finished he would stand by the door to watch everyone as they left and then joined those of us who had remained behind. This was again something we had not experienced before and it gave me intense pleasure and peace to share a few brief calm, satisfying moments outside the turmoil of war – such as the excessive pace and viciousness of the operation that was about to begin.

Transport had already driven the others to dispersal and it was always the padré himself who took the rest of us in his own jeep. And then within a short while we were taking off, returning after about four or five hours. The first faces to greet you were those of your personal mechanics. Generally I spoke with mine for about ten minutes, giving them a brief account of my activities in answer to their eager enquiries; I always considered this essential. A mechanic's unstinting efforts kept one airborne in safety. Your successes were also his successes; and if you came back with nothing much to report he was just as fed up as you were. So to give an account was one of the best ways I could repay them for what they did on my behalf.

Immediately upon arriving back at dispersal, the first port of call was to the bar for food and drink, all prepared for our return. I had looked forward to my favourite meal all the way home. A huge double-decker sandwich of 'Spam' and two fried eggs. The smell of it was my homing beacon. I never have lost my taste for it or the memories it recalls.

While eating, those who had a claim reported the details to the liaison officer and his assistant at a primary interview. The padré would be circling among us delighted to see the safe return of his 'flock'. Then it was back to the briefing room for post-briefing and official reports. Your day finished here – unless you had a second outing following immediately, in which case it was a trip to the mess for a main meal before returning to the briefing room, and the whole procedure would begin again.

From August 1944 I was always asked if I wanted to go on the next mission, especially as one of the leaders. But soon after our initial attachment to the group in May of that year, if either Zemke or Gabreski wanted me to fly their wing they needed to ask me anyway.

The manner of providing the necessary cover for bombers was as follows. The route of the bombers' flight path was first sectioned off into blocks. Separate fighter groups covered the bombers through their particular detailed block (45 minutes' flight time for each). Every fighter group knew from which unit they would take over and who was to take over from them.

Only the group commander and his deputy had a special channel to confer directly with the bomber commander in the air. Each separate day's cover meant a different sector from the last to provide escort. This meant that each group in turn had the opportunity to escort the bombers right to the target itself. In this sector fighters diverted the flak from the bombers by flying a few seconds ahead, weaving to and fro to avoid being hit and attracting the flak towards them, thereby enabling the bombers to take their straight course over the target as untroubled as possible. I always looked forward to covering this last sector for it gave the opportunity to see the actual result of the bombing raid.

The bombers were also able to bomb through clouds using the latest radar bomb sights. This would be a dreary operation for fighters as the Jerries would never intercept us in the air in bad weather, and it was too dangerous and difficult for us to go hunting in such conditions.

The normal operational height of the bombers was 24,000 feet; we flew between 27,000 and 32,000 feet. To check the wind variation at their height the bombardier used special white smoke bombs, dropping them before the target. If these were not used for testing they were automatically released with the main load, therefore making it possible to observe the flight of the bombs on to the target area.

After providing this cover (of any detailed block en route), and dependent upon weather conditions, we were free either to return to base or go hunting, which most of the time we did. We were not given any specific instructions for these diversions of where or what to go after except, of course, that they must be military targets. It was left entirely according to the situation we found after leaving the bombers. The results of these expeditions were superb and played absolute havoc on the German Air Force, for they were unable to take off or land without the continued fear of being attacked by the fighter groups. So, apart from the bombing raids, from the tactical point of view there was no specific plan, other than on special missions, except to release and spread the fighters all over enemy territory in every direction after the main object was achieved. Enemy transportation, trains, convoys and any military vehicles we saw were also attacked and in constant danger, forcing them to a standstill during the daytime. The Germans retaliated by arming the trains with three 40 mm Oerlikon guns on platforms: one at the front, one in the centre and one at the rear. This made attacks more difficult and dangerous, but it didn't put us off unduly; we simply changed our tactics accordingly.

By sheer chance we might happen to meet the complete number of our bombers – 1,000 or more – on their homeward journey. The sight they presented in the air was formidable and impressive, even though they had suffered damage or losses. I never could quite get used to this massive spectacle, even when I knew it was our particular job to meet and protect them through one of the blocks on their way back. Escorting a smaller number out could not compare with such a vast number all returning together.

We all had radio beams to assist with navigation. I personally never used mine and I presume it was employed mostly by bombers, as their individual navigation was less experienced than ours. As a comparison the British night bombers each flew separately, and navigation and timing was essential for 1,000 bombers to come over the targets at one-minute intervals.

Occasionally we were called upon to give assistance to the British Lancaster day raiders. In August 1944, on one particular occasion, we were asked to strafe the target area (an aerodrome between Ghent and Brussels) to divert the flak and attention away from the bombers, Polish aircraft were among them also, just prior to the actual bombing. Timing was essential. As we climbed to watch the individual bombing, the Lancasters came in immediately at no more than a 15,000-foot ceiling. Their accuracy was superb. It was interesting for us to observe this as we had only previously been used to seeing mass bombing from groups of bombers. One particular bomber, who apparently was highly unsatisfied with his final run in, decided to have another go. He was no sooner beyond the target than he made a sharp turn 'sitting on his tail' to make another pass, immediately ahead of the bomber following him that was already on his run in. It was well worth his meticulous effort. He dropped his bombs neatly on the target. Those of us watching above voiced our approval, but I can imagine what his chum called him for cutting in!

The VHF range was very short – up to 150 miles – so to assist us with radio communication on important operations, one of our own Thunderbolts would circle an area – for instance on the Dutch coast at 25,000 feet – to transfer radio messages between us and base.

Formation flying – called battle formation – was big and loose. Very close formation in various positions was not practised. Perhaps as the element of surprising the enemy was impossible with the large wave of bomber formations from East Anglia, close formation was considered of secondary importance. The difficulty came when cloud flying, night flying and low level were called for, as then one could only feel completely confident and in command with previous practice experience, particularly in watching your tail and everything else needing constant observation around your group.

The atmosphere was very encouraging from the youngsters, who were eager to fly and learn. Often too zealous in the battles which, without sufficient experience, had cost all too many of them their lives by colliding in the air; for instance by forgetting to watch each other's aircraft, intent upon their desire to shoot down the enemy. The best example was of the Lightning squadron (P-38s). Their air collisions occurred frequently. Whenever I heard that Lightnings would be within our aerial vicinity I kept as much a watch out for them as for Jerries. Later Lightnings were withdrawn from our operations.

Another reason for the air collisions was due to the fact that excitement drove these young pilots to attack an aircraft in 'packs', reducing their safety margin from any enemy interceptors to nil. Their whole attention riveted on the enemy directly engaged. They were the aggressors and behaved in that spirit. The individual score was also highly relevant; therefore one had to take part in the pack as they did, for there just wasn't an alternative if that was how the battle developed. For example, to order top cover while one section attacked was seldom called. The method was simply to pounce, one and all. The aircraft split in the air, diving and climbing all over the sky. If attacked on the way back to base, either separately or perhaps in small groups, they would just have to fight it out on their own without assistance, unless they were lucky with someone else in the vicinity to help.

This was really the reason why the battle was seldom directed by a group leader (or a deputy) except when he was particularly conscientious of this part of his duty towards his command. After Zemke and Gabreski left the 56th, this state of affairs often existed.

I was invariably the first to spot any German aircraft when I flew with the squadron. Further directions were inevitably expected from me. It surprised me when I first encountered this, as I was neither their group commander nor their deputy commander. But I did not stop to query it with Jerry diving at the group. I just got on with it. From then on it became standard practice for them to actually await my instruction in battle once I had detected the enemy. Even if Gabreski, for instance, sighted Jerry first, I automatically directed the battle if he or his deputy did not attempt to. This situation often arose, but I gained nothing materialistic as a result, such as decorations etc, and indeed expected nothing. My experience and past training dictated this responsibility when it was needed. I received friendship and trust from the pilots themselves and the ground crew. These things were more valuable and rewarding.

While operating over enemy-occupied territory the younger pilots needed to be controlled so as not to cause suffering to the civilian population if caught up in an attack – for example, when firing upon a train that was part goods and part passengers. On one such occasion, a few days after D-Day, we were operating deep into France. It was our job to stop all enemy transport reaching the front line, the trains obviously playing the major part. The squadron was out hunting for them after we had completed a dive-bombing raid, with 250-lb bombs on some tanks. I was leading one of the flights when we spotted a train, which came to a stop as soon as we flew overhead. I looked down and saw that it pulled three passenger coaches as well as goods trucks. Our job, of course, was to destroy the engine of any train – goods or passenger – and the trucks they pulled. But in such instances there was always the danger to passengers in the coaches. As troop trains were invariably heavily protected with guns, it was safe to assume that this one carried civilians, either French or slave labour. The boys were anxious to get on with the attack. I called to them to hold back, giving the passengers time to get away from the train. In that moment the doors of the carriages flew open and civilians poured from the coaches, running for cover, women and children among them. We waited until they were clear and then we attacked and destroyed the train.

Troop trains seldom moved by day and, later on, all trains came to a halt during daytime, except right down in the south of France. As soon as we had finished demolishing the train we re-formed and flew on. We spotted small flashes coming from a wheat field. Nothing could be seen among the wheat, only the flashes! We could only assume it was a platoon of German soldiers who had hidden themselves in the field at our coming, but stupidly attracting our attention by firing at us with their rifles. We went down and strafed the field and the firing ceased. It would have been a million to one chance for them to have shot one of us down, something they obviously hadn't stopped to consider before giving their hiding place away.

On another occasion, this difficulty of safeguarding the lives of civilians in occupied territory, while endeavouring to make our job effective, caused me a personal heartache and fury at having failed miserably. We came across a convoy of enemy trucks pulled up in an S-bend of a small village. They were protected by the village houses on either side, which the truck drivers had taken advantage of to camouflage themselves, hoping not to be spotted. I circled trying to assess the best way to destroy the trucks without causing damage to the village. The S-bend made any such likelihood impossible to achieve. Nevertheless, I made my run in for attack from either side of the S-bend road, giving short bursts on each heavy lorry without hitting any of the houses. I managed very nicely in this way to score direct hits to each and was just beginning to feel glad I had been able to accomplish it without damage to the village. But it looked as if I needed to come in again. As I climbed for the next pass and looked down, I was appalled to see that all the surrounding houses were being destroyed as each truck blew up in an enormous explosion. I had had no knowledge of what the trucks contained, but it was now obvious they carried ammunition. I swore to myself furiously at the sight below, which I had tried and hoped to avoid. I joined the boys who had been circling and watching from above. They sympathised and tried to cheer me up, but I was just plain depressed all the way home.

Chapter 18

D-Day

From the start of June our operations seemed to centre over France, from the coast to Paris and beyond. On 5 June our flight did a short operation – about two and a half hours – near Dieppe, and soon after landing we noticed the aircraft being painted with black and white stripes on the wings, around the fuselage and tail. This sight wasn't new to the Poles as we had experienced it previously, in August 1942 for the Dieppe invasion, and we guessed the long-awaited D-Day was about to begin. We were as excited and eager as any youngster at that moment.

Early that same afternoon the whole group was called by Zemke to the briefing room and we learned officially that the invasion was to begin the next day, 6 June. For our first flight we were to be disappointed to some degree, for it seemed to us that our part in the scheme of things was not really directly important to the invasion. The whole Channel had been sectored off and the job of the 56th was to patrol the sectors, four Thunderbolts to a square, flying at 10,000 to 16,000 feet. There were many gloomy faces!

Take-off was around 4 a.m., in pitch darkness. Our little Polish flight thoroughly enjoyed the spectacle of the resulting 'mess' of Thunderbolts and Mustangs (stationed 5 miles away), frantically circling and climbing in the sky trying to find each other to form up for the given sectors. Without constant night-flying practice it was not so easy to find your leader. It was a miracle no one collided. A few spun down at losing their speed, but recovered safely to climb again. The excitement of the day could be blamed for much of the confusion.

As I climbed I saw three silhouettes of Thunderbolts and joined with them. To my amazement they were all closing their throttles as no one wanted to be leader. So I naturally joined in the fun. Finally one gave up (Gladych) and set course for Dieppe and we took up our positions with him. On reaching 10,000 feet we switched off our lights; radio silence had already been observed constantly in the air. Reaching the Channel simultaneously, we all spotted an enormous black silhouette heading straight at us and we dived in unison to avoid collision. Fortunately, the Lancaster bomber hadn't taken the same evasive action. Lancasters were returning from bombing the landing beaches and we were meeting them en route. Dawn was breaking and we all gave a little shudder with relief at our near escape.

We arrived at our sector and our thoughts were towards the beaches, wondering what was happening and feeling peeved at having to patrol the squares allotted. Gladych decided we should go and take a look. Without breaking radio silence we flew off to satisfy our curiosity. The weather wasn't perfect, but we could see the heavy naval guns shelling the Normandy beaches and thousands of landing craft arriving. We returned to our sector satisfied that we had at least been there for a moment. There were no enemy aircraft to be seen at all. The new group arrived to take over from us at the set time and we returned to base.

On my second trip, south of Normandy, I found I was unable to use my oxygen mask due to a streaming nose and eyes from a bad cold; on the third time round for patrol I was unable to fly. During all three ops for the entire group, no contact or sight of the enemy was made. Apart from the excitement and activities of the day, it was uneventful for the 56th. This was the longest flying day for any of the fighter groups and for a good many pilots it meant twelve hours in the air.

In the following days we were taken off supporting the bombers and our job was now occupied in dive-bombing any military convoys. After that, the rest of the flight was spent strafing lorries, convoys, cars, trains, aerodromes, barges and marshalling yards. The RAF and PAF fighter wings were occupied in the same way. The enemy decided to move mainly at night. Within about two weeks it was very difficult to find a target to attack, as much had already been destroyed by this time. As for German aircraft, we seldom had the chance to find one.

Most of the bombs we carried were 250-pounders, and the Thunderbolt could easily carry 500 lb. The date of 13 June was to prove eventful for two reasons, and assembled for briefing we were informed that this particular operation would be rather interesting. Even though each mission varied anyway, from the sound of Zemke's voice it foretold some extra thrills. Two squadrons would be dive-bombing in pairs and in fours on various targets, and one squadron would keep top cover. The target for Mike Gladych and myself was an important bridge at Saumur about 30 miles west of Tours. We were to carry two 1,000-lb bombs. This meant that with our one extra drop tank under the belly we would be carrying 3,000 lb extra load. We were all surprised and excited, but our first remarks were to the effect that we needed to get off the ground first! The grass runway was really too short for that load, yet somehow, after eating up the runway, we all made it safely into the air, using water injection for extra power and with both hands pulling like mad on the stick to get our aircraft airborne.

Dive-bombing was a speciality that required particular training or, if possible, special aircraft like the German Stuka. Having had no practice at this we were all in the same boat and would learn as we went along. Surprisingly, the results were exceptionally good and justified our satisfaction in ourselves. We were told by the so-called experts that we should dive from approximately 10,000 feet, as our safety height for pulling out in this op with 1,000-pounders must not be below 4,000 feet. This was duly noted but was to come unstuck as far as Mike and I were concerned.

After leaving the others over the area, Mike and I received another shock – clouds with a base at 5,000 feet. We now had a decision to make – where else to drop our bombs, or try to drop them, in these conditions on our set target? Our safety height would be reduced considerably. We decided to try for the bridge, hoping for the best. We made a shallow dive and released our bombs from 2,000 feet. The force of the explosion immediately lifted us another 2,000 feet. Hardly what the experts intended, of course, but one way or the other we had attained the 4,000 feet they had specified! However, we both missed the bridge by yards! It was too much to hope for the direct hit necessary to destroy it – sheer luck had been needed under the circumstances. In the end we just had to leave it standing, although we had probably succeeded in causing it damage of some kind.

We carried out low-level bombing with ten-second-delay fuses on some missions. Again we had to learn as we went along. The bomb travelled the same speed as our aircraft. Unless it scored a direct hit it would skid and jump – looking rather like a dolphin – until it collided with a target or just came to a halt before exploding. Once, aiming for a lorry convoy my bomb merrily jumped two or three lorries before it finally stopped and blew up. Unfortunately, to my distress, a lot of cows and horses were slaughtered in our efforts to make contact with the targets. But on the whole, dive-bombing was good and more effective than the low-level attacks. The latter required intense practice that by now none of us had any time for. There were also missions carrying anti-personnel bombs (a load of twenty-four). These also had a ten-second delay and were used against trains etc, carried out in low-level strikes, with each bomb on the end of a little parachute.

Chapter 19

Loss

In general, Gladych and I had integrated with the Americans of the group more than the others, although Gabreski and Anderz were very friendly on the ground. They had similar characters both spirited and happy-go-lucky. Possibly the American boys found my Polish colleagues rather reserved. We were invited to the station mess parties and, as I often visited PAF Andrewsfield, I sometimes invited a few of my friends from there to these parties and they were made welcome.

But within our Polish flight we gradually hit a situation that originated from our former achievements or, in my case, the lack of them. Out of my five colleagues, I had previously only flown with Gladych and Rutkowski in the PAF.

It was a testing period for all of us in the 56th. Our actions, individual activities, participation and achievements were being observed, not only by the Americans in the group but also between each other. Due to the fact that we, as Polish pilots and officers, were not operating under our usual conditions – as in our own forces – if an error was made by any one of us and it was not mentioned within our flight, I did not hesitate to bring the subject up for discussion. And irrespective of who had committed it – which included me! It did not help to increase my popularity poll, but that was hardly the point; my ideas for participation within the 56th did not exactly top the bill either.

This friction wasn't pleasant and perhaps my tag of 'rebel' had been reinforced by any who wished to see it that way. It became obvious that my friends resented it if I pointed out to any one of them that they had made a dangerous error in the air – I was obviously getting 'too big for my boots'! A little extra consideration would have shown them that their safety, my safety and the safety of the group, was my only objective.

Unfortunately, when Janicki failed to return on the 13 June special mission it unhappily proved my case, particularly as I had warned him on two previous occasions that he not only endangered himself, but was also distracting my attention by struggling on my tail during those operations. Therefore his death was a very unhappy experience for us all. Because of previous actions, I had forecast this to him during a rather strong argument over the fact that he had positioned himself well behind my tail a couple of times. I pointed out that he was inviting the enemy to pounce on him. Also under no circumstances should he have distracted the attention of 'any one of us' in that way. He could easily have been mistaken for the enemy.

On the mission on 13 June we all carried two 1,000-lb bombs; Zemke led the group. When I noticed Janicki again in my mirror, for the same reason, I asked him over the radio if he was in trouble. This time he said he had engine problems. Zemke told him to return to base and detailed two Thunderbolts as his escort, ordering the three aircraft to get rid of their bombs. During this exchange Janicki had fallen back even further and I could no longer see his aircraft. Presumably he, too, had lost us. But his reply to Zemke was that he had decided to catch us up, stating that his engine was now all right. In such circumstances – carrying those bombs – it would have been by sheer coincidence for him to have been able to do so, unless he dropped them first to give his plane more speed. But nothing more was heard or seen of him. I can only assume that he was shot down, even before he had a chance to speak and, with that bomb load, no trace would have been left.

Back at base the Polish boys asked me to take Janicki's car and all his personal belongings and break the news to his wife in Blackpool. No one relished this type of job and it wasn't the first time I had had to do it. He also left children. But he had been the only one of our six who was married, and his death was the only loss in our Polish flight.

The only other incident came later, with Gladych getting himself fined £20 publicly for not reporting an attack involving our Polish flight of four and two Mustangs from 355 Fighter Group (their aircraft painted with yellow and black chequered noses). The latter had pounced us from behind. Mike yelled 'Bandits' and we broke like mad. Mike was promptly in position to open fire and his guns blazed. In that instant I realised who our 'bandits' were and I screamed at Mike to stop firing as they were Mustangs. Unfortunately, he had already hit the right wing as one of the Mustangs turned. They had obviously mistaken us for Fw 190s, an easy enough thing to do in the heat of battle, just as it was to confuse Mustangs for Me 109s, although not in this instance. Mike was our leader on this occasion and had chosen to say nothing of the incident upon our return to base. On the other hand, the two young pilots from 355 obviously yelled their heads off that they had been shot up by the red-nosed Thunderbolts of the 56th. That did it, for Zemke had an explanation demanded from him by the irate commander of the 355th. He was furious and Mike had to own up. Zemke would stand no nonsense and fined Mike for not telling him, however right he had been to defend the flight.

Chapter 20

Wingman

As I have indicated previously, Colonel Zemke began to ask me to fly his wing frequently. It gave me great pleasure and I appreciated it was his way of treating me as his equal. Gabreski, our squadron commander, came to me with the same offer. It was an honour from both of them and I didn't fail to realise it. But it also proved a little amusing, for it frequently meant that I needed to be able to split myself in half as I had the opportunity to fly two separate missions at once!

Flying Zemke's wing on one particular mission, we were taking off in quick succession two at a time, which was usual in good weather. Just as we two left the ground, Zemke closed his throttle for a brief second. Taken by surprise, my aircraft sped past his; I looked sharply into his cockpit rather anxiously to see what had gone wrong. Of course, nothing had – it was just his little joke. He was grinning gleefully at having duped me. On our next mission together I was prepared. I closed my throttle and it was his turn to get a fright and shoot past me, which – as was apparent – he hadn't anticipated. For his reaction was the same as mine had been previously. But I was leaning right over in my cockpit, leering at him and chewing on an outrageously long cigar in a Texan millionaire style. He choked with laughter and waggled his wings appreciatively. He may have been reserved and strict to a high degree, but he was equally full of humour and liked his little jokes, as any other. Regrettably I was never fortunate enough actually to be in an air battle under Zemke's direction. But without doubt he was one of the very best commanders in the 8th Air Force.

When Gabby asked me to fly his wing I did not have to accept, of course, as I was perfectly entitled to lead my own flight, something I was doing as commander of the Polish flight. But as his offer came more frequently after the first few occasions – partly as a joke and partly seriously – I suggested we should make it a mutual arrangement. And he realised perfectly what I meant. Briefly, I was indicating what he, as a commander, already knew – that every one of us must be afforded the same safety cover in formation and the same opportunity in the air. So, knowing his nature and his insatiable appetite and urge to pounce on a quarry, I put my terms to him. With regard to the above, and the fact that if, by any chance, we found ourselves alone – which was common, particularly due to the American pilots' general behaviour in aerial combat – and I judged the situation ill-advised to either make an attack on the deck or be goaded into a one-sided fight, I expected him to ignore the temptation also. For the safety of us both. He just grinned at me and nodded: 'Okay Lanny, anything you say.'

He didn't have to pick me especially. He had the choice of anyone from the 61st. But he seemed content with this arrangement. I, on the other hand, had no misgivings about not leading my own flight while I flew with him as his wingman. Perhaps he was remembering a day or so ago, for I had had to call him off an attack in which he apparently seemed unable to resist the urge to swoop down for a kill. I had no love for the Jerry he was after, but everyone was needed up top right at that moment and not on the deck where he was heading.

We had come across a formation of our bombers suddenly involved in a murderous attack from Jerries diving 'vertically' (in what can only be described as a suicidal manoeuvre, straight through the closed boxes of the bombers). In an attempt to break up their formation and get them at their mercy, it could only have been a terrifying experience for the bomber boys as these aircraft hurtled down directly on top of them.

As one Jerry dived through the formation and appeared again underneath the box, Gabby, without a word, suddenly flicked over and went into a screaming dive himself, down after his prey. As his wingman he was naturally expecting me to follow him down on the deck to cover for him in pursuit of this 'one'. I didn't agree with this sudden decision of his, so I yelled at him to get back upstairs where he belonged as commander of the squadron, as by this time we had already jumped into action to put a stop to the game that was in progress. On the deck we would have been at the mercy of anyone diving down after us. He acknowledged my call, pulled out and straight away climbed back up to us, just as happily as he had dived in hot pursuit.

I was lucky enough to have Gabby's personal aircraft after he received his brand new P-47, the latest-type Thunderbolt, which carried 100 gallons of extra fuel, increasing its flight range. His previous older-type P-47 was called 'Silver Lady'. She wasn't camouflaged at all, just gleaming silver and very highly polished. Her name was painted across the fuselage, with a large British royal crown on her cowling.

The engineering department on the station wanted to make a record of 500 operational flying hours on her engine. She had already just about reached 400 op hours and had 24 German victories to her credit, which probably was already a record by this time. But with the 500 hours they were aiming for she would then return to the States as a showpiece. When Gabby received his new Thunderbolt, I, too, was entitled to a new P-47. But when the mechanics asked me to accept their offer of 'Silver Lady' as my aircraft to complete the set target they wished for her, I was only too aware of the honour they were affording me and was very happy to accept. Of course, others flew her also, as was usual, but she was considered mine and I flew her more often than not. She was quite an aeroplane and gleamed conspicuously in the sky, and she flew me as wingman to Gabby. I was able to put in just over sixty-four operational hours in her, this not counting normal cross-country, which wasn't meant to count towards the target. I also added two more victories to her credit. But I didn't have the victories painted alongside the others that Gabby had attained. For that matter I didn't have any painted on my new Thunderbolt (after Silver Lady), or my name, as many of them did, including Mike. There was no specific reason for it. I just never thought much about it. But I had my own personal emblem on the new one.

After her arrival back in America, as far as I know they continued to fly 'Silver Lady' until she finally completed 1,200 hours without any major replacement of her engine since the time she was first built.

The date of 25 June was quite an eventful day, what with one thing and another, and the day I found the urgent need to use the water injection to get out of trouble quickly. It was a Ramrod operation, deep into France.

Gabby led the flight of four aircraft and I flew his wing. Each flight was searching for targets and soon our four found ourselves alone in the vicinity. We were looking for something worthwhile to strafe. By this period of the war targets of any note were becoming scarcer to find. Gabby, of course, was flying the new-type P-47 with extra fuel, and in his determination to seek something out we were flying further into France. Unfortunately, the other three of us did not have the advantage of the extra fuel and this fact obviously had escaped Gabby's memory until I decided to remind him of our position. For if he did not decide to turn back now, three of us certainly would not reach England on the amount of fuel we had left! Our only recourse would be to land on the emergency strips set up on the Normandy beaches for refuelling. But this we had been specifically asked not to do unless in a dire emergency. I had a sneaking feeling this was going to be just that!

So far we had been lucky – no interceptors, and it was just as well as we needed our gas! Nevertheless, Gabby said we should scout about for a few minutes more before heading for home. We were just about to turn back when we caught sight of a small marshalling yard containing two or three trains of goods trucks. With one brief look Gabby dived and I followed. But my sixth sense was telling me we were not alone up there! So I was watching the sky, my head on a swivel. We both strafed and scored hits, and although I had managed to put two trains out of action nothing really exploded, so they were undoubtedly empty trucks. I immediately climbed to follow Gabby who was about to go round again. But I stared in horror at four Me 109s above us. As I yelled their presence and position to the boys the Messerschmitts dropped their tanks, having spotted us – now as 'sitting ducks'. Gabby dived straight to the deck, opened up – complete with water injection – and we all took off likewise after him. But this wasn't going to help our fuel situation, Jerries or no Jerries. We were using up our precious fuel too fast. So I switched off my water injection as I flew on the deck. Soon I found myself way behind the others and, watching my tail, I observed we were not being followed. Obviously we had surprised Jerry by our speedy exit, as he had startled us. I called to Gabby to slow down and wait as we were not being pursued and we might need our fuel in case we got ourselves in a fight – we still had quite a distance to cover.

After ten minutes or so we all re-formed. Gabby then decided we should pull up to 10,000 feet and promptly began to climb – right into the centre of a German aerodrome. It really wasn't his day! I 'blessed' him with every name I could think of as all hell let loose around us. We were sitting really pretty, like trimmings on a Christmas tree and surrounded by 'lights'. But again we had stunned the German anti-aircraft gunners, this time with our 'incomprehensible' act. They were firing sure enough, but aimlessly. Fortunately, luck was with us and we all came out of that barrage unscathed. Moreover, luck took us to the Normandy beaches with whatever fuel we had left. Gabby still had sufficient but we three were more or less flying on fumes, or would have been over the Channel. So we came in to land for refuelling. Here I took not only my American compatriots by surprise but also the British mechanics who obviously thought I was about to pray to Allah. One Tommy muttered 'Blimey' as I went down on my knees and kissed the ground! Contrary to what it must have seemed to my friends, it was the first occasion I had set foot in Europe since 1940. As I looked towards the south I could see the horizon and nothing obscured my gaze for as far as my eyes could see. No hedges, no fences, no restrictions. Just open fields and wheat. I could breathe again and I felt free. All I could say in answer to their look of astonishment was that it was Europe.

The Tommies were anxious for us to be off and away. They filled up the tanks of three of our aircraft with 100 gallons each. We arrived back at base without further mishap. The two other boys then told me they had flown right under high-tension wires. We had all been very lucky indeed.

Two days later, 27 June, I flew Whippet White Two as wingman to Gabby again. I was flying Gladych's aircraft. After diving-bombing with twelve anti-personnel fragmentation bombs, we found ourselves between two German fighter aerodromes. Red Flight (our Polish flight) had reported four Me 109s in the vicinity. Gabby spotted some more and Whippet White Three and Four went down after them. Another P-47 joined Gabby and me, having lost his own element leader in the clouds. I recognised him as Patterson, one of the new pilots who had joined us from a bomber group. He had come to us in preference to being sent home after his bombing tour.

Light ack-ack suddenly started up and I turned sharply to the right and

Gabby to the left. At the same time I spotted three Me 109s in open V formation heading towards us at 2,000 feet below. I reported them and was checking for any more when Patterson – who had taken my wing – dived towards the three German aircraft. I followed to provide cover for him. He fired upon one, which began trailing white smoke from the cooling system that had been hit. Patterson pulled away believing he had got his man, without firing further. I went in and finished the Messerschmitt off. As I came in firing, the pilot was baling out. Gabby had taken on another, which he destroyed. I took on the third Jerry. He was already running on the deck and much too low for the pilot to bale out. He tried everything to shake me off his stern. I closed on him to 300 yards and was scoring hits all over his aircraft. He crash-landed. The three of us passed over him, firing shots at his plane for good measure. We were again short of fuel, but we made it to Dungeness to refill our tanks.

Patterson made his first claim that day. Only his excitement had caused him to overestimate the result of his shooting. I told him to make absolutely certain in future to destroy his enemy, especially when he was being covered – as I had covered for him – and the battle had not been a heavy one. The Me 109 was his. I had no intention of claiming the kill.

Our group was one of the few who would accept bomber pilots for converting to fighter aircraft. It was generally considered their reaction was too slow by many of the groups, and on average they were not successful as fighter pilots. But there were exceptions and Patterson was one of them, as he soon proved.

On 5 July there was a Ramrod operation to Châteauroux. I was Whippet White Two again to Gabby's Whippet White One. Gabby by this time was fast approaching his thirtieth victory. But until the post-briefing back at base after the following encounter, I couldn't satisfy myself that I had scored at all.

The mission was centred over France. Weather was perfect, but with six-tenths cumulus cloud at 5,000 feet. Suddenly Gabby thought he saw something near the deck. We both proceeded to investigate and recognised two Me 109s, promptly diving in to attack. Gabby took on one while I concentrated on the other. But he was to elude me, for after diving steeply he then climbed straight into the clouds. I followed but lost all trace of him. As I flew through this cover I could see 109s and a few Fw 190s scurrying from cloud to cloud. I had the distinct feeling of being a cat among a lot of mice with far too many holes to disappear into. As I called for assistance I sighted a P-47 with a white nose (another group, probably the 9th TAF) being chased by a Focke Wulf. I yelled over the radio for him to break away. But in my excitement I forgot he wasn't using our channel. In any case I was already diving to his assistance. But they, too, vanished into the clouds.

Still at 5,000 feet I turned again to the left and lined up in my gunsight a Messerschmitt 109, between 500 and 800 yards in front of me. Not to be outdone this time I immediately fired several long bursts and then he, too, was lost to view in the cumulus. I had no idea if I had scored any hits at all and I felt thoroughly frustrated.

At post-briefing I was just listening to the others who had claims to report. Then Gabby wanted to know which of us had been firing at the Me who had run into the clouds. I waited to see if anyone had had the same experience as me and, of course, it hadn't occurred to me anyone might have been upstairs at the time who would have seen what occurred. As everyone looked enquiringly at each other but no one answered, I said briefly what had happened to me. I was told to claim as Gabby had seen the pilot bail out and he could verify it in his report.

I wasn't flying on 20 July and the boys returned with some disturbing news: Gabby had crash-landed in Germany. Apparently they had been strafing on the deck and his propeller had hit the ground. But he had been seen climbing safely out of his aircraft and we learned later he was in a POW camp, where he remained for the duration of the war. Major Gordon E. Baker took over the 61st, a very nice person and a good commander.

August 1944 was an eventful month, at least for me and Gladych. By this time we were flying all over France, Belgium and Germany, covering for Liberator bombers and strafing every military target, moving or otherwise, dive-bombing, fragmentation bombing etc. Our invading forces were moving very fast, pressing on towards Paris.

On 13 August came an unusual operation. The target was a very large marshalling yard near Rouen. Our drop tanks contained a mixture of half (used) oil and half petrol, and for this particular mission two detonators were attached to each tank. This was the beginning of the use of so-called napalm bombs in Europe; the jelly type came later, in 1945. Some 98 drop tanks of 200 gallons, each exploding on the marshalling yards and goods trucks, produced a fire of 20,000 gallons of burning mixture. It was horrifying to watch, but an impelling sight.

A Ramrod operation was undertaken on 25 August, and on our return from covering bombers – flying at 23,000 feet – we met heavy ack-ack. My right drop tank was hit and I promptly released both of them when I noticed petrol leaking. I was lucky that was all they hit. As I peered down through a brief gap in the clouds I saw a very large town. I concluded it to be Bremen, so it was no wonder they were firing at us. A few minutes later when I looked again through another break in the clouds, I spotted a German aerodrome and also noticed a German twin-engined bomber just landing. I reported to Baker, who did not believe me for a moment, querying how the devil I could possibly see a German bomber landing down below when he couldn't even see the aerodrome. But nevertheless he agreed to let me go down and take a look. They would keep cover for me and I would check on the defences. 'If there's anything there,' he added.

I had Patterson flying my wing. We were firm friends by this time and we liked to fly together. We dived down at about 600 mph and strafed right through the aerodrome that did, of course, exist. By this time the German bomber had reached the sanctuary of the adjoining wood for camouflage. The defence was too heavy to stage an all-out attack. As I passed over the airfield I came immediately upon a main railway line and spotted two goods trains with a considerable artillery guard. I was already upon them and had no time to attack unless I came in again. From the direction we had come they hadn't been visible to us.

Immediately, I realised it was unwise to stay around here and I was busy reporting them and 'endeavouring' to call off young Patterson, who was behind me – and all while trying to stay out of trouble from the artillery platforms on the trains. Whether or not Patterson just ignored my urgent warnings or hadn't been listening I can't say as I never asked him later. He just kept on coming right behind me. As he swept over the aerodrome he blazed away with his guns and directly at one of the ack-ack platforms. He received a terrific shock as the thing blew up in front of him. The bodies of German soldiers hurtled past his aircraft. He returned to base with part of a German uniform caught in the engine of his plane. He was a very courageous boy and on this occasion a very lucky one! When we got back to base I had five or six holes in my wings from the enemy machine guns. The film from Patterson's aeroplane (which recorded automatically when the guns fired) was shown all over England and, no doubt, America also.

By the end of August we were taking off at night to arrive in Germany just as dawn was rising, in order to catch all the trains and transports that now moved only at night-time. We were on such a mission on the 28th. We were carrying fragmentation bombs and had been over the same area only the day before. But this time it was a surprise to come unexpectedly upon a formation of twenty-plus German bombers. As the weather conditions were bad they had given up their mission to bomb Paris and were returning to base, and we now met them on the way back. Sheer luck as it happened. They were flying right on the deck over Saarbrücken – a little valley surrounded by hills.

The boys had no sooner recovered from the shock of finding them, than with a yell of excitement they swooped down, completely uncontrollable, in attack. Nothing could have held them back and we created havoc among the Ju 88s and Heinkel 111s. It was sheer murder and not many bombers escaped the all-out attack. I found myself going after one Heinkel with two others with the same idea. It finally exploded after crashing right into the railway line. Many of the youngsters imperilled their own lives by almost colliding. Two actually did in their excitement. I withdrew my half claim to the Heinkel when I heard the two other lads from 63 Squadron had also claimed half each.

At the end of July our Polish flight had received news that we were to be withdrawn to the Polish Air Force in August. It was a sad prospect for us, and the Americans considered it a very serious loss to them. In the short space of time that we were with them they had come to accept us as part of their group. At the end of our attachment to the 56th the following letter was sent to Polish Headquarters through my squadron leader to Prince Karol Radziwill. It was from Colonel Hubert Zemke, commanding officer, 56th Fighter Group, United States 8th Air Force:

Of a recent date, the below-listed officers of your Air Force were transferred from this American Fighter Group to further duties with the Polish Units. It was with a certain downcast feeling that I saw them leave, for each and every one of them is, in my standard, a pilot and an officer. Not alone speaking of the valuable services they performed for us, but of their outstanding character and knowledge, I might say that if each and every one of my officers possessed the determination these Polish Officers displayed, a much greater material value and gain could be attained by my group. Their willingness to undergo long hours of dangerous work is a most fitting example of the men's desires for a new and greater Poland. The impression to this end had been instilled in each and every pilot of my group. May it ever continue.

The officers spoken of are: S/L. T. Sawicz. S/L. K. Rukowski. F/L B. Gladych. F/L. W. Lanowski. F/L T. Anderz.

This letter rather put me in the mind of what happened when Polish pilots were withdrawn from the RAF squadrons.

With the news of our pending departure from the 56th I was greatly surprised by the next occurrence. Colonel Zemke and Colonel David 'Dave' Schilling (Zemke's deputy commander, and commanding officer of 62 Squadron and an ace) approached me with the offer to stay with the group and actually 'join' the USAAF as an American commissioned officer. They put this proposition to both me and Mike Gladych.

I was left in no doubt that they were extremely pleased with my performance within the group activities and my participation in the training of their new young pilots. Experience was vital at this time for them, especially after D-Day when the great push was on. You couldn't be in the group and not know it. Nevertheless, I asked for time to consider their offer and they agreed – hopeful, they said, that I would say yes. I appreciated their offer in the spirit it was made.

Gladych and I naturally discussed the matter together. We thought, as a team, it would be nice to stay together if we were going to accept the offer. But first he would talk to Bayon and I would contact Brzezina to see how the matter should be arranged.

I made an appointment with Brzezina while, within a day or so, Mike went off to see Bayon, commanding officer of Polish Fighter Command at Stanmore. When he returned he gave me this account. Apparently he had asked Bayon if he (Gladych) was going to get a squadron when we all returned in mid-August. Bayon had told him 'Yes, in the near future.' Then he asked: 'What about Lanowski?' To this Bayon had given a sharp and definite 'No.' Obviously my sins were not yet forgiven! Gladych had stated he would only agree to take a squadron providing I was given the other squadron 'in the same wing'. Apparently Bayon was so annoyed he demanded to know if Gladych was trying to tell him what he should do. But Mike said it was to be this or nothing.

I informed Brzezina what had happened – from Zemke and Schilling's proposal to what I had recently learned from Gladych – and asked his views on the matter. For without the authority of my Polish Headquarters there was no real decision I could make without their approval. Nevertheless, it was still rather frustrating and maddening to know that upon my return the whole ghastly business in the PAF was going to start up again. Brzezina did not give me an answer straight away and I informed Zemke and Schilling I was awaiting news from the Polish high command before I could definitely respond to their offer. They understood and agreed to wait.

Brzezina informed me very soon that he had telephoned Bayon and had asked the same question he had done in 1943 – was there anything for Lanowski? Bayon gave the same answer as before. Disappointed, Brzezina then informed him that the American commanders of the 56th wanted me to stay with them and join the American Air Force and that I was doing very well with them. Bayon had put up no objection to this request and I can only imagine he was only too pleased to see the back of me! So Brzezina told me I could carry on and make my decision to join the American Air Force if I wished, providing that the British Air Ministry agreed – whose ultimate authority was necessary – and he would do all he could to assist me in the process.

The only possible way to effect such a transfer from the PAF/RAF would be the usual procedure of acquiring 'one year's unpaid leave' from the Polish Air Force. This would place me in the position of being able to apply for an American commission. But it would only be authorised on that condition alone. It would be an automatic transfer from one air force to the other, with immediate effect. Under these circumstances,

Gladych and I would be representatives of the Polish Air Force and Poland, even though we were to become officers in the American forces. It was normal procedure in our country and our forces, although unusual to Western practice.

With this information, Gladych and I went to see Zemke and Schilling with our answer. We accepted their offer but it must first be approved officially, as we had no authority to make our own arrangements until it was. We asked Zemke that he make official request to the proper authorities. He assured us this would be done and from then on they would deal with their side of the formalities. They did not anticipate any delays and, as the meeting closed, we were assured we would soon be American officers of the USAAF, and General Kepner, commanding officer of the 2nd Bomb Division would be informed. We had no reason to doubt their assurances, and letters in my possession verify that the official request for our services and transfer to the USAAF was made by the American military authorities to both the Polish military authorities and the British Air Ministry.

I had accepted their offer with only one aim in view: to continue flying and fighting, to the best of my ability, and to give whatever assistance was required of me within the group. Also to perform my duty honourably towards the forces I was soon to be commissioned into, and to uphold the honour and tradition of my own country and the Polish Air Force of whom I was a representative. I gave no thought to any other consideration. I based my decision on the offer made to me at that precise time. I already held a commissioned officer status and career in the Polish Air Force, therefore this was not a primary objective in my decision. I simply wanted to carry on fighting and flying and not sit behind a desk, as I was not cut out for that kind of thing.

The American commanders offered me an active job as flight commander and this fitted in with what I wanted to do – fight in the war to get it over with and to help in my country's freedom.

Sawicz, Rutkowski and Anderz left to return to the Polish Air Force units. Gladych and I remained behind to finish out the month of August. Sawicz was given a wing, and on 10 September 1944 was promoted to wing commander. Rutkowski was also appointed a wing and was promoted to wing commander. Anderz was soon after given a squadron and on 19 August 1944 was promoted to squadron leader.

On the occasion that I received an additional bar to the American Air Medal – I believe my fourth decoration out of a total of five at that time – the presentation took place in the mess as usual. The procedure for such occasions was that presentations took place after the evening meal. We dressed in our finest uniform; for me this meant my Polish best blue.

As far as I remember I was the first to receive the bar (a silver oak-leaf cluster) on that particular day. Ten other pilots were in the line, all Americans. It was my second bar in the month. As Zemke came forward to present the award he smiled and we shook hands, and he said how pleased he was to present it to me. He also told me he had submitted my name for a DFC. Verification came through the headquarters of the 8th Air Force shortly after, but the official presentation came in November 1944.

But, he added, he had some sad news to go with it, and another offer to me that he hoped I would accept. He had been asked to take over command of 479th Fighter Group, which was apparently in a very bad state. So having to leave the 56th he would very much appreciate it if I would go with him. I was surprised, and this time dismayed at his imminent departure.

Zemke had often shown he liked me and the respect was mutual. But I was shaken to realise the extent of his regard. He obviously knew of the plans for Gladych and myself to stay with the 56th and this was why he asked me to accompany him instead. But coming rather unexpectedly I asked to be allowed to think it over for a few days. When I gave him my answer I expressed my sorrow that I was going to have to disappoint him. I tried to make him understand that my position wasn't as secure as his. Here I knew everyone and they knew me. He also agreed the new and younger pilots trusted me during the ops, and that my job here was invaluable in helping to train them and lead them as I was doing. I was already established in the 56th whereas in the 479th I'd have to begin again and they wouldn't have the faintest idea who I was. On the other hand, they knew all about him.

We didn't discuss the fact that I wasn't yet an American commissioned officer and that it wouldn't help the situation until I was. It's just possible that I might have found myself becoming one during October 1944 had I gone with him. He had a way of arranging what he wanted, quicker than most. Perhaps a little selfishly I was thinking that if anything happened to him, what then, as far as my position was concerned. It may have occurred to him also. Possibly, too, he had a premonition that he wasn't going to be with the 479th very long. I only know his sadness and friendship and understanding of what I said showed plainly on his face at the impracticability of what he asked. On 12 August he left the 56th to take up his new position.

I was very depressed and had mixed feelings when I heard on 30 October 1944 that he had been forced to bail out of his aircraft over Germany due to bad weather conditions. We heard later he was taken as a POW. At the end of the war his camp was liberated by the Russians – who called him Tovarish (Comrade) Zemke – and I was relieved and delighted on seeing him safe and sound when he came to the 56th. It was then that he voiced his changed opinions about the Russians he had once admired.

By 28 August 1944 I had completed my first American operational tour, which made two tours, counting my one with the Polish Air Force. For this one I had completed 54 operations during 202 operational hours, and with the end of the month my attachment (with my five other Polish colleagues) was now terminated. In three and a half months I had completed the same amount of operational flying hours that it had taken me twenty-six months to complete in the Polish Air Force.

With regard to my service with the 56th, I learned later that it apparently flew under the name of 'Zemke's Wolfpack'. It was an apt description! I also read that great rivalry existed between the 'Wolfpack' and the 4th Fighter Group for the highest score. I had no idea of either of these things at the time, nor did my Polish friends. What I can state is that as far as the highest score in the air was concerned the 56th was unequalled in this by the other American groups – with 674.5 destroyed. The group's score was important to them, as it was in any American fighter group. But I never experienced any rivalry as such.

Chapter 21

September 1944

By the beginning of the month Gladych and I left Boxted to make formal applications regarding the offer made to us by the commanders of the 56th – that is, permission to rejoin the group and be permitted to become American commissioned officers. We went to the Polish Headquarters in London for this purpose and were told to make our request in letter form addressed to the C-in-C Polish Air Force, Brigadier General Izycki, through official channels. This was typed out for us in the adjutant's office and we added our signatures.

Group Captain Brzezina told us that this was a formality and that there were no objections whatsoever regarding our 'unpaid leave' to enable us to join the USAAF. We should then go to Blackpool for a short rest and to await formal permission to return to the 56th. This we did.

It wasn't long before our instructions to rejoin the 56th arrived, with the permission for one year's unpaid leave. We were requested to hand in our military PAF/RAF identity papers and asked to remove our flight lieutenant rank insignia from our uniforms before rejoining the 61st Fighter Squadron. This, too, we did as requested.

We were now on transfer from the Polish Air Force via the Polish Army, another formality, as the structure of our forces was the same as that of the United States Army Air Force. Our status upon handing over our identity papers was that of civilians, according us the status necessary to apply for the American commissions, which American regulations required. There is no doubt that I was a civilian from this time, as was Gladych.

Since we were operating from within Britain, the Air Ministry needed to sanction the requests of both the American military authorities and our applications through Polish military channels. Therefore it came about that authority was granted and we were 'assigned' back to the 56th. The terms of the 'one year's unpaid leave' were:

a) From the time it was granted one became a 'civilian' for the specific period.
b) No military pay was issued to that person during the specified period.
c) Upon completion of the period of 'unpaid' leave the person in question automatically reverted back to being a member of the Polish forces.

Granted under the conditions afforded to Gladych and me for transfer purposes were that:

a) The Americans were now able to commission us.
b) Payment from the Air Ministry ceased forthwith, as we were expected to be paid by the USAAF, who were commissioning us.
c) The moment our US commissions came through, the one year's unpaid leave became invalid and it was no longer applicable for us to be reverted back to the Polish forces.

There was nothing complicated about all this. I later discovered that American citizens of Polish descent, who came to England to join the PAF, underwent the same transfer action to enter the USAAF (after America entered the war) when they arrived in England. Moreover, the American pilots of the Eagle Squadron in the Royal Air Force 'transferred' to the USAAF on 29 September 1942. So it wasn't such an unusual occurrence. The only unique feature I can think of that varied from either of the above was that we were Poles and not American citizens. Perhaps it played its part in what was to result over the coming months.

Chapter 22

Back on ops

Before the end of September I returned to the 56th Fighter Group at Boxted. I was anxious to resume my job. I felt no anxiety about being commissioned as I was now released from the PAF, although the official documents stating as much had not as yet been sent to me. They would arrive soon. I had no idea what I was expected to do in regard to applying for a USAAF commission. I assumed this would be dealt with almost immediately.

The new CO of the 61st Fighter Squadron was Captain James A. Carter. Colonel 'Dave' Schilling was the commanding officer of the 56th, having taken over from Zemke after he left in August to command the 479th Fighter Group.

On 18 September the group had been assigned an important and dangerous mission of direct support to the airborne landings in Holland at Arnhem. The 56th had acquitted themselves outstandingly well against very heavy odds. Schilling commanded the group.

The presidential citation issued later read:

> War Department. Washington D.C., May 1945.
> The 56th Fighter Group, 2nd Bombardment Division, is cited for outstanding performance of duty against heavy odds on a danger-ous mission on 18th September 1944. The 56th Fighter Group, Lieutenant Colonel David C. Schilling commanding, was given the extremely difficult and dangerous mission of direct support of the airborne landings in Holland, where it was their task to attack and to silence enemy flak positions that would constitute a grave hazard to the aircraft and gliders making the assault. The area assigned to

the 56th Fighter Group was heavily defended by both light and heavy enemy flak positions, and the weather was so unfavourable that it forced the fighter airplanes to go direct to the deck and silhouette themselves against a low overcast, thus making themselves excellent targets for enemy flak and very dangerous to the pilots and aircraft of the 56th Fighter Group. Despite all the odds against them, this group, without hesitation and with complete disregard for personal safety, swept in ahead of the airborne armada and sought out and attacked enemy flak positions to destroy them even in the face of superior and concentrated fire. This mission was so successfully carried out against these heavy odds that the effectiveness of enemy flak against the airborne troops was greatly reduced. The 56th Fighter Group suffered heavy losses and severe damage (lost 16 aircraft out of 39 dispatched) on the important mission, but because of the devotion to duty and courage displayed by the group, the landings were a complete success and a great step towards complete victory over the enemy was accomplished. The great aggressiveness, courage, gallantry, devotion to duty and extraordinary heroism of the 56th Fighter Group, 2nd Bombardment Division, are in the highest tradition of military service and reflect great credit on themselves and the armed forces of the United States.

By order of the Secretary of War.

G.C. Marshall
Chief of Staff.

I doubt the pilots of the 56th in this mission had an inkling of the terrible toll extracted at Arnhem. They had done their job and given their utmost, as the paratroopers they were protecting were about to as well. I heard later from very reliable sources that when some of the wounded were brought out, the Polish paratroopers had been aware there would be virtually no hope of surviving the operation, having been told this soon after take-off en route to Holland. I understand they were the only paratroopers informed of the exact situation facing them.

This day, 18 September, included another important mission. Poland, too, had been in the throes of struggling to survive. On 1 August we had heard the news of the Warsaw Uprising. Every Pole had his own feelings and thoughts on this tragedy. These included anger, bitterness and a sense of utter helplessness of the situation. All those unnecessary losses – what could we do!

General Izycki, C-in-C of the Polish Air Force, called Gladych and me to London to ask that we use our 'influence' to secure American assistance in dropping supplies so urgently needed by the Poles in Warsaw. At the time it struck me as being a rather hopeful expectation, if not misplaced, in us seeking to 'influence' the high command of the 8th Air Force. But at that time the Polish high command was endeavouring to secure help for the Warsaw Poles in every direction from the Allies of the West. However, it was the considered opinion of the Allies at that moment that agreement must be reached with the Soviet high command before support of this nature could be affected. Russia, of course, was against the British and Americans making supply sorties to the Poles – the country kept its forces sitting just out of range of the Warsaw boundary until after Warsaw was forced to capitulate to the Germans. Whereby further slaughter took place as reprisals for the uprising. Then Russian forces entered the capital as 'supposedly' conquering heroes for the Polish people.

Much could be written on this subject but I think it should be stated that the Poles knew at the time who were their enemies: one had from 1939 occupied Poland; another sat outside its borders waiting to overrun it. Polish history shows that both Germany and Russia have always been enemies of that country. It was for this reason that I could never accept or agree with the timing, initiation or the carrying out of the uprising by the commanders responsible.

Nevertheless, supply sorties were made to Poland, and the Polish Air Force, Royal Air Force and the American Air Force participated in these missions. The latter particularly, after the necessary agreement and negotiations with the Russians.

All we could do after we left General Izycki was to inform Colonel Schilling and ask him to notify General Kepner of the Polish high command request. I can hardly imagine our small effort affected their decision to make the supply drop on 18 September 1944 in any way. We simply passed on the message of the C-in-C, PAF.

On 1 and 2 October I made three cross-country flights to get back into the routine after my month's absence from flying, and resumed operational flying the following day, 3 October. There certainly wasn't any feeling or thought that I should not participate. It was a matter of course that I came back to the 56th and simply carried on where I had left off.

The fact that Gladych and I were now with the 56th as 'civilians' hadn't impressed itself upon anyone insofar as flying with the group was concerned. Nobody called me 'Mr' Lanowski. I was 'Lanny' to them, as they were 'Dave', Tom or Jim etc, to me. Their only interest in our status was that it now put us in the position to apply for and receive American commissions.

But, of course, our Polish blue uniform bore no British rank, which jogged their memory that we had no official military rank until we received those given us with our commissions. To overcome this obstacle we were endowed with an 'honorary' American rank of captain, equivalent to the flight lieutenant rank that we had held under British command. But for some reason known only to Gladych he began introducing himself as 'Major', although he had not received promotion from the PAF any more than I had when we had finished our initial attachment with the 56th. Two official letters I have from October 1944 – from the RAF and PAF Headquarters – quote both our RAF ranks of flight lieutenant, and the procedure was that one could not be promoted to squadron leader until one was given a squadron. Mike had not been promoted, but perhaps he thought this was as good an opportunity as any to ensure this aspect of his career. He often proved a law unto himself both on the ground and in the air. I have no idea if Schilling intended him to be commissioned as a major, I only know we were told that we would receive American ranks equivalent to those we held in the RAF/PAF. It created no difficulty for me to adjust to my 'honorary' rank of captain – just a difference in the pronunciation from the 'kapitan' that had been my Polish Air Force rank.

Mike Gladych was asked if he would like to concentrate on forming a small flying training unit within the 56th, besides flying operationally, and to my knowledge he did so for a short period. I, too, was asked to continue training the new pilots and shepherd them during the operations themselves under my own flight. On being granted my commission I was to be assigned as a flight commander in the 61st Fighter Squadron, and this was the position I occupied from the moment of our return to the 56th. I continued to hold the post while my papers were orbiting the official American channels, and until I stopped flying operationally in April 1945, which was at the time the group itself virtually ceased operational flying.

The application papers were a nightmare to us, and enough to put any Pole off who spoke only simple English. To our great relief we found much of this taken care of for us. All we had to do was answer relevant questions about our past activities and show ourselves to be suitable for entry into the American forces as far as our character and beliefs were concerned. We went through the various inspections and apparently passed with flying colours! It was all a formality we kept being told. Don't worry, the commissions will be through in no time, and then our pay and uniforms etc would all be given to us. They were very adamant in their assurances and we felt no reason to disbelieve whatever they said. We looked forward to officially receiving our American wings, our new uniforms and also our pay. We couldn't live on air. We were being fed and we had quarters, but what few pounds we had was not going to last for any length of time.

When we were asked to sign the papers I noticed that we had been given our former British ranks (rather than being referred to by our civilian status of 'Mr') and Polish serial number, together with the wording 'Polish Air Force' at the foot of the page. We were, after all, with the group and flying operationally. It was necessary for these ranks and numbers to appear on the forms, but our documents would supply the necessary information that we were in fact eligible as civilians to be acceptable for American commissions. I saw no reason to disagree with this, and it never once occurred to me that this very fact of including this military status would imperil my commission or be used against me in the future.

A slight complication arose when it was realised that we did not have any document to prove we were on unpaid leave from the Polish Air Force. I decided that instead of waiting for such a document to be sent to us from Polish Headquarters I would go myself and procure the notification! I went to the Polish Minister of Defence, Lieutenant General M. Kukiel on 24 October 1944. Without any difficulty I received the necessary statement (it cannot be called anything more than a chit of paper) declaring that both Gladych and myself were authorised to join the United States Army Air Force and verifying our one year's unpaid leave.

We included this document and a letter I received from Lloyds Bank, RAF Pay Department – informing me that the Air Ministry had notified them to cease my pay with effect from 1 October 1944 – with the application papers that were dated October 1944. On the following day, 25 October, in the station orders (S.O. 201) it detailed verification of our fresh attachment to the 61st Fighter Squadron from PAF Headquarters in Blackpool.

I was not aware at this time that confidential official papers were circulating between RAF authorities, PAF Headquarters and the USAAF, dating from September to October 1944, concerning our transfer to the American Air Force. Or that consultations were taking place between the Polish military authorities and American military authorities confirming and verifying our move. Previously I had asked Zemke and Schilling to make the formal approaches through the correct American channels to the Polish authorities. The letters show this was done. But I did not ask Schilling either in October or afterwards if they had done so – I simply took it for granted they had. The fact that I had been permitted to rejoin the 56th and given permission to receive an American commission seemed adequate proof.

Naturally, neither the RAF nor the PAF would just take our word of an offer to join the American 56th. They wanted evidence and all the necessary details to ascertain this for themselves, as they were hardly going to allow us to go as civilians to fight a little war all of our own with an Allied force.

On 7 October our mission was to cover Liberators all the way to their target, which was to be Magdeburg, 80 miles from Berlin. We were to sweep ahead of them just prior to the bombing of the target to direct the anti-aircraft radar away from the bombers and divert the flak towards our aeroplanes. We found the defence fantastically heavy.

I led my own flight. There wasn't a cloud in the sky and not one enemy aircraft came to intercept us. The bombers came in just behind us, dropped their bombs and then turned for home. I decided to take my flight just ahead of the target to observe the results. It was perfect bombing and nothing much left by the mass of Liberators. I then instructed my flight to head back for base. Turning left I saw some of our bombers going down after being hit. There was one in particular, obviously crippled but still trying to fly back home. One of his right engines was on fire and one on the left smoking. I began circling him to see what he was deciding to do. He was not mortally out of action and could still possibly make it with a bit of luck and some help. The pilot feathered one engine and succeeded in putting the fire out. He still had three engines going, but there were still 300 miles of enemy territory to cover and virtually no hope of calling for any protection.

While we had been circling him (my flight of four aircraft) all the others had left the vicinity, heading back towards base. We were now alone and could only do whatever was possible to get him home safely. When I called my pilots over the radio that we should give protection to the stricken bomber, there came back unanimous agreement. He certainly needed it. He was in a most vulnerable state. There was no question of leaving him.

Now came the problem of just how to get him home and, more difficult, how to make him understand what I wanted him to do to get on course for England. I had no radio contact with him at all as we were not on the same frequency. The answer was to use sign language and this too presented a complication.

The bomber's speed in his condition was by now lower than our critical speed for stalling. To communicate with the pilot I had to come to his wing and fly alongside him while we had a 'chat'! I moved forward with flaps and dive brakes out and hung on to his wing. My three boys were circling us all the while.

I could see the crew of the bomber – about ten of them in all – waving and smiling and cheering. They were obviously so relieved at our company they were even offering me cigarettes to demonstrate how they felt. Still hanging on beside them, I showed them an American packet of cigarettes, took one out and lit up, to their approval. I got the thumbs-up sign! But what I wanted to know was if the pilot knew his course for home. It occurred to me that even if he did know, he may not admit it for fear we may decide to leave him. Somehow I got him to understand my question and he shook his head vigorously – he didn't know which way to head. I gestured that I intended to fly in front of him, pointing in his direction, and for him to set his compass on course. We would then circle around him on the journey back to England. The pilot nodded his comprehension of what I was indicating. I inclined my head in reply, opened up my engine, positioned myself right in front of the nose of the Liberator and flew in this position with him for a few minutes.

As I couldn't maintain this manoeuvre indefinitely, I then banked away to join my flight who were circling above. To my horror I found he was trying to follow me! If I had done aerobatics he would have done them too, or had a damned good try. I muttered, 'Wariat'! (he's crazy) in astonishment. I waved my wings to indicate this was not what I wanted of him. My sign language had failed, obviously. I circled and pulled up alongside him again. His crew were in hysterics at their pilot's enthusiasm to stay with us, and my frenzied gesticulating that I wasn't his 'Mum'. Eventually he got the message and we tried the manoeuvre again, this time successfully.

We were so lucky during this flight. Not one intruder came into sight. No one took a potshot at us, and all the while we flew slowly but surely towards home, circling the Liberator to keep at its speed.

In a sense, my ambition was being fulfilled in a more personal way than one expected. One of our main important duties was to escort and protect our bombers. I believed completely in this responsibility. And now here I was with my own little bomber to shepherd home. But like the bomber crew and my boys, I thanked God when we reached England's shores. It was the longest flight I had experienced because of the circumstances. It took almost six hours and it seemed incredibly longer.

I flew again to the cockpit window to bid him farewell, as he now was safe and would reach his base without mishap. The pilot and crew were desperately gesturing that we fly on with them to their base for 'drinks'. I thanked them, acknowledged their offer, but shook my head in refusal. We gave a final greeting and set course for Boxted. I knew if we had gone with them none of us would have been fit for the next day's operation.

As it happened my next op didn't come until 12 October. A letter arrived from the CO of the bomber squadron, expressing his thanks for his men's safe return. We were invited for a special air crew party to be given in our honour. They were waiting for us when we arrived and we were bombarded the moment we entered the officers' mess. Brushing aside all objections I found myself hoisted shoulder high while they voiced their appreciation. I, too, was filled with gratitude and pleasure. My three young pilots had no less a reception. The party was one to remember.

There were other parties on other occasions – those at Boxted station – where I was to feel equally embarrassed, this time in the manner that Schilling introduced me to the guests.

As the war progressed, I flew with Schilling commanding the group more than I had done previously under Zemke and Gabreski's command. Our friendship was strengthened and we appreciated each other's skill and experience in the air. As a result Dave would seek me out to meet his friends or those who came to Boxted and insist that I was the finest pilot he had ever flown with and then go into elaborate details about my 'incredible' eyesight. That was his description, not mine.

What actually happened was that whenever I flew with the group I was invariably the first to spot either enemy aircraft and/or our bombers if we were flying to cover for them. Moreover, when I reported what I saw, the others were unable to observe anything even though I had given the exact position, for instance on the occasion I spotted the bomber landing on the German aerodrome (25 August). In the beginning I wasn't believed. They thought I was seeing things. It wasn't until I was proved right time and time again that finally whoever I flew with simply took my word for it – including the group commander – and a change of course was given accordingly, either to rendezvous with our bombers or gain the advantage over enemy raiders. This was in spite of the fact that it took them a few minutes before they, too, sighted the situation for themselves. Sometimes clouds obscured momentarily what I saw. But not for long and the positioning was more or less accurate. For this reason my colleagues were prepared to believe I could even see 'through' clouds. This, of course, was ridiculous and I have never claimed any such thing. But it didn't stop them from asserting it, and they maintained they had never experienced anyone before with such a 'gift'. I was promptly adopted as their 'mascot' and many came to tell me they felt 'real safe' when I flew with them. It was all very gratifying and I was happy to be of service. But what was the actual truth?

There was no magic, no phenomenon, and many accomplished pilots who experienced this for themselves knew the answer. In my case, as undoubtedly in theirs, I was just a born aviator. During the many years I had been flying I had piloted many different types of aircraft and in this circumstance more than the average American airman or commander. Zemke, for instance, was the only pilot in the 56th when we were there with him who held the Senior Aeronautical Badge (which was later awarded to Gladych and me). The badge defined one's flying skill. In the Polish Air Force we had five separate grades of such an award (the first class was attained only during war). Therefore, one's airborne experience helped towards the ability to pinpoint oneself on a target in the air. Clouds (unless impenetrable) or no clouds, I instinctively knew where to look in the expectation of finding something. Especially the enemy, and there they would be. Also I felt no worry or fear in setting my aircraft for steady flight, which enabled me to scan the skies continually. This, too, only came with constant practice and past experience. The former was something the Americans were not very partial to or had no time for. I say this because there were those who just could not fathom why one should want to practise, however many times you had flown. Either they would understand or they would dismiss it. Practice also depended upon other factors – such as time.

There was a final thing I had to my advantage – my past sporting background, particularly skiing. It's a matter of life and death within seconds when skiing with great speed cross-country, especially in forests. One of my skiing friends was killed this way. It was a fact that the Germans selected pilots from skiing competitions. One of the most important holiday pastimes for pilots in both Poland and Germany was skiing. It wasn't meant as a holiday, but rather to add to their abilities and requirements as pilots, such as developing instant reactions, stamina, will power and speed.

So, in other words, I possessed a combination of the above requirements. I was also fortunate to have perfect eyesight from birth.

I began operations again on 3 October. I was with the Group officially, yet I was not holding an official military status either on the ground at the base or – more importantly – in the air while I flew with them. This was a fact. But it was also a fact that I looked upon myself, as Gladych did, as a military man 'on transfer' from my own forces to the American forces, and have no doubt that this is what both the British and the Polish military authorities considered we were. For this is what the Americans had requested of them. Our civilian status – as our unpaid leave – was nothing more than a mere formality.

In the early days of November the realisation that we held no official documents of any kind – especially when we were flying – to proclaim who or what we were impressed itself upon me. Gladych and I needed an official military document or we would be dead ducks if we were shot down over enemy territory and captured. There would be only one fate for us. We would be considered spies.

With this problem in mind I went to see Schilling. He told me to go to the station adjutant and see what he could fix for us in the way of an official identity.

First we had our photographs taken, ghastly looking images where we stood like a pair of criminals holding our numbers up in front of us. Then on small white cards was typed our names, 'honorary' rank and vital statistics (colour of eyes, hair, weight etc). We added our signatures and Major Virgil H. Durrance (adjutant) included his. Our cards were initially stamped on the reverse side by the Colchester Police – I can't think why! – before our photographs were glued over these stamp marks and the 'official' stamp seals of the US Army were franked on top. Anyone who looked at these 'identities' eyed them with horror. They would have been our death warrants had we ever found ourselves in the hands of the enemy. Nothing looked more conspicuous and amateurish. But at the time it was all we had and were only too pleased to have something.

I wasn't especially worried about the identity card, for two reasons: I didn't think I would have to use it for very long; and I never thought about the possibility of being shot down. Not because I didn't believe it could happen to me, for I often had the feeling that on a particular trip I would not return. Perhaps I just felt I would be killed and not taken as a prisoner. I don't know. One can't really explain such feelings that appear contradictory. Anyway, I flew quite happily with this 'identity' of sorts. Only later as time progressed did I begin to look at it and my position in a different light. For until a month or so after the war ended, this was the only identity as such that I had.

As I was now 'officially' with the 56th and part of the group, despite the outstanding issues, I concentrated fully on the job detailed for me, that of a flight commander. More than ever now my interest was in helping the inexperienced pilots, and to the best of my ability I applied myself to this responsibility. When I first came to the American unit with the other Poles, one of the first noticeable facts one discovered about them was the importance they attached to individual scores – and this included the flight commanders. Everyone aimed at attaining the highest score possible. I would say that Zemke was in a minority who thought the importance was in teamwork as opposed to the individual approach. This wasn't new to us coming from the Polish and British Air Forces. We had our 'aces', of course, and no one would want to deny it. But when the majority established their records it was at a time when they had very little choice in the matter during the Battle of Britain, and previous to that in France in 1939–40. Afterwards, the emphasis fell on the squadron, or wing, as a whole, and was not centred on a few specific pilots. Now, for us, we experienced the position in reverse.

Out of the six Poles who joined the 56th it was Gladych who seemed to adopt the American attitude towards his score the most. I'm not suggesting he was wrong. That was entirely his business. But he was the only one of us who chose to do this.

There had been nothing to stop the rest of us from concentrating upon scores for our personal advantage. But we hadn't. Neither had I when I found myself flying more and more with the American pilots, especially the younger and inexperienced ones when I led them into battle. The reason for this was simply that I didn't happen to believe in it – I was a team player – and my past training had instilled this belief in me both as a sportsman and a pilot. Moreover, a leader's responsibility was to his pilots, first and foremost. Those who needed assistance in conquering their fear should be able to obtain it from their commander – who in turn should know instinctively who required help and when it was wanted the most. He should also have the ability to inspire confidence in the air. If he didn't have this, he had no business being a flight commander in the first place, any more than he had if only interested in pushing up his score to the expense of his flight.

With this belief I had applied myself to my job as a flight leader. My personal score suffered as a result but frankly I wasn't interested if it did, as long as I got the boys back home safely and with a score they could be pleased with, having earned it for themselves. If they needed a bit of prodding one way or another to ensure a definite 'kill' in the air, I gave it. It wasn't done with any intention of personal gain – or to show that I was better – neither was I doing the pilot a favour by not claiming half. He had earned his victory and he came home safely afterwards and the battle had been a good one. At the same time I assisted in the planning of the freelance bombing and strafing after the main objective of our operations was completed. The planning of this naturally came from Headquarters.

The young pilots were eager – very much so – but as a result they lacked co-operation in giving support to each other. For everyone in the air wanted a fight of his own. This could have unnecessary tragic results. Fortunately, by this period the German Luftwaffe were bleeding so heavily and otherwise engaged that they were unable to take advantage of many aerial mistakes. Nevertheless, danger was always prevalent.

The reason I stress the importance of practice training is because I had come from the school whose system acknowledged its importance at all times. It was invaluable. Therefore I could never really accept the American reasoning that there was a lack of time. For it certainly was not the case, or to the degree they would have you believe. Of course, they were able to replenish their ranks constantly, something we could not afford or had the means to do. In both the PAF and RAF, practising was a part of our activities that was considered vital, and quite rightly. Whole squadrons would be taken off operational duties and replaced by others, while we went for rest periods in which we engaged in air-to-air and air-to-ground target practice, prearranged attacks on some aerodrome or other, and target shooting on certain areas of beaches along the coast or at old shipwrecks. We also practised night flying, low-level flight including shovelling – not at all easy or to be taken lightly, executed on the deck – and formation manoeuvres. The RAF even had a Fighter Leaders' School in operation, which I had attended.

When I had been 'A' Flight commander in 302 Polish Squadron at Northolt, we practised at every available opportunity and the squadron was soon recognised as having exceptionally good pilots. Those who did not come up to standard quickly found themselves out of the squadron. Whenever there was an attempt made to relieve us of some of our pilots – the capable ones – the CO took himself off on urgent business somewhere at my suggestion, leaving me to handle the matter. We held on to our pilots after I had given my answer in no uncertain terms. As a result the pilots kept themselves up to scratch. They knew I would have them out if they weren't.

There was no reason why the American boys could not have used the time they were not on ops for training. But I was in no position to detail such flights. Therefore, I could only pass on my experience and advice during the actual operations after having gone over the points beforehand back at base. Possibly it was due to the different system why Gladych's training flight petered out after a while.

But although it was not possible for me to help these young aviators in the way I would have preferred, nevertheless I was rewarded to find that they followed my instructions completely when attached to my flight, and I had no losses. Their navigation showed itself to be pretty hopeless, especially when flying at low level. But at least they could always fly north-west and they'd be sure to hit a familiar landmark and be home sooner or later. This often explained the reason why they linked themselves to my flight. When I asked what they were up to they'd say I was taking them home. I'd tell them to find their own way but it didn't make any difference. I might just as well have saved my breath.

I got similar treatment on the base, which I often found very embarrassing. I would suddenly find a few of them joining me wherever I went. Mary's little lamb had nothing on some of these boys. It was simply their way of showing how they felt and I was glad of their company and their tremendous sense of fun.

A previous mention of 'shovelling', or slotting-in, at low level recalled an occurrence that took place while I was stationed at Northolt. It impressed itself in my mind and showed the degree to which our training had become part of us.

Our normal procedure after take-off was to fly at treetop height all the way to the South Coast in battle formation (the Polish battle formation was introduced and accepted by the RAF and later the American Air Force). After our arrival and re-forming in England, our formation was that each flight of four aircraft flew in finger-four formation, and each squadron of three times four flights tiered up, with the highest four flying opposite the sun. The same principle continued up, with additional squadrons within an entire wing. This formation differed from the British who had been flying line astern and line abreast, which we as Poles would not adopt as we considered these formations to be dangerous. The stretch of the wing was quite considerable, approximately 2 miles in width.

Upon reaching the Channel and leaving the coast, dependent upon the weather and the calmness of the sea, we would fly so low we could see our own shadows reflecting on the water below. The reason for this manoeuvre was to avoid being picked up on enemy radar. They couldn't detect us below 300 feet. On these flights it was vital we were notified at pre-briefing of any convoy positions in the Channel, as they carried barrage balloons up to 500 feet in the air to stop enemy low-level attacks. We didn't want to get caught up in our own defences!

On this particular day the whole wing received a dreadful shock in suddenly being confronted with a British convoy directly in our flight path. We were streaking across the water and there they were, complete with balloons to safeguard them. Of course, to succeed in our operational mission over enemy territory we were maintaining the rule of strict radio silence, and no one even now attempted to break it to issue curt instructions for dealing with the situation. I can only say that every pilot must have spotted the one gap right in the centre of the convoy – the only way through. And every pilot knew what was expected of him to enable us to get through that gap intact. The manoeuvre itself took only seconds to accomplish but required a split-second decision within the wing to compact itself – like a pack of cards – which called for exceptional skill and experience. The leading squadron climbed slightly to allow the squadron on the right to slot in directly below them and those on the left to slide into position directly above, thirty-six aircraft in all. To the onlookers – the convoy – this must have presented one of the best displays of formation flying they had seen, and must have looked so easy and simple.

We achieved a three-fold success in those few moments: we remained at low level and undetected by enemy radar; executed a completely unrehearsed manoeuvre (as a wing), which until this moment had been unnecessary to perform; and maintained our radio silence throughout, relying on training and instinct to accomplish a very difficult feat.

But we had not done it without sweating a great deal with the concentration it required. Fortunately we had taken the convoy by surprise. For it was not until we had flown through their line could they realise we were not enemy aircraft.

Once through the gap we resumed our normal battle formation. We climbed to our operational height of 25,000 feet, and only then did we finally break radio silence. Normally we would have continued observing it to confuse the enemy of our identity for as long as possible. But we were not superhuman and it was asking too much in the circumstances. So break it we did and with a vengeance! It's not surprising we have been tagged with 'those crazy Poles'. It would have confirmed those opinions for anyone listening to the excited babble at that moment.

We maintained that keeping perfect formation, and radio silence, assisted in gaining the initiative over the enemy in the air. It carried with it a psychological effect. For upon seeing such a formation in the sky immediately created a doubt in his mind as to whether to attack or not, or if he had actually been seen. Being unsure, if and when the enemy did finally decide to strike, his confidence was already undermined.

There was also the satisfaction of knowing that he knew who we were. The famous 'White Service', who listened to German conversations in the air, would confirm to us through our Northolt controllers that the Germans had spotted us and knew we were Poles.

Only the understanding of teamwork and constant practice could produce flying of this quality and achievement.

Between August and October the group received orders to look for General Patton, commanding the American Army moving south and then east around Strasbourg. Apparently Patton's army was moving incredibly fast, without opposition, and Eisenhower had no knowledge of his exact position. Patton's aim was to get to Berlin before the Russians. Unfortunately he was short of maps and fuel (or so we heard) but his messages were constantly behind his exact position. With the outcome of his advance one can only conclude he realised he would be ordered to halt his progress, so he was pressing on hoping he'd reach Berlin before his fuel gave out or the order to stop caught up with him.

I remember that once we spotted his army racing ahead down below. All we could see were terrific dust trails on the fields heading east. It just could not have been anyone else. I personally was delighted at his speed and his aim.

Chapter 23

Hanau

I recall the first time I saw a V2 shooting up past our aircraft. We had no idea what it was and within seconds it had vanished from sight, streaking up into the atmosphere. When we reported it we were told to record the exact timing to the second of launching. I personally was able to do this only on the one or two occasions that I saw them. But the first time came as a shock to us. On 18 November came an eventful operation and my part in it unexpected but not unusual. Our mission was to the east of Hanau (near Frankfurt), and our target was oil storage depots. Before we took off, at the briefing we had been told to strafe the oil tanks by diving vertically to encompass as many tanks as possible by spreading our firing over as wide an area as practicable. We had not done this before and to my recollection we didn't do it again. No one had been trained for it, so it was decided that each flight must watch the flight diving to ascertain the results and if necessary alter the positioning of the dive to effect the destruction of the oil tanks. Our squadron commander was Captain James Carter. I led my own flight (Whippet Yellow). Over the target area cirrus clouds covered the sky at about 25,000 feet. Our top cover (Platform) was to be 62 Squadron. Therefore we could concentrate on the demolition of the target.

On my first dive-strafe with my flight we attained excellent results. But even though I knew 62 Squadron was covering for us I still scanned the skies – just in case!

I took my flight down for a second attack, succeeding Blue Flight. We were all taking it in turns to dive-strafe the target, going down one after the other. Following strafing I climbed up to join Whippet Leader (Jim Carter's flight). As I did so I immediately saw above, at one o'clock high, approximately sixteen aircraft flying from the north-east to the south-west. Just for a moment I took them to be our top cover (62 Squadron), but in that instant, to my horror, they dived and I recognised them as Fw 190s. They were heading straight at Whippet Leader's flight (White), situated north waiting to dive next on my turn. I screamed 'Break – 190s' and in a few seconds a deadly dogfight developed between Whippet White and the enemy aircraft at about 8,000–9,000 feet.

Almost immediately I observed one P-47, which I believed to be DeMars (White Three) being shot up by two attacking Focke Wulfs, who had straight away got on his tail from their attacking position. I promptly yelled for 62 Squadron to come to our aid. Everything was happening at once. I had already begun to dive to the assistance of DeMars, who was in the midst of the battle. I was getting no answer from 62 Squadron. Yet in those moments I was registering the situation in the air.

Red Flight had just completed strafing and were ascending. Blue Flight were behind me also heading towards the battle. At the same time Jerry had cunningly split up into two sections. One half of them had climbed up to wait and watch, ready to pounce for a kill. These were the ones worrying me; I couldn't afford to take my eyes off them. I sensed who and what they were and their intentions. They were the experienced ones – the aces – and I didn't like what they had in mind!

As I came in firing on the two Fw 190s to break them off the P-47, I could already see they had scored hits on his aircraft and DeMars had baled out. I reached the battle with my boys just ahead of Blue Flight. The dogfight was raging furiously with aircraft twisting all over the sky. I was still yelling for 62 Squadron and issuing directions and warnings to the pilots. So far Jim Carter had given no instructions concerning the battle and was still silent.

I had no time to hang around to see if I had scored any hits on the two enemy aircraft I had been firing at; I had to pull out quickly. I was checking to see who needed assistance. Suddenly the 62 Squadron leader (Major Leslie Smith) called: 'Where are you, Lanny?'

'Over the target, where do you think!' I answered. Apparently they had gone off strafing something and had lost sight of us until they heard the battle and my calls to them. I reported the enemy aircraft, sitting like vultures above, and their position for the 62nd to engage them. They were still distracting my attention.

I was already pulling up to place myself where I could engage the enemy aircraft if they made one move towards us. As I did so, I spotted the 62 Squadron P-47s climbing furiously, black smoke pouring from the Thunderbolts – everything going flat-out to intercept for us. Smith called: 'Don't worry Lanny, we'll take care of them. You carry on with your battle.' Relieved, I turned my attention immediately to the dogfight in progress. In that moment I saw everyone was now fully occupied with someone and I was left with no one to engage for myself. I felt like Napoleon!

Then a Focke Wulf was turning sharply and evasively – these German planes had the advantage in this manoeuvre over our aircraft. I fired instantly with a 90-degree deflection at about 500 yards range, but I wasn't satisfied at all with this impossible attitude, and he'd gone in seconds. One thing Jerry didn't dare do was to dive into battle with Thunderbolts, for these could out-dive them in seconds and they would already be dead. Another Focke Wulf appeared in the next moment in exactly the same position and again I fired automatically. The same thing happened and I felt equally frustrated. My head on a swivel, I saw another, this time being chased by two Thunderbolts. But the German pilot was out-manoeuvring them beautifully and there was nothing they could do about it. Cleverly he turned sharply, causing the P-47s to whip past him. I knew just how they felt. But he had inadvertently placed himself in exactly the right position for me to have him. I dived and opened fire from approximately 300 yards, closing fast, and dead astern.

I scored hits directly on his fuselage and cockpit. There was a light explosion and white smoke came from his cockpit. The propeller turned slowly and my speed now took me to his wing. As I drew level I looked over into the shattered cockpit. It was covered in blood and I felt slightly sick. My feelings were suddenly a confusion of intense hatred and over-whelming pity for the pilot. I involuntarily felt that he was just a young pilot involved, like myself, in this 'dirty war'. The next moment his air-craft fell out of the sky straight to the ground and exploded.

I looked around; I was the last one to have been engaged as the boys were now already forming in a line above me. I called to them that it was all over and climbed up to join them and collect my flight. But the pilots of the 61st all formatted behind me. I asked them what was going on.

'Okay Lanny. Take us home,' was the reply. 'Oh go away. Find your own way home,' I said. Not that it made the slightest impression. It was then I realised that Jim Carter was not with us. So I brought the pilots back to base.

From the moment I called the warning I was the only one doing most of the talking over the radio, except when 62 Squadron answered me, or the pilots who responded to the directions I had given. So I didn't know what had happened to Jim Carter from the time I saw his flight of four about to be attacked. In fact he returned to base after we had already got back, and made one claim that had apparently taken him to the deck where he had chased it until he finally shot it down.

From the time that Zemke had left the 56th post-briefings no longer took place. So upon our return we were met by the intelligence officers to make our reports. Everyone was in high spirits as the mission had been very successful and the battle had been a good one. The group had only lost two pilots against those claimed of enemy aircraft shot down. These totalled thirteen in the air. Not an unusually high number for the group as they had scored as many, if not more, on previous occasions. But it was a good total around that time. Therefore, the pilots were very happy with the score. The dogfight itself became a great topic of conversation and they were openly congratulating me for the part I had played in conducting it. In fact they were calling it 'Lanny's battle'.

I was as pleased as they were, but the most important thing to me was that we had come back with a minimum of losses, and this had been my main concern – as it always had been.

Jim Carter did not profess to controlling the battle as he had stated that he had been chasing his claim on the deck. Schilling was delighted at the results and, other than the fact that they still continued to discuss that particular mission for a few days after, I did not give it any more thought.

It was two days later that we went off on another dive-bombing mission near Bonn. After bombing our target we turned left to come home and found ourselves being shot at by artillery. Schilling (who was commanding the group) called over the radio: 'It's too hot to investigate. Let's get out of here.'

But on my turn, my flight was nearest the ground, and through a large gap in the clouds I saw tanks, lorries and everything one expects to see at a front line. I reported to Schilling and said I wanted to go and check, as I was sure we were over the German front line. Schilling immediately replied: 'Are you crazy Lanny. If you say we go, we all go.' We dived down and it was as I anticipated, the German front line and enough targets for one and all. The boys were wild with excitement at the unexpected find. They immediately went into action without waiting to be told. In the midst of the ball they were having, one or two Mustang groups passed over and, seeing the time we were having, joined in. The German defence was heavy but we obviously did considerable damage for I, personally, destroyed three heavy lorries and damaged one. It was not possible to estimate the result of firing on the enemy tanks.

We returned without losses. It proved it was possible to succeed against all the odds, providing the attack was a surprise and, in these circumstances, unplanned with 100-plus aircraft attacking from all directions. There were no claims to report as we had engaged no enemy aircraft. Nevertheless, we were all satisfied with the outcome of the operation. Schilling came to me with an enormous grin on his face and admitted I'd taken him by surprise. 'I thought you had gone crazy for a moment Lanny. I couldn't see anything. But I guessed it must have been something important to make you want to go and find out. It was a damned good show!' He expressed the opinion of every one of us.

While I was with the group I noticed they viewed the destruction of enemy aircraft on the ground in the same manner as we had in the RAF and PAF. It was the period of the war when one could see hundreds of German aircraft stationary on the airfields, often with no defence at all. On most occasions they could be shot up and destroyed at random. These claims were not compared in the same category as those destroyed in the air in battle. They were not considered 'victories' as such and by now these aircraft were not going to be used against us anyway. So we were more interested in the targets that could still cause damage. But hundreds of aircraft on the ground were destroyed by the Allied air forces and to my knowledge the 56th claimed 327 of these. Some other American groups considered their totals of aircraft destroyed on the ground in the same vein as those in the air. It was a matter of opinion I imagine. To me personally the ones in the air were the more important and the more difficult as claims. Strafing on the deck at low level required experienced practice and was not to be taken lightly or it could be hair-raising when undertaken. As the American pilots found insufficient time for practice, low-level bombing and strafing did not come easy to them.

The following week we heard that Jim Carter had been awarded the Silver Star for his action and leadership on the mission of 18 November. Somehow it did not come as a surprise to me but unfortunately it caused a great deal of anger to the boys of the 61st Squadron whom he commanded and with whom I flew. They went around voicing their disapproval in no uncertain terms and came to me both embarrassed and considerably bitter on my behalf. It was a very unpleasant situation for a time, as a good deal of their anger was directed at Schilling himself, who had recommended the award. I had the difficult task of placating the pilots and I told them that as everything had gone well during the mission, that had been my only interest. I wanted a finish to the ugly atmosphere the award had created and it had not been particularly easy. Jim Carter obviously felt very uncomfortable and for a while he didn't come to speak with me socially, which I could understand in the circumstances. The matter was never mentioned after that time.

It is only recently that I came across a reference made to that mission in the 56th Fighter Group's unofficial historical record book, published just after the war. At the end of the hostilities Schilling continually promised me that I should have a copy of this book, but for reasons I could not then understand he failed to keep his promise. The 18 November 1944 operation is picked out in the book as one of the important missions for that month, and would pass unnoticed as anything except the account of an especially good mission accomplished with honours, even though there was more to it than that.

As it happened I hadn't thought about any awards after we got back and there certainly had been no time to think of any during the battle itself. It always surprised me the way they continued to add one bar after another to my American Air Medal with amazing regularity. The last one I received from them was the second silver oak-leaf cluster to the medal – making eleven air medals in all. After August 1944 those awarded to me were granted when I was a civilian. But as I was on transference from the Polish Air Force to the USAAF I naturally considered myself to be military personnel as much as my commanders did in this respect. Therefore I had no qualms about accepting the military awards they gave me, including being numbered among those permitted to wear the Presidential Citation (three in all). This was an honour reserved for whole units for special services, and all the unit members were entitled to wear it.

On 25 November 1944 I was awarded the American DFC. I was equally pleased that my personal mechanic was being decorated with a special award (the highest the ground crew could get) for exceptional service. To my deep regret I have long since forgotten his name, but never him personally.

The day was bitterly cold as we stood to attention on the parade ground. It was a special event for those who were receiving the decorations, with most of the group on parade. I was the first to be presented with the award that day. For the occasion I wore my air force 'blue' (my one and only uniform). It did not bear any British rank on the jacket but I had retained the three stars that denoted my Polish Air Force rank of kapitan. The British only recognised their own rank status, so the above rank was as unofficial as the 'honorary' rank given to me by the American commanders. I was referred to as Captain Lanowski as General Auton congratulated me on my award. It was a momentous occasion for me especially, considering the circumstances under which it occurred.

At the end of the ceremony I went off with my mechanic and we had our photograph taken wearing our new decorations, and feeling rather pleased with ourselves. I liked him very much and I was not the only one who considered him to be the finest mechanic on the station. I felt very fortunate to have him looking after my interests. He had my life in his hands and I valued the concern he took to that end as I had done previously towards my Polish mechanics in the not so distant past.

Apart from various incidents concerning my position, until we were to become officially American officers, I felt very much at home in the group. Gladych had Americanised himself very effectively and had acquired a most convincing American accent. The pilots were inquisitive about Gladych, particularly wanting to verify if he had ever been to the States. Knowing Gladych I told them their guess was as good as mine.

For a while Gladych's various accounts had not affected me personally except on the occasion he had got cross over the 18 November mission. I heard he had gone to the pilots asking the exact details of that day and had subsequently written an account of it for the *Polish Wings* publication, which I didn't see or know about until much later. As he now spoke a good imitation of the American accent it was not difficult for the pilots to distinguish between our voices. My broken English didn't seem to bother them at all and I had no difficulty in being understood either on the ground or in the air. They knew immediately who it was without the necessity of me giving my call sign.

Besides Gladych and me there were two other pilots – Americans of Polish descent – in the 61st who spoke Polish. Their names were Winski and Murajda. The others of Polish lineage only spoke English. One of these boys was very upset at not being able to speak Polish to me as his parents had never taught it to him.

Financially we were in a very difficult position. The last time we had received any pay was in September 1944. Of course, any money owing to us by the time our commissions were granted would be paid as back salary. This we were told by Schilling, who realised our difficulty. But we were by now short of cash for our personal requirements. Fortunately I didn't need much. Cigarettes were only 3d a pack, which we bought on the camp. I hardly drank at all and even when I did spend an evening with the boys, who knew our situation, they were adamant about not allowing me to pay for the usual round. They meant well, but it was hardly a pleasant position to be in. Therefore I looked for other ways to spend my spare time that did not create this state of affairs.

But, naturally, we had to have some money. We just couldn't be without any and Schilling came up with an idea. He didn't tell us about it at first until we pressed him to know where the money came from that he gave us in the last few days of the month. It was about £15 to £20 for each of us and no signatures were required on any receipt. He just handed it to us and told us to take it. At first I thought it came out of his own pocket, but then we learned that apparently he had asked the boys of the 61st to donate something towards pocket money for us and this they had done. It was a shock and we felt uncomfortable about it, but it was insisted we take it. I thanked Schilling and wished him to understand I could only take it providing he understood I intended to repay their kindness as soon as I received my pay on commission. Afterwards I went personally to thank the boys themselves as I appreciated very much their gesture.

In December the amount of missions flown began to drop off, due principally to bad weather, and thereafter the termination of hostilities was already in sight. Nevertheless, various operations were made, mostly covering our bombers for the final finish of Germany. When we escorted bombers in these last stages not one enemy fighter came into the sky to intercept. They were all standing idle on the aerodrome waiting to be destroyed by Allied aircraft.

Come Christmas it was decided I should have some leave. I didn't mind, although I had nowhere particularly to go and I couldn't really afford it anyway. Another collection by passing the hat around was made for us at the end of December. But I didn't especially feel like celebrating by this time and the money would not have lasted the next month if I had.

While I was on the camp I was provided with quarters and food. On the camp itself some of the boys actually gave me items of clothing that I could wear. Other articles I paid for out of the money they had donated to us. But in actual fact my personal effects were extremely limited. Certainly not anything like those the American boys had and were provided with, such as uniforms etc. Off-site I wore my British/Polish uniform, my one and only. I didn't wear it often for the simple reason I didn't go out of camp very often. When I did wear it I put on it the American wings that someone on the base gave me. I wore them on my left breast together with my Polish wings, an eagle clutching a laurel wreath, suspended on a chain. My blue peaked cap still bore the Polish badge.

As far as leave was concerned for the pilots on the base they had a very good arrangement. They clubbed together to afford a flat in London, which was stocked with food requisites etc from the camp. It was kept fully supplied at all times. The key was then handed to whoever had leave to spend in town. Therefore they always had their own place to go to. Possibly I could have used the flat also, no one would have objected; I just didn't want to encroach upon their good nature any further. Fortunately I was not completely without friends to visit, and it was good to exchange our news and relax into our own language.

A week or two before Christmas there was great activity on the station. Glenn Miller and his band were visiting Boxted to give us a concert. Naturally ops for the day were out of the question. Fortunately the weather agreed with us when nature made it her business to provide unsatisfactory flying conditions. For once we were all glad of her 'co-operation'.

Glenn Miller's aircraft, a Liberator, was specially equipped for his use and painted with yellow and black stripes – looking much like a Colorado beetle.

The stage was in the centre of the hangar. Everyone was present for the show and wherever one could find a good viewing position one stood, sat, hung-on to, or straddled. This included the girders of the hangar. Whichever direction you looked, someone was sure to be. It was the most marvellous morale booster that I could imagine and the best entertainment from a wonderful person and his band. Perhaps it was just the time and the place, but it had an enormous effect on everyone, including myself. Ever after, to hear one of Glenn Miller's records instantly transported me back to that day in the station's hangar, when I recalled old friendships and times without feeling any of the bitterness that the period brought to me.

A week later we were all stunned and horrified to hear that his aircraft was missing over the Channel. A very great loss was sensed by all who had been entertained by him.

I was due to go on leave for Christmas in a few days' time when Dave Schilling called me to his office. I found him in a very excited state about a proposed mission. He was feeling particularly proud to confide to me that the 56th had been chosen for the operation as 'the best outfit in the United States Air Force'. He had every right to feel that way, it was no small acknowledgement and the 56th had long since proved itself time and time again. He was so delighted at the honour we had received that he almost forgot to tell me what it was all about.

So giving him a gentle prod I brought him back to earth. 'All right Dave, now tell me what it is,' I said, smiling at his boyish grin. 'Come on,' he replied, 'I'll show you.' He pulled me into an almost empty room except for a large table in the centre. On it stood a model of the target – 6 feet in diameter – detailed to perfection.

'Look at it, Lanny, it's an oil and rubber synthetic plant. The bombers have tried to knock it out but they haven't succeeded.' It had received a very heavy pounding but the whole plant stood intact. The surrounding area had received the weight of the bombing intended to destroy the plant. The defence was obviously so strong the bomber boys just couldn't get at it.

Dave was rattling on with the ideas he had in mind. The operation looked to be for the next month (January 1945). I was just standing gazing intently at the model – thinking. Apart from all the secrecy surrounding such an operation it was a mission that demanded extensive low-level bombing practice. With this in mind I wondered instantly whether Schilling realised exactly what it involved. I also speculated whether those at Headquarters realised it also. It seemed to be their way to imagine that these things could be undertaken without a great deal of practice and instruction first. Certainly Schilling had not so far mentioned the intention to train the boys for it.

So I asked him if he realised what this kind of attack demanded. Yes, of course he did. 'What do you think of it, Lanny. You'll come with me?' 'Not on a suicide mission,' I answered, and he gazed at me astounded. He was too excited and I knew why. It was an operation that if successful would bring recognition to the group and the individuals who took part in it. This would include the highest decorations and, I thought, posthumous ones at that. I had no intention of throwing my life away on these grounds. A fat lot of good medals would do anyone dead. If they wanted to attack the oil plant they should do it properly or not at all. They had given it over to the bomber boys to destroy and they hadn't been able to. So now it was the turn of the fighters to attempt it – at this stage of the war, when it really didn't matter very much, and the boys would lose their lives for nothing! With these remarks I had unintentionally sobered Dave up, and he stood there contemplating what I said. 'You want my opinion?' I asked him. 'Of course Lanny,' he nodded. 'What do you think?' I started to list the points.

The most important thing was the row of thirteen brickwork chimneys, about 300 to 500 feet apart. Our job was to destroy the line, including the power station at its head, attacking at low level. Dave said he would lead one flight, I another, Gladych the third and so on.

We needed to fly at our normal height, showing ourselves on the enemy radar conspicuously on a false direction, but not too far from the actual target. The reason for this was because we would be carrying two 500-lb bombs each and because of this only one 200-gallon drop tank, cutting our reserve fuel and leaving no margin for errors even though we could land in liberated countries for refuelling.

Then we would have to dive right to the deck in order to disappear off the radar screens, and fly at treetop height to our target. There should be no guesswork at getting there, so navigational abilities required improvement at low level.

In the final stage, we would form line abreast and (the most important point) fly right between the chimney stacks at right angles, dropping the bombs for a direct hit at the correct speed and at the right moment. Schilling confirmed the fuses would have a ten-second delay.

I had no idea what Headquarters' plan had been to attack the target but apparently my suggestions more or less agreed with what they had in mind, according to Schilling. I then pointed out two very important points regarding practice for the mission, and a third – most vital of all – on the expected defences:

1) There was a necessity for low-level bombing training. (For until now ours had been mainly guesswork and a 'finger to the wind' principle).
2) No one had had experience to fly between chimneys such as these were placed, and under the conditions one would expect to find for defending them. It had to be done line abreast and all going through at the same time – and this is what I told Schilling. Being shot at in that vital moment was not going to be funny. So it had to be practised until perfect. It wasn't a joke and had to be considered seriously. Air crew lives depended on it.
3) We had already been informed of the maximum defences the enemy used for high-altitude bombing, and it had been very successful at that, but what did anyone know about the defences for low-level bombing? There appeared to be no information on this point! I was convinced – knowing the Germans – that there

would be such defences in place for low level that none of us would come back alive. I expected to find nets, rockets, cables on parachutes etc – everything known and probably a good deal unknown.

If it was on the books that the operation stood after all this was taken into account, I would do what I could to help train the boys for the mission. I would fly them until they were sick of the sight of chimneys. I'd take them up north where the brickworks were and have them going through them non-stop, and low-level practice all the while.

The job should have been carried out at least two years before, when it was important, but providing they did it the way I had outlined it, I'd go. But I wanted results not wishful thinking or just for a few more medals all round.

Anyway the whole plan had yet to be confirmed. They had sent it to Schilling for his reaction, I suppose, and his opinion. There were no hard feelings about it because I respected his leadership and he knew it. But I had my own opinions, which I believed in and stood by.

The result was that after Christmas, and come January – when it was meant to be put into operation – we had heard nothing more about it, and I had already decided I would not go if they left it too late to get organised. Schilling too seemed surprised not to hear any more and we concluded they had reconsidered the subject at Headquarters and we shrugged it off.

After the war ended the station chief intelligence officer went to Germany to check on the groups' activities, i.e. to calculate and verify the results of our missions. When he returned one of the first things he did was to call me to his office. 'Do you remember the mission to destroy the oil and rubber plant, Lanny? You were absolutely right in what you said. None of you would have got through. The defences were fantastic.' It was both interesting for me to be assured, and for those in charge to realise it would have been no picnic. There was a time and place for unplanned attacks. We had all done them at one time or another. Some things had to be trained for in detail, and they must have realised it because Headquarters had scrapped the whole idea.

However, the intended target was seriously damaged afterwards by the Royal Air Force and they made a thoroughly good job of it. Even so, it was still in a fit enough state for the intelligence officer to ascertain what the defences had been for low-level bombing. The group were also to attack a synthetic plant at Zeitz but apparently this, too, was also bombed by the Royal Air Force.

The brief summary of the mission planned for the 56th Fighter Group in January, that Schilling had discussed with me, made for interesting reading:

Target:	Luena Synthetic Oil Plant Refinery: Mersburg, Germany.
Pilots.	61st Flight: D. Smith, also J. Perry.
	62nd Flight: D.C. Schilling, H. Stovall, P. Fleming, R. Winters.
	63rd Flight: H.E. Comstock, J. Fahringer, W. Grace, A. Andermatt.
Description of target:	50,000 tons of oil per month. 475 heavy guns, 375 light guns.

I don't know if this was the information they had before or after the war. It is interesting to note that only the names of two lead pilots of the 61st Flight are detailed. The other two, of course, were to have been mine and Gladych's.

The intelligence officer also brought back with him a Heinkel 111 (for us to fly) – and a German fighter ace. The German was in full dress uniform complete with Iron Cross set with diamonds. The objective seemed to be to enable us to 'talk' with him and ask any questions we wished. I attended this 'show', staged as only the Americans could stage it, complete with high-ranking generals. I listened to the questions and I listened to the answers. None of it seemed very real to me. I had an absurd feeling that in a moment I would wake up and find it hadn't happened. I was wondering what question I – as a Pole – could put to him that he – a German – could answer 'honestly' and 'directly', at such a time and place, and in such company. There was none.

Chapter 24

1945

January turned out to be another one of those months as far as our commissions were concerned, and we received rather a surprise. A request for our complete release from the Polish forces came from the American military authorities. It seemed their regulations required this, although it was something they would have got the moment they granted our commissions.

One of the generals along the way had decided our one year's unpaid leave still tied us – as military personnel – to the Polish Air Force, and perhaps he didn't like the wording on the certificate: 'to join the United States Army Air Force for a period of one year, during the term of their unpaid leave from the Polish Air Force'. I can't imagine why else our 'complete release' could have been requested as we were already civilians and had been since the previous October. We already fulfilled the requirements of their regulations. Unless he thought we only intended to become American commissioned officers for just one year. Which, of course, was nonsense. The wording used was only a formality. They had undoubtedly gone through this procedure before with the American citizens who had joined the PAF and the RAF and later transferred to the USAAF when it arrived in England.

Moreover, the Polish and British authorities would have released us completely in the first instance had this been the only method by which we could have received USAAF commissions. They were not entirely unfamiliar with the procedure. It had been done before.

There was something more to it than that obviously. But to us it looked like a lot of unnecessary red tape. Perhaps they were beginning to feel more secure about things in general so they decided to tidy the system up a bit. Unfortunately they 'forgot' or 'overlooked' the fact we were active with the group (56th) – operationally active – and were not just sitting around doing nothing. We may not have been flying operationally as much as we had before, but then nobody else was either. Nevertheless, we still ran the same risks as before every time we flew over Germany. Our position had not improved. In fact it had got worse. Much worse.

Schilling asked if we could obtain the release the authorities wanted. He was fed up with them playing us around, as we were, but again he said everything would be all right. It was a formality and once they had the necessary documents we would be commissioned and our back pay would be forthcoming. This was fast becoming of vital importance to Gladych and myself.

At first I wasn't quite sure how to go about getting this release paper. The Polish authorities, having already granted us the year of unpaid leave, considered us civilians, which we were. So there was only one place I could obtain the necessary document and that was from the Polish government. So off I went to see a Polish minister I had once met. He could advise me and tell me what to do. He suggested the Polish Consul would be the right person for me to see. He telephoned the Consul, Dr Karol Poznanski – also a minister in the Polish government – and arranged for me to visit him the following day.

On 5 February 1945 I went to keep the appointment and explained the position to Dr Poznanski. Without any hesitation he promptly arranged for me to be given a certificate of complete release and one also for Gladych. I left his office with the certificates in my pocket. We were now civilians in the full sense of the word. Again, it was granted only for the purpose of performing my duties in the forces of the United States of America. The certificate was valid until 5 May of that year, long enough, one would have thought, for the American authorities to get their system functioning properly and commission us, which was now thoroughly overdue by four months. One could only hope this would be so, as three months was the normal time for any department to arrange official matters. It didn't necessarily mean that after that date I couldn't join the American forces, simply that they, the Polish authorities, expected me to be a member already.

I handed the document over to the Americans at the unit. It appears they made a copy of it for inclusion in my application papers. They did not make out any fresh application papers. Had they done so I would have had to sign as before. Presumably the same ones were sent round again, dating from October 1944.

By the end of February two things occurred that I found necessary to deal with. First I put a stop to the monthly routine of passing the hat round for our benefit. I don't know what Gladych did about it but I declined any further offers from the pilots to help me out temporarily with pocket money. I had witnessed the procedure and I had never liked the idea in the first place, but I didn't wish them to think I was being churlish. But now it had to stop if I was going to retain my self-respect. They understood and I think they too were relieved at no longer having the responsibility of partly keeping me. Why should they have to do it anyway? My position was nothing to do with them, the pilots themselves hadn't caused it.

Next, I decided to move off the camp. By this time I could feel that a great deal of embarrassment was being felt at our being there, living with them but not being one of them. So I thought it best to live close by instead. Everyone still believed we would be commissioned and therefore so did we. Why not!

I called in at the local butcher's shop, the only shop in Langham village owned by a Mr Thorpe. He was a very cheerful and helpful person and I asked him if he knew anyone in the road (which was virtually all the village was) who might consider letting me a room. I had to be as near as possible to the station. He suggested I went to see a Mr and Mrs Jack Dear. They lived in the 'Hollands', a little house whose back garden faced on to the runway. I went to see them feeling a little anxious. I wasn't quite sure how I was going to put my situation to them. I wasn't seeking charity, but that is what it looked as if it was going to be. I couldn't afford to give anyone very much, especially now I had stopped the money from the pilots. I could, of course, borrow from Peter to pay Paul. We would have to see what they said first.

I was greeted by two of the kindest and gentlest people it has been my fortune to meet. They were not swept away by any temporary feeling of wishing to help me for the moment, which would fade as quickly as it came. They listened quietly and patiently in their tidy sitting room where we sat, while I explained the circumstances that I was placed in at that time. My heart warmed to them the moment 'Mother' Dear opened the door. She was soon to become 'Mother' Dear to me and has remained so ever since. Her husband Jack had suffered from shell shock in the First World War (as her father had done) and he was a typical country person whose basic interest and love was for the land. He could grow anything in his garden and it would appear under the expert guidance of his green fingers. At the same time he was not immune to raising rabbits and slaughtering them for lunch. And a jolly good meal they made. He was a very honest and sincere person and full of fun, and incessantly teased his wife. Once I came to live under their roof, I in turn teased him. When he worried if I didn't return from a mission, for instance, he would suffer from shaking, although the worry itself would never be allowed to show on his face.

After they had listened to my tale, without any hesitation they offered me the hospitality of their home and I knew it came from very sincere genuine feelings. I soon moved into their home with my few personal belongings and I was made to feel welcome in the homely atmosphere. I paid them what I could, which wasn't much and certainly not adequate for what they gave me in return. I brought what I could from the camp to help with the food problem, for although I was really a civilian I had no ration cards or any of the amenities usual for civilians. To be able to have these I needed a civilian identity and this was something I had not been given. This is not surprising when it is realised I was expected to be commissioned almost immediately upon being released – both in October and again in February – and so become part of the military system.

Mother Dear and Jack had adopted two young girls as their own daughters, who were now working on the land. They were extremely nice young ladies and we all got on very well together as the proverbial happy family. They made my Polish friends welcome who came to see me, and my cousin Manek, who at the end of his visit flew back to his army unit in Scotland in a converted Thunderbolt.

To ensure I arose early in the morning I listened subconsciously for the sound of the engines running – about 4 a.m. I dressed quickly and left the house silently so as not to waken the others. Poor Mother Dear would watch for my aircraft to land with the rest of the group, and if I failed to return with them – which I did on a couple of occasions, landing elsewhere first to refuel to bring me on to Boxted – she worried dreadfully until I came flying directly over the rooftop to let her know I had arrived back. It gave her a shock until she realised it was only me.

For the first time since I had left Poland I experienced what it was like to live in a home again. I can't explain what I felt, simply to say that the kindness and affection the Dear family gave me, and comfort in the anxiety I was feeling at that present time, was overwhelming. My faith in the Americans was beginning to be shaken but not sufficiently for me to leave them. But later, when I realised that their red tape was holding up my commission – which even now may take ages to come through – the enormity of my circumstances really hit me and I felt bitterly angry and distressed. Then Mother Dear and Jack came to my rescue with their warmth and feelings on my behalf. Without their encouragement and constant friendship I don't think I could have borne the situation as I did. But most of this was still to come.

In December 1944 the mechanics picked out another Thunderbolt for me as 'Silver Lady' had gone and the new P-47s had not yet arrived. They selected HV-V and kept her in tip-top condition. So much so that one particular day when I walked over the tarmac to check on her for the next day's op she wasn't where I expected to find her. I naturally asked where she was and my boys told me that she needed her engine changed. Fair enough, I looked around enquiring which aircraft I could take in her stead. This apparently was adding insult to injury. 'You'll have your own', I was informed in no uncertain terms, 'even if we have to work on her all night.' Next day there wasn't time to check her out before we took off so I carried out this procedure on the way to the target. It didn't occur to me not to take the plane without first inspecting her. Nor was it blind faith. I was just perfectly satisfied the ground crew knew their job. I never had cause to complain before and I certainly had no cause for it on this occasion. She purred sweetly all the way there and back home again, with never a hint of trouble.

I was extremely lucky with my mechanics. I had two exceptional friends looking after my welfare – what more could any pilot want? We became a team. But this didn't stop me from teasing them with my remarks about our Polish mechanics who I also had cause to be grateful to. They had looked after me while I flew with the Polish Air Force and they had a record to be exceptionally proud of. So I related various instances to my American crew. They would grin broadly, half in disbelief and sure that I was telling a tall story just because they were Poles and my countrymen. On the other hand, when I visited Andrewsfield, which at the time was a Polish station, I would be asked about Boxted and naturally I sang the praises of my current mechanics. This, too, was met with scepticism, this time by the Poles. This was going to be fun! Flight Sergeant Korczowski – former mechanic to General Rayski – offered a wager to my American crew that he could completely change the engine of a Thunderbolt even though he had never worked on one before, and within a specified time limit – which sounded quite unbelievable. Especially that he intended to do it all by himself; moreover the Americans didn't know the Polish mechanics and how they could work.

I informed my crew of his challenge and they stared in disbelief, but willingly took on the bet, convinced they were going to make easy money. I flew Korczowski over to Boxted. My crew had laid out every tool he required to change the engine and Korczowski set to work. We left him to it. To the utter amazement of my crew and others who had heard about the wager, Korczowski finished the job with perfection and with fifteen minutes to spare! He was genuinely applauded for the 'feat' and taken off to celebrate his success. Up the Poles!

It took about ten minutes to fly over to Andrewsfield and I visited them often. The Poles there had established quite a nice little going concern making cigarette lighters from Polish and American gilded buttons. I acted as the go-between. The boys at the 56th couldn't buy enough of them and, whenever I flew over to Andrewsfield, even before I landed I could see the Polish mechanics rushing towards my place of landing all ready with a fresh supply of lighters.

I once invited the sporting officer to visit Boxted in his little Auster aircraft. When he returned to the Polish station he took with him an enormous amount of sports equipment – jamming his aircraft tight – which the Americans had donated to the Polish airmen.

It made a very pleasant atmosphere between the two stations when my Polish friends came to Boxted parties at my invitation. There was a lot of good will on both sides and the Americans had the opportunity of appreciating the effort of the PAF in the war – besides their own – and were able to acquire a broader view of the situation in general, instead of being able to judge only from those few of us they had known on their base.

In mid-January I received the P-47M that we had been waiting for; they had slightly increased power and the extra tanks. They were the exact type of P-47 being used in the Pacific. Z (Zbar) was the code – the same as I had used previously. I don't remember if it was intentional or quite by accident. For the first time I agreed to have an emblem painted on my Thunderbolt, as the others had on theirs. I chose the one that had been designed by a Polish friend of mine and myself that we had used on the front cover of our Polish magazine published in England in 1940–41. It had never been used for any other purpose other than on the magazine so I adopted it. The station 'artist' painted on the cowling the Polish Air Force insignia – a red and white four-square check (bordering the square with a thin outline, white against red and red against white). In the centre of the emblem was a steel knight's gauntlet crushing a Messerschmitt. The gauntlet represented the famous battle of Grunwald of 1410 when Polish and Lithuanian forces destroyed the German Army, consisting of the famous German Teutonic knights. On the side of the cockpit, I put a small aluminium racing horseshoe. I never was very keen on talismans, for I always felt that if one forgot it you felt jolly uncomfortable until you got back home safely.

I also had a small replica of the emblem painted on cardboard, and stitched this to my leather flying jacket. My friends stared at it in horror, convinced I would pay for it with my life if I was ever shot down and caught. Well it didn't seem to matter, the same fate would have befallen me anyway as we still only carried our 'famous' identity cards given by the station adjutant. If that didn't cook my goose on its own account, nothing would. (In 1955/56 my wife saw a similar emblem displayed prominently at the start of an American film based on the USAAF. The difference in the two was that they had replaced the Messerschmitt for a 'bolt of lightning'.)

Schilling left the 56th in late February/early March. But before he went he told me he wanted to put our names down for the American Senior Aeronautical Badge. At that time the rules stipulated that you were required to have a minimum of 5 years' service and 15,000 flying hours. Schilling himself had this decoration, which, I believe, he was given after Zemke already had his. The other point about this badge was that it carried a monetary payment according to the rank you held. It was also a military badge awarded only to military personnel. This was rather an interesting situation, particularly as neither Gladych nor I held any rank at that time in any government's military forces. But this again didn't occur to us at the time. It was simply indicated to us that it was virtually 'in the bag' that we would be commissioned soon.

The honour had to be sanctioned from the Washington War Department itself, unlike some of the decorations. On 11 April we were officially informed the award was granted from Washington. In effect it meant that Gladych and I were the 'youngest' officers in rank, as captains – honorary or not – to hold this award. We felt very pleased with it, but as we still hadn't been commissioned officially we did not have the corresponding wings to mark the event. I added an American silver star to the American wings I already had had given to me. This likened the wings to the actual decoration, when we would eventually receive it. We also looked forward to the extra funds it would provide, and felt much happier with our position now.

Lieutenant Colonel Dade took over from Schilling, who became assistant director of intelligence at the headquarters of the 8th Air Force (AAF Station 101).

It is possible that in the month of March, either our commission papers had come back for some reason or another, or it was decided that as Schilling was leaving the group the station administration department had better complete an entirely new set of papers for our application for commission. I only know that the documents had to be retyped and newly dated for 1 April 1945, and that Gladych and I had to sign them once more. Dade fulfilled his part by recommending the commission wholeheartedly, and so did everyone else on the station whose authorisation was required, such as the intelligence officer, the CO of the 61st (Jim Carter), the deputy commander and the operations officer.

We were not very happy about this unnecessary delay. There was another certificate that orbited the channels along with these new papers, dated 24 April 1945. It referred to the certificate issued to me on 5 February of that year, enabling me to join the forces of the United States. It confirmed that this permission was granted irrespective of whether I was enlisted into the United States forces as a 'private', 'non-commissioned officer' or a 'commissioned officer', and was signed by the Polish Consul, General Dr Charles Poznanski. This little document was one of the mysteries of my case, and impossible for me to recall why it was ever requested and by whom. I remembered my only visit to the Consul General's office had been on 5 February, and this document obviously had been sent to me by post. But upon whose request I never discovered. But it accompanied the application papers, becoming enclosure number 6.In the meantime, on 19 April, I flew my last mission with the group, in the vicinity of München (Munich). Again I do not recall if it was because I just decided not to fly on operations any more or if the powers that be asked me not to participate in them.

One thing they had forgotten on the station when they completed the application papers, was to make out a new medical form. The last one had been completed on 8 February 1945. The last and only time I had been examined by the American doctors on the camp was in May 1944 when first coming to the group with the other Polish pilots. The omission resulted in the papers heading back to Boxted from Major General Kepner's headquarters in the 2nd Air Division on 8 May 1945, drawing attention to the fact that the medical had expired (that day), valid only within a ninety-day period. By this time the war in Europe was already over.

The station officers were furious at the added delay. A new form was freshly typed and the whole lot sent out once again. What was not realised then, either by any of the commanders – or by Gladych and myself for that matter – was that the certificates I had obtained from the Consul General, dated 5 February, had also expired under the same ninety-day rule. After that date it transpired that I was still a 'civilian' and that we had reverted back to the one year's unpaid leave that had been granted to us in the first instance. So one way or another we still qualified to be commissioned into the USAAF. Had the date on the former document come to the notice of the various commanders of the headquarters of

the 8th Air Force and the TAF, it would have been necessary to acquire
a fresh civilian certificate of complete release. As it was, no one noticed
it, and when it reached Washington with my other papers they didn't
notice it there either. But the action they were to take was completely
unjustified in every sense of the word.

After the forms had come back to the station for a new medical I was
by that time thoroughly fed up with the whole business, and I don't doubt
many would consider me to have been mad to stay on with the group
after all that had taken place. I had been borrowing money from my Polish
friends to keep me going and had to rely on the hospitality of Mother
Dear and Jack to allow me to remain with them until this 'so-called' commission came through. Even so, everyone was still convinced we would
be commissioned. No one doubted it for one second. It was simply one
of those things, they said, and nothing but a lot of red-tape rubbish 'bot-
tling up the works'. I was no longer sure and, if it came to it, I no longer
cared if they commissioned me or not. But I couldn't make any plans
for myself as the application had still to be authorised and until we heard
I didn't really know my position at all.

I already knew I couldn't return to Poland, as was the case for the
thousands of other Poles who had had to watch their country being given
over to a domination far worse than the one she had already suffered.
Not one of us could pretend we didn't mind, or understood about the
fate of our country, and no one should expect us to. We had fought for
Poland's freedom and we had been made to stand and watch her being
enslaved for the second time during the Second World War.

The West liked to think that the Poles in Poland were Communists,
but no Pole in his or her heart is Communist – or ever will be. They
may have to have appeared to be so for they had no option and were
given none. They had their own beliefs for our country's survival as
Poland. She had weathered many a storm of aggression from her neighbours from far back in history, and she never entirely surrendered and
came back to establish herself in her own right once more. Unfortunately,
there were many Poles in the West who fondly visualised a free Poland
to which they could return and take up the threads as before. This, of course,
was a dream that could never become reality and it was as well that it would
not, as the Poles in Poland are the masters of our country's destiny. Only

they could make of her what they would. One could only hope one day she would attain the freedom she so rightly deserved. As for me I could never completely visualise myself back in my own country, not even when the war came to an end. Very few of us could.

After I finished flying ops in April and prior to the war terminating, I found little to do on the station. In practice, as a flight commander, which they had detailed me to do from October 1944, my job was now completed. Although no doubt it would have stood officially when the commission came through, as this was the position recommended for me in the application papers. Nonetheless, I continued flying right through May, June, July and August, even if my trips were only cross-country and local. On 21 June I flew formation for one hour, but other than that I no longer took much part in the group's activities. The very last aircraft I flew, on 24 August, was a German Messerschmitt. The last date I flew a Thunderbolt was on 16 August 1945.

I did not consider myself as anything but one of the members of the group, although there was little going on during this time. It was simply a case of waiting until we were officially accepted. But it was a very trying period for everyone concerned.

One day I was called to the station adjutant's office and handed a decorative sheet of paper, which I read to be the 'Fighter Pilots' Creed' of the 65th Fighter Wing. My name was printed especially on the front in the same manner as the rest of the wording in the creed, so it obviously was meant for me. It was written:

I resolve that I will:
Know my airplane perfectly.
Know all enemy airplanes thoroughly.
Be a superior gunner.
Be an outstanding pilot.
Have the will to fight.
   Capt. Witold Lanowski
   56th Fighter Group.
. Certified: signed Jesse Auton
   Brigadier General, USA
   Commanding.

On the reverse side of the creed was defined specifically:

1. Know my airplane perfectly.
   I will know in detail the mechanical workings of every part.
   I will know every flying characteristic, both good and not so good.
   I will know every new development that may affect my airplane.
   I will know the limits of stress and power of my airplane
   and engine.
2. Know all enemy airplanes thoroughly.
   I will know their flying characteristics, speed, armour and
   armament in comparison to my airplane.
   I will recognise each of them at the first glance.
3. Be a superior gunner.
   I will know my guns and sights completely.
   I will practise firing and sighting at every opportunity, with every
   weapon available.
   I will make every shot an aimed shot.
   I will take enough lead to centre every shot in the target.
   I will never waste ammunition back of effective firing range.
4. Be an outstanding pilot.
   I will always maintain combat formation team work.
   I will keep myself in perfect physical condition.
   I will use my radio sparingly and confidently.
   I will develop my flying technique to perfection in every
   manoeuvre.
   I will out-fly every other pilot in smoothness, judgement and skill.
5. Have the will to fight.
   I will seek out the enemy always.
   I will never be deceived by enemy tricks.
   I will see the enemy before being seen.
   I will close quickly on the enemy, destroy him, and break away fast.

I certify that Capt. Witold Lanowski, P.0711, 61st Fighter Squadron,
56th Fighter Group is eligible to sign this creed by his ability as a
fighter pilot.

It was signed again on this side by General Jesse Auton and I was asked to add my own signature above the typing of my name, i.e. Witold Lanowski, Captain, Air Corps.

I was very surprised to receive this document and the honour it obviously intended to bestow upon me. I was pleased naturally, but also confused. Much of what they did confused me now that I had time to think about it. Everyone was treating me as a commissioned officer in the USAAF already. They were including me in the various awards and giving me those intended for one of their personnel. Yet a doubt had arisen in my mind as to whether the commission itself would actually come about. Particularly after it had been jeopardised, as it so often had, by the way it was being handled.

Between 9 and 11 August I was called to Lieutenant Colonel Dade's office. Dade looked uncomfortable and embarrassed. I soon knew why. He had the unpleasant task of informing me that my commission had been refused! I don't recall if Gladych was there at the same time or if Dade decided to see us separately. Oddly enough, I remember very little of that particular day except being told I hadn't been accepted. Somehow I had been expecting something on these lines, but all the same I was stunned. I just couldn't believe it. It didn't make any sense at all. I don't know what Dade actually said except, no doubt, that he was sorry. The meeting didn't last long as there didn't seem much to say and I knew it was pointless to argue. What could he do? One thing I asked and that was about our pay, and what he said came more of a shock to me than actually being refused the commission. He was very apologetic but could do nothing personally to reimburse me for the back pay I had lost. He had no authorisation to issue any remuneration to me as I would not have been included on their payroll until I became an American military personnel, and this was now out of the question.

When I left his office I was feeling very angry and bitter. I was even kicking myself for not ensuring that my commission was granted by personally taking my application papers to the necessary channels and getting the signatures required. There had been nothing to stop me from doing this. Ever since I had been with the Americans I had found myself free to fly anywhere – at any time – in any aircraft on the station. There was never any question of anyone stopping me flying or going where I wanted to go. I never experienced anything like it in the PAF or RAF stations, but then the Americans were different in so many ways. Had I taken the papers myself I could have flown to Germany and much of the red tape could have been bypassed. I discovered when it was too late that it only required the final sanction of Eisenhower himself to commission me, without the papers having to go to Washington. Eisenhower was in Germany and I would have been able to fly there. But, as in many instances, one finds out the hard way.

I realised now that I had been kept dangling on a piece of string – or was it red tape – when in fact the procedure could and should have been made easier, as it had been in cases before of those who had transferred previously to the USAAF from the RAF and PAF. It made little difference that they had been American citizens; the procedure had been the same, just simplified to effect a rapid move. They had joined the Polish or Royal Air Forces and then later transferred to their own forces with no difficulty. I witnessed Czech officers who were relocating to the USAAF collecting their American uniforms from the PX in 1945. I happened to be in the PX at the time and I saw it for myself.

The incredible fact was that we had been specifically asked to join the Americans; the request had not come initially from us. It just didn't seem to make any sense at all.

There was also the case of the Eagle Squadrons of the RAF who transferred in September 1942 to the United States Army Air Force. The description of this occasion in the fighter group's war record book (published after the hostilities) was that they had been 'activated' to the USAAF as an entire fighter group, to become known as the 4th Fighter Group, who became the 56th's greatest rival group as far as the scores in the air and on the ground were concerned.

Funnily enough, before we actually heard of the result of our commissions, Zemke had visited the 56th after arriving in England on his way back to the USA from his incarceration as a prisoner of war. I hadn't bothered to tell him that I still wasn't commissioned and I don't know if he made it his business to ask Dade. If he did he certainly didn't let on to me that he knew. Anyway why should he think about it – he had had enough troubles of his own. At least I hadn't been a prisoner of war like so many others had been.

But the most important thing I had to do first was to set about acquiring the finances due to me, under the terms of the agreement. I had no way of knowing how long this was going to take me but the authorities' action had instilled in me a determination that they must pay up in the end. While I felt bitter, I still couldn't quite believe that there hadn't simply been a misunderstanding somewhere. I couldn't think they would be as stupid as their actions implied or that they were capable of playing such a dirty trick. In my opinion they had represented what one expected democracy to be.

I had to plan what to do next and who to see to assist me in my claim. As the war had ended, on the camp everyone was already thinking about going home and preparing for that eventuality. They didn't know how lucky they were. You needed to have both your home and your country taken from you before you could really appreciate that fully.

I was given all the original documentation concerning my commission, as well as copies, but they didn't even try to arrange any kind of official identity papers for me. They just were not interested. Since this problem hadn't particularly caused them any anxiety even while I flew with them, why should they worry now that I was no longer part of the group?

When I looked through the documents I saw that everywhere I was consistently referred to as Flight Lieutenant Lanowski, P.0711, Polish Air Force. Other than the fact that my release papers came under the heading of 'enclosures', nowhere was any attention drawn to, or stated, that I was a civilian. Nowhere did it mention that I was not being paid while I served with them. Finally I came across the refusal itself; this came from the adjutant general's department of the Secretary of War, Washington: 'Inasmuch as the services of Flight Lieutenant Witold A. Lanowski, P.0711, Polish Air Force, are not needed by the Army Air Forces, request for his transfer to the Army of the United States in the grade of captain is not favourably considered.'

Perhaps for the first time I realised the damage this unofficial military status had done to me. Not only were the authorities apparently of the opinion that I could easily return to my own Polish unit, as I was obviously still a Polish officer, but that also they preferred to believe that the British or Polish Air Forces had been paying me while I was 'attached' to the USAAF. They didn't state as much but the papers I held in my hand seemed to infer this was their viewpoint, and why should they commission me now? The war was over and they no longer had any need of my services (they said this much at least) – I could now go back to where I had come from.

Also in the papers I saw no mention that the commanding officers of the 56th (Zemke and Schilling) had formally asked Gladych and myself to join the USAAF, although our experience and value to the service was stipulated.

On 13 August I decided I must act swiftly if I was to catch the various commanders it was necessary for me to see in England. Therefore I notified the CO of the 61st that I intended to fly to Bovingdon (before travelling on to Pinetree at High Wycombe, the headquarters of the American Air Force in this country). As usual he raised no objection to me taking one of the aircraft. He simply informed the mechanics to prepare one for me. I took a P-47M (HV-A) and went to the control tower to tell them where I was going. I was told the weather was exceptionally bad and all flying had been stopped. But they didn't exactly try to stop me or object when I waived their weather predictions to one side. I wasn't interested in how bad the weather was, I intended to go to Bovingdon even if I had to fly on my nose, and that was virtually what I found myself doing. They had simply said to me: 'If anyone can fly in this weather – you can Lanny. We'll let Bovingdon know you're on your way. But they won't believe us.'

I had to fly at treetop height all the way to Bovingdon; I couldn't see a thing. The skies just emptied every drop of rain they held. Clouds were more or less right on the deck. Normally it wouldn't have been attempted, especially as there were little hills surrounding the High Wycombe valley and Bovingdon, too, was situated on rising ground.

The American personnel at Bovingdon control tower stared in disbelief that anyone would attempt or want to fly in such weather. They were even more amazed by the fact that I had been given permission. What permission? No one had tried to stop me! I told them the truth. I didn't need permission to fly, incredible though it may have sounded. But then everything about my whole situation was far-fetched and it hadn't been me who had made it so. Seeing my so-called rank of 'captain' they obviously thought I was some kind of a crank. But nevertheless they telephoned for a staff car to come and take me up to Pinetree where I said I intended going. I travelled the 20 miles relaxing in the general's chauffeur-driven car. I felt they owed me that much after that flight!

The headquarters were underground, situated in the heart of a hill, which was entered through massive steel doors. Military police stood guard every few hundred yards. It was a maze of corridors in which it was quite possible for one to get completely lost if it hadn't been for those guards. It was like a miniature city, very self-contained.

I didn't leave the headquarters until 16 August. I was first vetted in the underground labyrinth. Then while arrangements were made for me to see someone who could assist me, I stayed the night. On about the second day of my stay I was finally received by the commanding generals. I don't recall who they were, I only know they were high-ranking generals of the US Air Force. Oddly enough I can't even recall where I slept while I was there. I do know I was taken to a very large state house where a few generals received me. They seemed to be aware of my case, but their attitude astounded me! They didn't seem in the least put out by the fact that I – a civilian – had been with their air force group at Boxted flying operationally, ostensibly accepting it as an everyday occurrence. I could almost see them dusting their hands very nicely together, having won the war for us. Decorations had been handed out all round and everyone had had a thoroughly good time afterwards. Now here was this man saying he hadn't been paid! Poor man! We must try to do something for him.

I felt that first I should have picked up a brick and thrown it through the window; perhaps that would have woken them out of their complacency. Certainly I would have got myself arrested as a madman. That would have assisted me no end. Instead I listened as patiently as I could to them cogitating over what I should do. Obviously, they concluded, I must put forward an application through the proper channels. It would be dealt with accordingly and I would receive my 'money'! Then it was thought that perhaps I should have some legal advice on the matter of how to go about such a claim. It didn't seem to occur to anyone simply to authorise the appropriate department to pay me and have done with the whole nasty business. I could see that securing what was owed was not going to be easy. While at Pinetree I engaged with everyone I possibly

could, including their legal department, but no one was terribly helpful. Everyone was of the opinion that I must first enter an proper claim
through the official channels. This had to be done from Boxted station
so I returned there on 16 August.

The refusal to grant the commissions caused embarrassment to both
pilots and mechanics alike in the 61st. Those who knew Gladych and myself
well were upset; others who had joined the group later did not completely
understand our position.

My friends now seemed to have split up into two different camps.
The pilots felt I should go to America and try my luck in their country;
the mechanics and engineers were convinced that was the last thing I
should attempt. They came to me intent that I should not even contemplate such an idea. They felt that neither my character nor the type
of person I was could adjust to the American way of life. I just wouldn't
be happy there. I appreciated their concern and respected the advice they
offered. I couldn't exactly see myself adapting, but this didn't stop the
pilots from writing home enquiring after some kind of job or sponsor
for me in the States, and I had a few letters of introduction that would
have secured me a position of sorts, such as a farm labourer, had I
decided to go to America.

Had I really wanted to go I would have done something very definite
about it, but I didn't. If I had actually been commissioned into the USAAF
I don't doubt for one moment that I would not have gone; my intention
was to continue my military career as a regular serviceman. My main
concern was to continue flying and fighting in the air, which I had been
unable to do in my own services. In a letter to me from a member of the
congressional staff in Washington, sent in 1964, it was inferred that the
prospect of going to America and becoming an American citizen had,
in fact, been a consideration which had prompted me to apply for an
American commission. This statement was included in a detailed
explanation endeavouring to prove to me what I must not expect in the
way of reimbursement after having my commission refused.

I found a great many things I had to settle for myself, not least the
question of my pay with the American authorities; I still wanted to see their
legal advisers. It never occurred to me at the time to go immediately to

a civilian solicitor. I considered it a military matter, to be dealt with accordingly. I intended to go to see General Kepner; I felt certain he could help and advise me in some way about the reimbursement.

Officially I did not exist, so I had to acquire some form of status and identity from the British authorities; I had to try and get back into the Polish Air Force. But according to my complete release document this I could only do through the Polish Consulate and they were no longer of the Free Polish government. It was the Communist government that was now officially recognised and I could expect no help from them to secure my re-entry into the PAF in Britain. It was the prevailing opinion that Polish personnel must now return to Poland, but however much I wanted to go back to my homeland I could never reconcile myself to the new regime. Therefore my survival would be in jeopardy. Many of my compatriots, including Michowski, who did return to Poland were shot under the Stalinist regime. I heard that the Czech pilots who went home after the war were imprisoned immediately by the authorities there as a threat to security. What a joke!

Gladych, at this time, had already decided to go to the States. He intended to marry a young Canadian or American girl from the WAAFs who he had met. Until now I had seen very little of him and even less as time passed. He was a complex character and made his own friends. I was often asked to confirm various accounts of his exploits he'd given about himself and his activities in the air.

When we had discussed the matter of our forthcoming commission he had seemed certain that it would be granted. He often told me he was 'arranging the matter'. I never took what he said very seriously, especially when he left it to me to put together the various documents we were asked to acquire from the Polish authorities. Then when it came to the point of pressing for our pay Gladych showed no determined effort to support me. He seemed more content to wait until he got to America, convinced he could deal with the matter more successfully there. So as he appeared to be otherwise engaged it was obviously better for me to concentrate on my own plans.

On 20 August a bomber arrived at Boxted en route for Nuremberg. It appeared a very good opportunity for me to fly to see General Kepner, commanding general of the 9th Air Force at Wiesbaden, later to become the headquarters of USAAF in Europe. I asked the pilot if he would take me along as a passenger and he agreed instantly. They expected to be there for several days (it turned out to be a week). As I wanted to get my pay claim started straight away I had very little time to get it organised, especially since the station headquarters were already preparing themselves to leave the base and England.

Setting out the application for my pay claim for official consideration was undertaken by the adjutant's office. It was an amazing coincidence that the bomber had come to Boxted and I had to make a very quick decision to ask them to take me. On this same morning I was called to the adjutant's office to sign the papers for my pay claim, with just two of my documents attached to support it. Whatever else I had I took with me to see General Kepner. It was thought that my application would be favourably considered, even though I did not have time to go over it in detail as the plane was waiting for me. I had no option but to leave it in the hands of the official station offices, as I had done with the commission papers, and this was the normal procedure.

However, the application made out for me was not factually correct, and contributed to further delays and confusion. I was given a military status in the PAF/RAF that I did not hold. They had done the self-same thing in my commission application. But I knew they were no longer interested and my position was becoming more of a nuisance and embarrassment as each day passed, so I had finally signed the document and hoped for the best. I didn't expect any substantial help to secure reimbursement through the 56th Fighter Group and I did not get any. They did all they thought they could and left it at that. If I could make more headway with General Kepner's help, all the better.

We landed at the station in Germany, where to my surprise I found all my former friends of the 9th Air Force. The last time I had seen any of them was when I had been intelligence officer with them during March and April 1944 (354th Fighter Group). We were all delighted to meet up again after so long and they wanted to 'show me the town'. I said it would have to wait until I had seen Kepner, but it was a while before this could be arranged. Meanwhile, I visited the damaged ruins of Nuremberg accompanied by my American friends. Devastation of the area was widespread. Some of the smaller towns were wiped out completely. Nuremberg itself – especially the old city – was practically destroyed. One could still smell the stench of dead bodies. According to what I heard the Germans said 10,000 had died there. I was also told the Nuremberg trials were already in preparation.

While I walked through the bombed streets with my friends I was particularly interested to discover how strong was the German morale. So I was watching for something particular that would prove to me what state it was in. My American 'buddies' noticed my strange attitude and finally they asked me what exactly it was that I was looking for. I told them that I had been searching for just one dirty child among the population and the ruins. I had failed to find one. They were all scrubbed clean and were spotless in their dress even though many were clothed in rags. Even then my friends didn't understand what this meant, and I pointed out that this was the nature of the German race and in a very short space of time they could expect to see Germany on its feet again, just as it had happened previously.

Then something else happened to amaze them. I was wearing my leather flying jacket as usual, as I had little else to wear. I had been left with only the clothes I stood in (other than my 'blue' uniform) – and, of course, my Polish emblem was very conspicuous on the side of my jacket. Whenever we entered any shops in the area, the German customers took one look at the emblem and hurriedly left the shop. This brought a look of surprise on my companions' faces for they said this hadn't happened to them before. Why was everyone running away? I said I would explain outside the shop.

We were in the heart of Hitler's domain and in the stadium the biggest speeches had been made. The concentration of Hitler's movement was in this city, and in Munich close by, and here I was sporting my emblem on my left breast as one of the victors whom they had endeavoured to crush for all time. The effect it had created could only be expected. It certainly cleared the shops in seconds!

The Americans raved over the German equipment they had found stored away as they entered Germany stage by stage. The engineers, particularly, at the precision and make of the tools. They were works of art.

Our stock – as pilots – came upon inspecting the flying equipment of the Luftwaffe. I recalled how often we had been told in the RAF/PAF that all German forces' equipment was 'ersatz'. I hadn't believed it then when I remembered the time I and my friends got to a crashed German bomber before anyone else reached it – there had been nothing 'ersatz' about what it carried for the crew's use. Now we could see for ourselves how beautifully they had been equipped.

I was given a pair of German flying boots and gloves that would have delighted me had I had anything like them when I had been flying during the war. The gloves were of very soft skin, lined with angora wool fur, with thick cuffs. The boots were excellently made. Fur-lined soft leather, like ski boots, fastened with a strap across the arch of the foot and a side zip. Best of all, both gloves and boots were equipped with electrical heating. There was no doubt about it, of the 'rubbish' these boys had, many of us – as we froze in our aircraft (in the RAF and PAF) – would have given our eye teeth to be wearing.

On 24 August it was arranged for me to see General Kepner. At the base they offered me the use of a Me 108 to fly to Wiesbaden and the 9th headquarters. It wasn't a very long flight and it amused me to fly over Germany in one of her own aircraft. (But I was secretly glad the war wasn't still on!) The choice had been between the 108 or a rather dilapidated 109. The Americans were using them for convenience between the smaller aerodromes, although they also had their own familiar Mustangs.

General Kepner received me in his office and was obviously very pleased to see me again. He took the opportunity to thank me personally for sending him the picture of the Thunderbolt – the aircraft he was so fond of. Then he asked me what he could do for me. A very leading question! I told him as briefly as I could what had happened regarding my American commission. My papers for commission had naturally passed through his office en route to the higher authorities, and they had received his sanction, especially as he had been aware of the situation from the outset. But other than commending me for commission he obviously was not aware that it had been refused. He expressed great shock as I explained these matters. I don't think he could believe it at first. When he spoke he openly disagreed with the decision. He certainly did not mince his words. I went on to explain about my pay and this caused him equal concern. I showed him the papers I had with me and a copy of a Lloyds letter, which proved I had received nothing from the RAF.

General Kepner found himself facing a very disagreeable situation. He too was angry and very disgusted. He wanted to help me all he could and we talked awhile. I learned from him that he did not intend to stay in the USAAF. I had the notion that his feelings went deeper than just my case. For the first time I felt I was facing a man who really was concerned about what his military authorities had done to me. Finally he said he intended to give me a letter that should without doubt verify my unusual services. He asked if he could send it to me to England, as it wasn't the type of letter that could be dashed off in a few minutes. He sincerely hoped it would prove effective in helping me to receive financial payment and he was deeply sorry for all that had happened.

I thanked him for appreciating my position. He felt particularly responsible as he had given his authorisation for Zemke and Schilling to approach me in the first place with the offer to join the Americans. I felt that if the American authorities did not take notice of his commendation, then the situation was indeed going to be difficult. General Kepner was a famous commanding general in his own right in the United States forces and was very highly regarded.

I left Wiesbaden feeling a great deal happier. I was now anxious to return to England. The B26 bomber that had brought me to Germany took me back to England on 27 August. General Kepner's letter arrived in the early days of September, dated 30 August 1945. I was very touched and honoured by his words.

To date, whatever I had done regarding both the commission and the pay claim I had also included Gladych in the discussions I had with various military departments. But as Gladych was preoccupied with getting to America he took no active part in contacting anyone who may have been able to assist us, and more or less went his own way. When he knew where I had been he was interested to know the results, but I believe he did not hear from General Kepner, who I had seen only on my own behalf. He was certainly surprised at the contents of the letter. However, I think he believed he would achieve more success with the authorities in America itself.

Chapter 25

September 1945

In September I decided the best place for me to acquire an identity would be from the Colchester police. They had known of me from the time I first came to Boxted station, and it was common knowledge that Polish pilots were flying with the American group.

I went to see the chief of police personally and explained the position. He listened sympathetically as I asked his advice about the best way for me to get an identity card. He was very shocked at the unpleasant situation and could not understand the military officials' decision any more than I could, or the attitude they took towards me generally. He offered at once to give me an alien's papers, which should enable me at least to prove who I was and to draw the ration cards and clothing coupons that, up until now, I had not been sanctioned to do. All this caused some concern to the Home Office later on, as apparently the police chief had had no right to issue me with any such papers since there was nothing to prove I had ever landed in England!

Nevertheless, he filled out all the necessary details and for the first time since September 1944 (exactly one year on) I was again in possession of an official identity. Or, at least, so I believed. I began to feel human again and a little more secure.

On the 1st of the month I had brought my pilot's logbook up to date. It was signed and verified – including the flights I had made after I had been told about my commission being refused – by the CO of the 61st Fighter Squadron, Lieutenant Colonel Gordon E. Baker. He had superseded Jim Carter, as Dade had already left the group at the end of August and Renwick had then taken over, with Carter as his deputy. The group expected to leave in the near future.

Strangely, they gave me a fresh pilot's flight record sheet for September 1945, even though I did not make any further flights after my logbook was signed on 1 September. It was an odd situation and debatable as to the exact date I was deemed to have left the 56th. I can only imagine that as my pay claim went through the station's offices they considered I was still with them until I heard the result. The flight sheet certainly infers I was a member of the group for September 1945.

As the Americans had not yet left Boxted, I continued going to the station. They were in process of packing everything up or destroying what was no longer required. The wastage of good material was enormous, the place looked a wreck. Whatever could not be taken away was destroyed completely or burned. The base had to be left exactly as they had taken it over from the British.

Some of my pilot friends were still endeavouring to persuade me to go to America with them, but I refused. However, as Gladych needed a passport to enter the States and the only place he could get one was from the Polish Communist Consulate, he suggested I went with him to obtain one for myself in case I changed my mind at the last minute. We told our Polish friends where we were going and I went along more out of curiosity than for a passport.

We found the Polish Consulate in just as big an upheaval as anywhere else I had visited. They were in the midst of organising themselves. Much to our surprise we experienced no difficulty in procuring the passports. Perhaps they were under the impression we wanted them in order to return to Poland. We left as easily as we arrived, despite stories of people disappearing mysteriously on entering an Eastern bloc consulate or embassy. Now I had a civilian alien identity card plus a Polish passport, which was more than I had had a few weeks before. But I never made use of the passport then or in the future. I don't recall what happened to it as I considered it of no use to me.

In mid-September the group finally left Boxted and before they went – leaving only a skeleton staff behind – I visited them once more to say goodbye and we wished each other good luck.

On my last visit to the camp, I had returned to me the papers on my pay claim. It seemed I had to furnish whatever particulars were required. They had no records at Boxted. It all seemed rather typical of the general attitude. I read in the papers that the headquarters of the 8th Fighter Command were requesting orders and information from the 56th Fighter Group to substantiate my claim for reimbursement. The 56th passed the buck to me with the request that I submit any such orders I had in my possession, to prove my claim. No orders of the nature required were available at their headquarters as they were in the process of returning to the US and their files had been turned in to the AGD, Inactive File Bureau, APO 319 (American postal number). These instructions were dated 24 September 1945. Briefly, the view of the 8th Air Force headquarters was that the claim would not receive any consideration from higher authorities without sufficient evidence in the form of supporting documents, upon which the claim was based. Such evidence was believed to be with either the 56th or the 65th Fighter Wing headquarters. They required any written orders or authority that officially attached me to the 61st Fighter Squadron, as well as full statements from everyone concerned, before contemplating any form of payment, even if it was authorised. It would also probably require 'special Congressional consideration', the first time such action was alluded to, and this was in September 1945!

All this may have looked very plain sailing, except that no one had thought to mention any of this to me when I had gone specifically to Bovingdon itself to learn what was required to secure my pay, and at a time when I could have acquired the necessary information. Now it was a bit late in the day with everyone gone and the station packed up. One can only wonder why these matters were not delved into at Bovingdon, the USAAF headquarters.

Then again, Pinetree was responsible for the consultations and agreements made on our behalf with the Polish and British authorities. They were the commanding generals and only they had the jurisdiction to make such agreements. Therefore any such records and information that would assert the evidence required could only be held at Pinetree. Copies were no doubt sent to the 56th and the 65th Fighter Wings, but they were only copies. The officials must have known the 56th were leaving Boxted and most of the commanders had already gone. Again none of it made any sense. For that matter, what was stopping the 8th headquarters from checking with the British Air Ministry or Polish Air Force if there really was any doubt in their minds. No one attempted to do this at any time other than to confirm the agreement back in October 1944.

It was so obvious they were stalling for time and didn't want to pay or acknowledge responsibility for the broken agreement. I had in my possession a letter from one of their own generals of the USAAF and I could already see, before I even submitted it to the authorities, that it was likely to be worthless in assisting with my remuneration.

Many years later, in 1966, a friend of mine in London mentioned a visit from a gentleman who had been an adjutant of the 56th in 1944/45. On discussing my case the man stated that no one in the group had known I had not been paid or they would have been able to reimburse me at the time, as, apparently, there had been ample funds available to enable them to do so. I was very surprised to learn of his remarks, which I considered in very bad taste and a pack of lies – an effort to save the face of the 56th commanders he had once served. Everyone had been fully aware of our position back then. We were not unknown. We stood and were held in the same regard as their famous aces and there were hardly any who could match our experience and training, which contributed to the acknowledgement paid to us. But I had had plenty of time over the years to study the facts of my case, and I now fully understood the behaviour of this gentleman's military and governmental superiors, and the attitude taken against me.

I recall the difficulty I suffered from the American military authorities to obtain due payment. I don't doubt that there were funds available. In fact, in January 1946 General A.C. Kincaid, Chief of Staff to the US air forces in Europe, considered I should be compensated for my services if funds were obtainable in the European theatre. However, a reply to this instruction was that there were none (letter dated 16 February 1946). The difficulty was in ascertaining exactly when money ceased to exist or was no longer available for such use.

On more than one occasion from 1945 onwards I expressed the opinion that it would be better for all concerned for them to pay me quietly, without any further claims being made that could only reflect badly on them sooner or later. But all such arguments fell on closed ears. The truth was they were hoping I would give up my claim.

So when I finally left the station I was in a dilemma as to what to do next. I could not obtain the information that was required.

I stood on the streets of Colchester with nothing more than the clothes I stood in – no money and little or no hope of securing any that was rightfully mine, and no home I could enter with any self-respect. There was no status that I could officially claim that would protect me in the situation I faced, and certainly none that had any official validity.

By this time my one year's unpaid leave had come to an end. My complete release document had long since expired, in May 1945. Therefore, according to the terms of both these documents I was once more automatically a member of the Polish forces. But no military status had yet been given to me and I wasn't sure if one would be forthcoming from the Polish forces, who were still under the command of the British.

So this episode of my life story came to a close, the next few years consisted of legal battles with the USAAF, the US government and the Polish Communist embassy in London, trying to have my claim settled, my identity verified and a chance to carry on my flying career.

Eventually, in 1949 I was granted British nationality and applied to join the RAF, being successful on my second attempt. In 1951 at the reduced rank of sergeant pilot I started my short career as an official RAF pilot. But that part of my life, and the following early 1960s flying in the Congo with Jan Zumbach in the 'Katangese' air force, is another story!

Final statement

'I keep my "skull and cross-bones" formations ready to kill, without mercy or pity, men, women and children of Polish origin and who speak Polish. That is the only way for us to get the living space we need. ...'

On 22 August 1939 Adolf Hitler made this declaration on behalf of Nazi Germany against the Polish nation, and within two weeks had begun to execute that part of his fanatical resolution.

However, by substituting the Polish nationality with any other one, this statement could apply to any country, depending upon where and towards whom one's hatred lies. Add to this a national leader with the necessary strength to accomplish the task, and any nation on earth stands in peril of annihilation. Such an aim found agreement and mass support in our recent history, and could easily do so again, however much this may shock and alarm.

Further affirmation of Nazi maniacal hatred was given in Colonel Wagner's diary of 8 September 1939: 'It is the Fuhrer's and Goering's intention to destroy and exterminate the Polish Nation.' And in October of that year Heydrick declared: 'Let the small fry off, but nobility, the papists and the Jews must all be killed.'

Catastrophic and horrifying as the last war was, with its greater implications had we not defeated the common enemy, must surely serve to remind us of the power that just one man can evoke in millions of followers who do not wish, or are afraid, to question his policies. For even today we accept too readily what we are told. Which, in itself, is easier for us, in blaming someone else if things go wrong.

The grim statements of Hitler and his commanders shocked me when

I read them almost forty-eight years after the event. Not of the hatred itself, for we Poles were all made thoroughly aware of that. It was the intensity, the all-consuming detestation that had existed against the nation and people of which I was born – Poland.

I did not know of these declarations at the time I fought in the Second World War. Now the mere thought alarms me that had I known perhaps I might have descended to that level, in retaliation. And if that were possible, what reaction would have come from an entire race of people – in wreaking revenge – if such hatred was directed at them?

To my knowledge, not only was I not aware of either this mass extermination policy towards the Polish people or of the intensity of the destructive emotion behind it, but neither were my colleagues with whom I fought in the Polish Air Force. In fact, prior to the onset of the Second World War, we – as our counterparts in Great Britain – believed that the war in the air would be conducted like that in the First World War as fought in the West, in which honourable behaviour, during and after aerial combat, had generally been observed. Our disillusionment in Poland was therefore swift and effective, serving to reiterate our national instinct and wariness of an age-old invader of Poland.

We felt anger and rage – and if rage and bitterness combined is hatred, then we have hated. Being aware of these feelings and the actions such feelings create, collectively and individually, particularly under the extreme conditions of war, is to understand the power that hatred can weald. A prime example of this, of course, is the abomination exacted against both Jews and Poles in this period, especially in the concentration camps.

As a result, it is with some sense of frustration that I frequently witness the attitude to push aside the deeds and knowledge of what has gone before, often as though it never existed, and with it the achievements and the sacrifices of that not so distant past.

These are some of the reasons why I am not able to brush aside past events shared with so many others, many who were my close friends, who never lived to see the end of the Second World War. Certainly not when the very aims of that struggle are diminished by lack of knowledge, understanding, or, what often seems, deliberate, deception. For then the price paid by so many becomes worthless.

Like a great many of my countrymen I chose to live in the West. Having left Poland as most of them did in 1939, I was one of the thousands of Polish servicemen who on the downfall of our country continued fighting in the West with the Allies, eventually reaching England in 1940 and residing here ever since. In 1949 I obtained British nationality.

Those times and its consequences had a major effect on my life, which made them difficult to forget. There are many others like me who, also, would not or cannot dismiss those times as part of a past best forgotten while we continue to face the same conflicts. I also believe that what happened then, or occurs now – or even in the future – is no more than what we ourselves are responsible for creating; and therefore cannot disown or pass that responsibility on to others however hard we may try; and that from our mistakes in the past, as well as those in the present, we can learn.

From the lessons of history we can acquire answers to present-day problems. Even if looking back frightens us or makes us feel guilty for what took place, the past also contains the hope of freedom and peace that is still desired today.

In relating my own experiences, therefore, I can only sincerely trust that it will help, however slightly, to broaden our understanding of each other. Not just as different nationalities but as people occupying the same world. This inevitably must concern the past as well as the present. For whether we are willing to accept it or not we are dependent upon each other and responsible to each other, and particularly to the future generations yet to come.

Perhaps then, one day, words like these will never again have cause to be said by another human being because of the brutality of man: 'Can I taste a piece of bread before I die?' – spoken by a seven-year-old child prisoner in Auschwitz – or those of a dying woman who asked to feel a pair of shoes: 'Thank you for finding them; I hope those who walk in them will find happiness and peace.'

The Polish motto, under which we Poles have so often fought, would then be truly representative of what it says, and the aim accomplished: 'Your Freedom, and Ours'.

Appendix 1

Combat Claims

Two kills were with the Polish Air Force. Source: 'Lista Bajana' (recognised official Polish claim records) and 'Aces High' publication, author Christopher Shores.

Claims with the 56th FG were:
1 FW 190 on 22 May 1944 flying HV-E (P-47 'G')
1 Me 109 on 27 June 1944 flying HV-M (P-47 'D')
1 Me 109 on 5 July 1944 flying HV-Z (P-47 'D')
1 FW 190 on 18 November 1944 flying HV-Z (P-47 'D' 'Silver Lady') which was the strafing mission to Hanau with all three squadrons of the 56th taking part. Lanny engaged a total of three FW 190s that day but only claimed 1 as he was unsure of hits for the kill on the other two. This kill was whilst flying 'Silver Lady'.

He also destroyed a Messerschmitt Me 109 on 27 June 1944 flying HV-M (P-47 'D') but did not claim the kill. Lanny gave full credit for this kill to his wingman, Patterson, after he had initially fired on the Me 109 on his first pass scoring a few hits but the Me 109 turned away trailing white smoke and was chased and destroyed by Lanny.

He also destroyed a Heinkel He 111 on 28 August 1944 flying HV-G (P-47 'D') but did not claim the kill.

Flight Records

Polish Air Force:
Combat hours: 220hrs
Number of operations: 97

Total number of hours on Spitfires Mks II, v, vb, IX = 475 hrs 40 mins

56th Fighter Group:
First operational sortie: 15 May 1944
Number of sorties flying 'Silver Lady': 21
First flight in P-47 'M': 20 January 1945 (HV-M, Mike Gladych's Thunderbolt)
First flight in own personal P-47 'M': 23 January 1945 (HV-Z)
Number of sorties flying P-47 HV-Z: 16
Number of flights in P-47 'M' model: 24
Total operational hours: 202 hrs 5 mins
Other flying hours: 122 hrs 50 mins
Total hours: 324 hrs 55 mins
Number of operations: 81

Grand Total Combat hours flown: 422 hrs 5 mins
Grand Total Combat Operations flown: 178

Second World War Decorations

General Service Medal
War Medal 1939 – 45
Air Crew Europe Star 1939 – 45
French 1939 – 45 War Commemorative Medal
Polish 'Cross of Valour' & Bar
American Air Medal with 2 Silver Oak Leaf Clusters
American Distinguished Flying Cross

Copy of records for US medals given by month:
A few Air Medals are missing between #7 and the 2nd Silver OLC but the records may be incomplete.

May 44	Nothing listed
June 44	Nothing listed
July 44	22 July General Order #62 HQ VIII Fighter Command
	Air Medal
	Oak Leaf Cluster To Air Medal
August 44	6 August General Order #70 HQ VIII Fighter Command
	Distinguished Flying Cross
Sept 44	Nothing listed
Oct 44	Nothing listed
Nov 44	14 November General Order #301. 2nd Bombardment
	Division
	4th Oak Leaf Cluster to Air Medal
	5th OLC
	6th OLC

7th OLC

Dec 44	Nothing listed
Jan 45	Nothing listed
Feb 45	Nothing listed
March 45	Nothing listed
April 45	28 April 45 General orders #151 HQ 2nd Air Division 2nd Silver OLC to Air Medal.(10?)
May 45	Nothing listed

Index

A

B

C

D

E

F

G

K

L

M

N

O

P

R

S